Extreme NXT: Extending the LEGO MINDSTORMS NXT to the Next Level

Second Edition

Michael Gasperi and Philippe "Philo" Hurbain

Apress®

Extreme NXT: Extending the LEGO MINDSTORMS NXT to the Next Level, Second Edition

ISBN-13 (pbk): 978-1-4302-2453-2

ISBN-13 (electronic): 978-1-4302-2454-9

Printed and bound in the United States of America 9 8 7 6 5 4 3 2 1

Trademarked names may appear in this book. Rather than use a trademark symbol with every occurrence of a trademarked name, we use the names only in an editorial fashion and to the benefit of the trademark owner, with no intention of infringement of the trademark.

Java™ and all Java-based marks are trademarks or registered trademarks of Sun Microsystems, Inc., in the US and other countries. Apress, Inc., is not affiliated with Sun Microsystems, Inc., and this book was written without endorsement from Sun Microsystems, Inc.

Lead Editor: Tony Campbell
Technical Reviewer: Philippe "Philo" Hurbain
Editorial Board: Clay Andres, Steve Anglin, Mark Beckner, Ewan Buckingham, Tony Campbell, Gary Cornell, Jonathan Gennick, Michelle Lowman, Matthew Moodie, Jeffrey Pepper, Frank Pohlmann, Ben Renow-Clarke, Dominic Shakeshaft, Matt Wade, Tom Welsh
Project Managers: Beth Christmas and Debra Kelly
Copy Editor: Nancy Sixsmith
Compositor: LaurelTech
Indexer: Carol Burbo
Artist: April Milne

Distributed to the book trade worldwide by Springer-Verlag New York, Inc., 233 Spring Street, 6th Floor, New York, NY 10013. Phone 1-800-SPRINGER, fax 201-348-4505, e-mail orders-ny@springer-sbm.com, or visit http://www.springeronline.com.

For information on translations, please e-mail info@apress.com, or visit http://www.apress.com.

Apress and friends of ED books may be purchased in bulk for academic, corporate, or promotional use. eBook versions and licenses are also available for most titles. For more information, reference our Special Bulk Sales–eBook Licensing web page at http://www.apress.com/info/bulksales.

The source code for this book is available to readers at http://www.apress.com.

This book is rededicated to my dear wife, Jayne. Thanks for putting up with the mess I made on your desk . . . again.

——Love, Mike

I dedicate this book to my wife, Annie. She puts up with the pervasive invasion of LEGO and electronics parts everywhere, as well as with LEGO models "decorating" most of the shelves of our home.

——Thanks and love, Philo

Contents at a Glance

Contents

Foreword

I am convinced that the developers of the LEGO RCX could neither have imagined the extraordinary success of their product, nor were they able to predict that the Programmable Brick would constitute a worldwide community of adult fans collaborating with—and to some extent, competing with—one another in miscellaneous domains, such as the creation of highly sophisticated LEGO robots or the design of astute sensors and actuators.

For almost a decade, this community has established itself and constantly grown. But during the last months it has gained strong impetus with the appearance of the LEGO NXT. Many members of the community are known to be excellent MINDSTORMERS, but only a handful of people have acquired the overall accepted—although unofficial—status of a master MINDSTORMER.

The authors of this book are approved masters!

Michael Gasperi is one of the pioneers of extending the RCX functionality. Known as "Mr. Sensor," he initiated the development of compatible sensors. He also started a well-visited web site, sharing details of his projects with RIS fans and setting up a collection of chosen links to other people's sensor pages that he was able to grab on the Internet. Meanwhile, Gasperi's "LEGO Mindstorms Sensor Input Page" has become the reference par excellence concerning the creation of homebrew sensors for any LEGO robotics amateur. With his experience and his ability to explain things clearly, Michael also participated as the coauthor of one of the best MINDSTORMS books: Extreme MINDSTORMS: An Advanced Guide to LEGO MINDSTORMS (Apress, 2000). His famous RCX input multiplexer has been published in the U.S. electronics journal Nuts and Volts. These are the ideal prerequisites for continuing his work through this new book that is dedicated to the LEGO NXT. However, Mike felt that he would need the help of another MINDSTORMS geek.

Philippe "Philo" Hurbain is in fact the absolute opposite of a "geek." He is an enthusiast, for sure, and certainly one of the best LEGO experts, but he also is an active member of the MINDSTORMS community, lending a helping hand to anyone who is in trouble with his or her robot project. Philippe is a gifted photographer and has a particular sense of precision. Combining all his areas of expertise, Philo has created the neatest MINDSTORMS web site, and has a long list of the most remarkable accomplishments. He has won a lot of prizes in LEGO extreme building contests; for example, with "Pimousse": a heavy-weight–lifting robot that is able to lift 44kg (97 pounds)! Philippe says about himself that his best programming tool is the soldering iron. He certainly is too modest here because besides his extraordinary electronics skills, he also is an excellent MINDSTORMS programmer.

This book is the absolute must for any advanced LEGO robotics enthusiast who intends to become a master MINDSTORMER using the NXT. Compared to the RCX—already an outstanding device—the NXT sets the standard for the next generation of robot kits. By analogy, Extreme NXT represents the advanced part of the MINDSTORMS library and should not be missing on the specialist's bookshelf. Being lucky to have seen the book before printing, I was deeply impressed by the creativity and ingenuity of all of the chapters. First of all, the NXT MINDSTORMS kit is presented in a form that's typical for both Mike and Philo: all the sensors are taken apart so that the reader gets an insight into their interior and participates in reverse engineering. Remember that in the beginning of MINDSTORMS, it was a real surprise for LEGO to see adult freaks hacking its products, sharing their discoveries in open source projects, and thus becoming the real motor of the RCX's enormous success. That's certainly why LEGO voted for an ambitious business strategy of sharing most of the NXT internals with the community, and even selecting 100 members of the community to be part of the MINDSTORMS Developer Program (MDP).

This book starts where its predecessors ended. The authors come right to the point with their central message: "Explore your NXT, play with it, and participate in unexpected experiments!" During the course of the book, you'll learn by playing with problems—one of Seymour Papert's constructivist postulates. You're asked to make your own NXT connector . . . and learn about how NXT talks to its sensors and motors; measure the salinity of water . . . and discover electric resistance; observe melting ice . . . and investigate the secrets of electronic temperature measurements; play music with Léon Theremin's organ . . . and understand the functioning of Light Dependent Resistors.

Like their Broom Balancer, the authors maintain the equilibrium of being explicit enough without ever getting lost in details. The practical, well-illustrated descriptions capture your attention with a note of humor. While explaining powered sensors, they introduce a Hall Effect Sensor and demonstrate its function with an NXT Robot Mouse seeking magnetic "cheese." The NXT edition of Mike's good old differential Light Sensor is converted into a sundial.

Later in the book, you're introduced to the secrets of the solderless breadboard and the PC board. To help you to overcome your hesitation to plunge into the complex world of integrated electronics, the book presents a most exciting experiment: an electronic whistler using a common light bulb filament! In another workbench project, a medical syringe and a pressure sensor serve to verify Boyle's Law. But even with these higher-ceiling projects, the authors stick to their rule of keeping things comprehensive and clear while using the NXT unexpectedly.

The authors investigate NXT output functionality through Button Pushers, Knob Twisters, Switch Flippers—names that reveal the authors' love for playing. In parallel, you learn how to change mechanical rotation into translation. You discover that you can use lamps, LEDs, Muscle Wires, electromagnets, and solenoids; finally, you build your own kinetic sculpture and a panoramic photographer robot. The I²C bus is explained on the basis of an absolutely amazing Magic Wand project, a reincarnation of the Simon game, a second edition of Philo's Color Sensor that's incorporated into a colored-brick–sorting robot, and an NXT version of the world's first video game, Pong. The NXT data-logging features are explored through measuring a hand warmer's temperature; Bluetooth is used with a remotely guided robot photographer.

Extreme NXT is a goldmine! Reading this book—and even more, working with it—will certainly produce new MINDSTORMS masters. By the way, the torch is passed to the NXT generation.

Claude Baumann

About the Authors

Michael Gasperi When I was growing up in the 1960s and '70s it made sense to build things, such as computers, from component parts. In fact, you could build all kinds of electronic products, including television sets, this way. Not only does this not make any economic sense now, it is also physically impossible to deal with the tiny electronic components. Back then, magazines such as Popular Electronics provided all kinds of projects for the electronic hobbyist to experiment with. One of the regular columns was written by Forrest Mims III, and I eagerly anticipated reading his latest monthly installment. I always thought, "What a cool job this guy has; someday I'm going to do something like that."

I went to Purdue University, got an engineering degree, and ended up doing industrial research at Rockwell Automation. However, a part of me still yearned for the dream job of cooking up interesting projects and telling people how to do them. Back in 1998, LEGO introduced the MINDSTORMS Robotics Invention System. I naively bought a kit for my daughter Audrey, but quickly got swept up in the network of adult hackers trying to unlock the product's real potential. Through a simple personal web page I started publishing how the LEGO sensors worked and how to build new ones. This led to being invited to appear at MIT's MindFest and eventually to coauthoring a book on the subject, Extreme MINDSTORMS: An Advanced Guide to LEGO MINDSTORMS (Apress, 2000). Now that LEGO has introduced the next generation of MINDSTORMS, I felt compelled to experiment and write again.

Philippe "Philo" Hurbain (also the technical reviewer of this edition) Like Mike, I grew up in a time when electronics hobbies were widespread, and finding components and magazines was easy then. I built lots of gadgets, and also measurement instruments. One of my biggest projects was also my first robot: a wall-avoiding car that was wire programmable, using components unsoldered from old IBM mainframe boards.

While studying engineering at École Centrale de Paris, I assembled my first "computer" in a time when 16K was considered a huge amount of memory. After I got my degree, I worked a few years for a French computer startup; then I created a small design house with three fellow students where I designed communication boards (ISDN and then ADSL).

About 25 years ago, I discovered LEGO Technic, which I used to build an equivalent of my old wall-avoiding car. That was my first LEGO "bot." However, there were no standard LEGO parts for what I needed, and I didn't have time to learn how to build complicated LEGO models, so I tired of it. But then the Robotics Invention System 1.5 reached France and it looked wonderful, so I bought one for my daughter. Of course, I ended up playing with the set a lot more than she did. I was hooked!
I started describing my constructions and RCX electronics add-ons in a web site, which got me some recognition from fellow builders and even from LEGO, which chose me as one of 100 beta testers for its new NXT robotics set. In this book, I share some ideas, tips, and tricks learned during this exciting period.

Acknowledgments

This book wouldn't have happened without my friend Dave Baum. Back in 2000, Dave got me started as a writer by convincing me to coauthor with him on the Extreme MINDSTORMS book. When LEGO announced that it was introducing a new generation of MINDSTORMS, it made sense to write a similar book. Fortunately, Dave received one of the early release NXT kits, and he generously loaned it to me so I could jump start the book development process. Thanks again, Dave.

Michael Gasperi

The true father of this book is Mike. He had to convince me that we should coauthor a book on our common passion: hacking the new NXT. So, thanks a lot, Mike, for leading me in this adventure! I'd also like to thank LEGO for creating this outstanding product and for choosing me as a beta tester.

Philippe "Philo" Hurbain

Introduction

Before you get overly involved in extending the NXT, you need to understand the history of the MINDSTORMS concept, and the hardware and software that is available for it. In Chapter 1, we discuss what comes inside the NXT kit and the RCX sensors that are compatible with it. Let's void the warranty by taking them apart and seeing what's inside. We'll also provide a brief introduction to NXT-G and NXC, along with three alternative programming languages. Chapter 3 covers the ins and outs of the NXT and how to connect to it.

The simplest types of sensors to homebrew are generically referred to as passive sensors. Contact, resistive, potentiometer, and voltage sensors usually only require a single electronic part, but despite their apparent simplicity, they can be used to create some interesting projects. Chapters 4, 5, 6, and 7 contain plans for projects such as a surfboard game, an antenna sensor, an Ohmmeter, Temperature and Humidity Sensors, a theremin musical instrument, a model of Braitenberg's vehicle, a digital protractor, two joysticks, and a battery tester.

The 4.3V-powered sensors aren't a lot more complicated than the passive ones, but you can build even more interesting projects with them. In Chapter 8, you'll look at the Hall Effect, infrared rangefinder, and differential Light Sensors. With them you can build a robot mouse that looks for magnetic cheese, a vehicle that follows walls, and a digital sundial.

Things get a little more complicated when you look at two-wire powered sensors in Chapter 9. They have a higher power supply voltage that allows you to use integrated circuit operational amplifiers to measure very small voltages. The projects include a half volt voltmeter, hot wire anemometer, and calibrated pressure sensor. Chapter 10 shows you how to add LED control to your homebrew Light Sensor projects.

Not every extension to the NXT requires building new hardware. The NXT can control appliances by using its motor to push buttons, turn knobs, or flip switches on them. In Chapter 11, we'll show examples of operating a wireless remote control to make an NXT version of the Clapper, turning the knobs on an Etch-A-Sketch to make an Etch-A-NXT, and flipping a pneumatic switch to open and close a simple robotic gripper. We'll also show you how to connect LEGO's new Power Functions motors directly to the NXT.

By Chapter 12, you'll be ready to go beyond LEGO motors. Some new outputs are easy, such as lamps, LEDs, Muscle Wires, and electromagnets. Others, such as relays and power amplifiers, allow you to connect the NXT to much bigger loads. The projects in the chapter include a decision maker, kinetic sculpture, and RC-Servo motor controller; and you'll learn how to connect two loads to the same output.

The ultimate interface to the NXT is its I²C bus. It allows the NXT to be connected to intelligent sensors and expanded to have practically unlimited inputs and outputs. In Chapter 13, we'll go into the details of building a benchmark I²C port. From there, you can build a Magic Wand display, Simon game, relay output, keypad interface, stepper motor controller, Color Sensor, and several more projects.

Chapter 14 is a collection of cool projects that involve combining the NXT with other things. You'll use spreadsheet programs, other NXTs, LEGO trains, and digital cameras to conduct a data-logging experiment, remotely control a vehicle, automatically control a train station, take some panoramic photos, and play a game of Pong.

Constructing electronic projects like the ones in this book might be new to you. Appendix A will show you how to build an electronic circuit on a solderless breadboard and then how to move it to a printed circuit board to make it permanent. It even takes you through the basics of soldering. Appendix B has sources for components, web site links, and other references where you can learn more. Appendix C has the full listings of the programs only partially shown in the chapters. The book web site in the Source Code/Download area of http://www.apress.com has the programs and CAD drawings of the projects for you to download.

CHAPTER 1

■■■

In the Beginning

LEGO launched the MINDSTORMS NXT in the fall of 2006. But the story really begins eight years earlier in the fall of 1998, when LEGO introduced the first MINDSTORMS kit:The Robotics Invention System (RIS) with the Robotic Control Explorer (RCX) programmable brick (see Figure 1-1). It represented the evolution of five decades of modular construction techniques from LEGO, with years of computer-based education methods from the Massachusetts Institute of Technology (MIT).

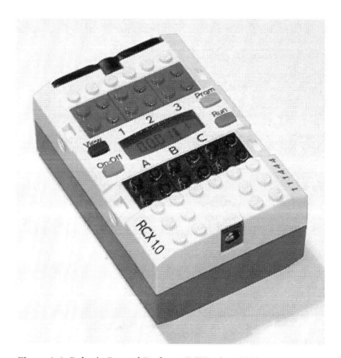

Figure 1-1. *Robotic Control Explorer (RCX), circa 1998*

1

LEGO had been producing construction toys since the late 1940s, starting with the familiar interlocking building blocks and ending with today's highly technical pieces that include beams, motors, gears, and pneumatics. Although the style of building has changed, the new pieces are designed to be backward compatible and interoperable with the old. These compatibility features, and the huge inventory of parts, are some of the reasons why LEGO is such an attractive choice for construction.

MIT had been investigating the use of computers in education from the late 1970s. The name MINDSTORMS was actually taken from a book title by MIT computer scientist Seymour Papert. The work involved the concept of not just using computers to deliver tests and evaluate children but also for children to use computers for problem solving and invention. The original computers were so large they had to be external to the inventions, but as technology allowed, they became a part of the creation itself through a myriad of prototype programmable bricks.

The RCX and the Robotics Invention System

The Robotics Invention System (RIS) was revolutionary because, for the first time, people could easily share complex inventions. Everyone could build exactly the same invention without traditional skills such as carpentry, metal working, electronics, and programming. It was also a boon for educational institutions that needed a durable and reusable platform for engineering lab projects. Figure 1-2 shows the more than 700 parts included with the RIS.

Figure 1-2. *The original Robotics Invention System (RIS), circa 1998*
Photo courtesy of LEGO

The RCX had an eight-bit computer, three inputs, three outputs, infrared communications, a speaker, and a four-digit LCD display. It was programmed on a personal computer with a simple graphical language that vaguely resembled the stacking building blocks. The seriously simplified language was useful for most elementary designs, but lacked the high-level functions found in most computer languages. People immediately started to reverse engineer, or hack, the product. The shortcomings of the minimal number of inputs and outputs of the RCX also put pressure on the effort.

Back in 1998, the Internet was still relatively new. Most people accessed it through slow dial-up connections, and the main collaboration tools were newsgroups and e-mail lists. People around the world started feverishly exploring the RCX, discovering and then reporting to everyone on the Internet what they had found. Despite limited communications, the effort pioneered by Kekoa Proudfoot and Russell Nelson led Dave Baum, Ralph Hempel, and Markus Noga to introduce alternative languages; and Michael Gasperi to publish designs for homebrew sensors within months. Eventually, LEGO embraced the effort by publishing Software Development Kits (SDKs) and other documentation to make the RCX a more open platform. They were even present when MIT hosted a gathering of the early hackers in 1999 called Mindfest.

Following the RCX, LEGO introduced a more limited programmable brick called the Scout in the Robotics Discovery System (RDS). It was targeted for a younger audience than the RIS, who had less interest in programming. Because its operating system was in unchangeable read-only memory (ROM), it was doomed to be ignored by the hackers. Even more ignored were the more limited Micro Scout and the Droid Developer Kit, which wasn't much more than a programmable motor. Although Vision Command offered some sophisticated image-processing capability, it was really a Windows application and only used the RCX as a kind of output device.

It all felt as if LEGO was going in the wrong direction. Instead of constantly improving, the new MINDSTORMS products were getting less sophisticated and more limited. In a world in which electronics become obsolete in months, the RCX stood virtually unchanged for eight years. Embraced by the education community, it became a classroom fixture, serving as a platform for teaching programming and a wide range of engineering topics.

The MINDSTORMS NXT

The MINDSTORMS NXT (see Figure 1-3) is an enhancement in every aspect to the original RIS.

Figure 1-3. *MINDSTORMS NXT*

In particular, the NXT programmable brick shown in Figure 1-4 has a 32-bit microprocessor, 4 inputs, 3 outputs, Bluetooth communications, a speaker, and a 100x64 LCD display. Also, the NXT includes three powerful motors with built-in rotation sensors. The graphical programming language, NXT-G, is simple but complete enough to be quite usable.

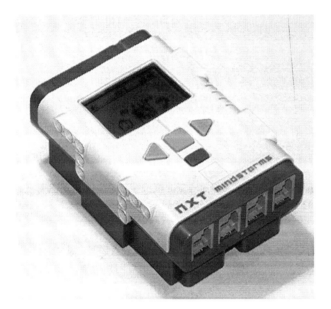

Figure 1-4. *The NXT programmable brick*

LEGO didn't just improve on the product; it went about improving the product launch as well. One hundred NXT kits were distributed months ahead of the major launch to a hand-selected group through the MINDSTORMS Developer Program (MDP) to work out any remaining issues. LEGO even provided detailed product documentation and SDKs well in advance. Aftermarket sensor manufacturers and software developers were able to have products available immediately, as opposed to months later for the RIS.

There was only a small network of NXT hackers because the product was very capable right out of the box. Its programming language is quite usable; there's an extra input, three sophisticated motors, and more types of sensors; and it is well-documented. Not that there aren't ways to go beyond what comes in the MINDSTORMS NXT box—LEGO couldn't possibly provide every sensor or actuator that could be used for building inventions, and that's where this book fits in.

In 2009, LEGO freshened up the NXT kit with an improved NXT2 (see Figure 1-5). The NXT2 has enhancements to the software as well as a Color Sensor to replace the original monochrome Light Sensor. The second-generation kit no longer includes the Sound Sensor and it has a slight change in parts inventory to reflect the four new construction plans. The MINDSTORMS product continues to be a very popular consumer item as well as a major tool in education. It has even been chosen as the computer for the *FIRST LEGO League* and *FIRST Tech Challenge* robotic competitions.

Figure 1-5. *Steven Canvin, Marketing Manager, LEGO MINDSTORMS, holding the very first NXT 2.0 kit*
Photo courtesy of LEGO

The Sensors

Sensors provide feedback to a system telling it where it is or how it's doing. The NXT has several types of sensors designed specifically for it and backward compatibility to the old RCX sensors. All the sensors are well documented by LEGO, but we'll provide additional characteristics and show the internal construction of the sensors.

NXT Sensors

The original NXT came with five types of sensors: Touch, Light, Sound, Ultrasonic, and Rotation. The NXT Rotation Sensor is conveniently built into its motor so shaft position and speed are always available to NXT programs. Second-generation NXTs replaced the Light Sensor with one that could additionally discriminate color and eliminated the Sound Sensor entirely.

Touch

The NXT Touch Sensor is shown in Figure 1-6. A nice feature of the Touch Sensor is its cross-hole that allows you to connect the sensor operator directly to other assemblies.

Figure 1-6. NXT Touch Sensor

Internally, the Touch Sensor is a printed circuit board (PCB) mounted push button and a connector, as seen in Figure 1-7. There's also a resistor in series with the switch so it won't create a dead short if it's accidentally connected to an output port.

Figure 1-7. Touch Sensor breakdown

Light

The NXT Light Sensor includes a red light emitting diode (LED) light source that can be turned on and off from software (see Figures 1-8 and 1-9). The LED allows you to measure either the reflected LED light shining back from an object or the ambient light falling on the sensor.

Figure 1-8. NXT Light Sensor

In Figure 1-9, you can see the LED, phototransistor, and connector mounted on the top of the PCB. All the small surface-mounted electronics are on the bottom of the board.

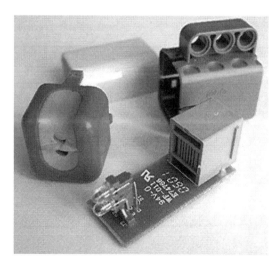

Figure 1-9. Light Sensor breakdown

The phototransistor in the Light Sensor is far more sensitive to the infrared colors of light than the relatively narrow visible spectrum we see. This can be confusing because it sees hot light sources such as incandescent light bulbs as being much brighter than we do. Figure 1-10 shows how the transistor's spectral response overlaps the human eye.

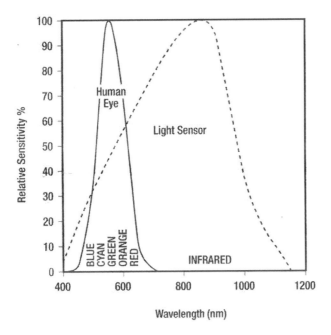

Figure 1-10. Light Sensor spectral response

We'll discuss light sensitivity in more detail in Chapter 5 when we make our own Light Sensors. (Looking ahead, Table 5-1 has the average light intensity of various locations.)

Figure 1-11 shows the sensitivity of the NXT sensor over a wide range of light intensities, which is usually measured in units of lux (lx).

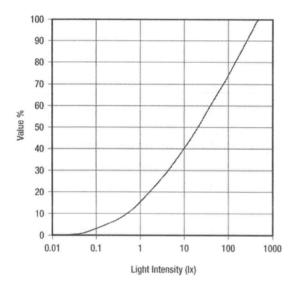

Figure 1-11. *Light Sensor sensitivity*

Sound

Surprisingly, LEGO didn't provide the RCX with a Sound Sensor and dropped it with the NXT2. Because it's such a natural type of input, the Sound Sensor was one of the first sensors to be widely homebrewed. The NXT Sound Sensor (see Figure 1-12) is constructed much like the Light Sensor.

Figure 1-12. *NXT Sound Sensor*

In Figure 1-13 you can see the microphone mounted in plastic foam, a capacitor, and the connector on the top of the PCB with the rest of the electronics mounted on the bottom.

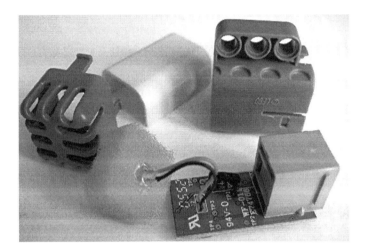

Figure 1-13. *Sound Sensor breakdown*

Sound volume or sound pressure level (SPL) is measured in units called decibels (dB). Instead of an absolute measurement such as lux, decibels measure how much a sound level is relatively louder or softer than another sound. In this case, 0dB is the faintest sound that an average person can hear. Table 1-1 lists some typical dB values.

Table 1-1. *Sound Pressure Levels*

SPL dB	Source
90	Loud noises
80	Shouting
70	Talking
60	Office/talking at a distance
50	Quiet living room

Figure 1-14 shows the NXT Sound Sensor sensitivity.

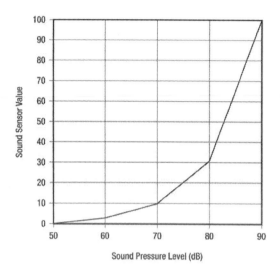

Figure 1-14. *Sound level value versus sound pressure level*

Looking back at Figure 1-10, you can see that human vision has peak sensitivity to green light and drops off to zero toward both blue and red. Human sound sensitivity also has a peak. It's around a few kHz and drops off to zero toward both 20Hz and 20kHz. The Sound Sensor can be put into a dBA mode, in which the sound reading more closely matches that of the human ear. A rough idea of the frequency response of the Sound Sensor in the two modes is shown in Figure 1-15.

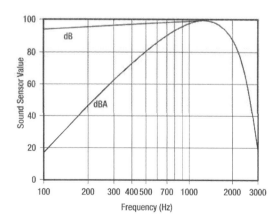

Figure 1-15. *Approximate sound level value versus frequency*

Ultrasonic

Avoiding objects is one of the first objectives for a robot. Most of the time it's better not to even touch objects, and that's where the NXT Ultrasonic Sensor comes in (see Figure 1-16).

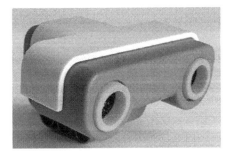

Figure 1-16. *NXT Ultrasonic Sensor*

The guts of the sensor are shown in Figure 1-17. The two cylindrical objects connected with wires to the PCB are the ultrasonic speaker and microphone.

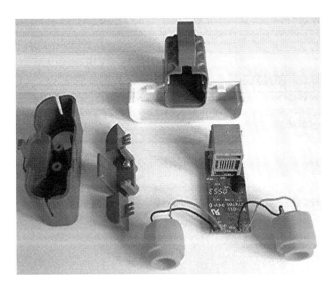

Figure 1-17. *Ultrasonic Sensor breakdown*

It's such a complex sensor that it needs its own microprocessor. Because of this added intelligence, it reports distance in absolute units instead of on some relative scale like the Light and Sound Sensors. The sensor works just like sonar by sending out a short burst of ultrasonic sound at 40kHz. It then measures the time it takes for the sound to travel out to an object, reflect, and travel back. If there's only one large object, such as a flat wall, in front of the sensor, the measurement is quite good. However, if the scene becomes complicated, such as with many small objects, it isn't as reliable.

Color

The LEGO Color Sensor was added in 2009, along with other upgrades to the NXT software. In addition to being a Color Sensor, it also duplicates the functionality of the original NXT Light Sensor. The sensor detects color by sequentially measuring the amount of light reflected from red, green, and blue LEDs. The three measurements are compared to determine the rough color values shown in Table 1-2. When reproducing the Light Sensor, it uses only one of the LEDs (or none of them) when making ambient light level measurements. The tricolor LED can also be used by itself as a colored lamp for aesthetic and debugging purposes.

Table 1-2. *Detected Color Values*

Value	Color
1	Black
2	Blue
3	Green
4	Yellow
5	Red
6	White

Figure 1-18 is a photograph of the Color Sensor. The small spherical dome on the front of the sensor below the letter R is the phototransistor, the one below the B is the tri-color LED, and the bottom one is actually just a decoration.

Figure 1-18. *NXT Color Sensor*

Internally, the Color Sensor looks like Figure 1-19. Most of the electronics are on the bottom of the printed circuit board with the LED and phototransistor on the top.

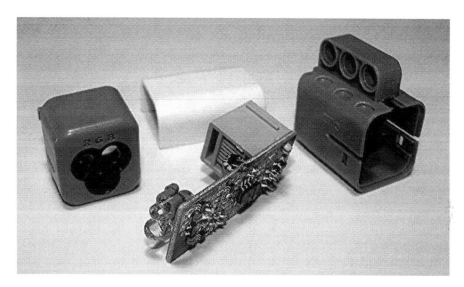

Figure 1-19. *Color Sensor breakdown*

NXT Temperature

Also introduced in 2009, the NXT Temperature Sensor (PN #9749) is intended for the education market and is not supported by the consumer version of the NXT. The sensor can read from –4 °F to 248 °F (–20 °C to 110 °C), which is a much wider range than the original RCX Temperature Sensor we will cover later. Figure 1-20 shows the sensor with its long metal probe. It has an integral cable because the standard connector could be damaged during an experiment.

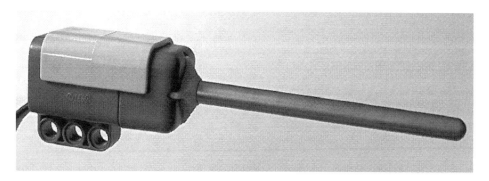

Figure 1-20. *NXT Temperature Sensor*

15

RCX Legacy Sensors

The Robotics Invention System included two Touch Sensors and one Light Sensor. There was also a Temperature Sensor that could be ordered separately. The Rotation Sensor had to be ordered separately, too, and this was a serious drawback because Rotation Sensors are critical to building complex projects. It also consumed one of the three RCX input ports, unlike the NXT built-in Rotation Sensor. All the RCX sensors require the conversion cable (LEGO #8528) to connect them to the NXT.

Touch

The RCX Touch Sensor (see Figure 1-21) uses the same conductive rubber technology found in the buttons of calculators and remote controls (see Figure 1-22). The operator lacks a way to connect directly to it, and it also doesn't move back and forth very far, which makes constructing reliable bumpers difficult.

Figure 1-21. RCX Touch Sensor

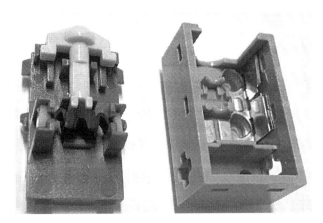

Figure 1-22. Touch Sensor breakdown

Light

The RCX Light Sensor also contains an LED light source, but it's always turned on (see Figure 1-23).

Figure 1-23. *RCX Light Sensor*

The sensor is built into a brick, and you can see its internal construction in Figure 1-24. It uses a phototransistor like the NXT Light Sensor and has similar infrared spectral sensitivity. The light sensitivity is also comparable to the NXT, but partly because of physical placement of the always-on LED and the phototransistor, the RCX Light Sensor has notoriously poor sensitivity to low light. It seldom has a light reading below 10.

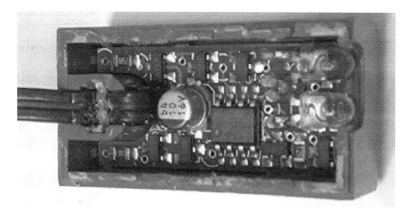

Figure 1-24. *Light Sensor breakdown*

Rotation

The RCX Rotation Sensor resolves 16 locations per rotation or 22.5 degrees (see Figure 1-25). Internally, it detects the vanes on a rotating shaft with two opto-interrupters. An opto-interrupter is a phototransistor and an LED that are pointed at each other with a small gap in between. The RCX or NXT watches the states of the two interrupters to determine which direction the sensor is rotating, and increments or decrements a counter accordingly. Unfortunately, at low speed, the sensor has some problems with losing counts.

Figure 1-25. RCX Rotation Sensor

You can see the vanes and the electronics on the PCB in Figure 1-26.

Figure 1-26. Rotation Sensor breakdown

The RCX Rotation Sensor has one big advantage over the NXT. Because it hasn't been combined with an elaborate gear train and electric motor, the RCX Rotation Sensor rotates almost without friction. If you want to measure the rotation of something like a hamster wheel, you need the RCX Rotation Sensor.

Temperature

The RCX Temperature Sensor looks like a brick with a short metal tube sticking out of it (see Figure 1-27). The temperature transducer is located inside this metal tube. We'll discuss the sensor in great detail in Chapter 5 when you make your own Temperature Sensor.

Figure 1-27. *RCX Temperature Sensor*

The NXT Motor

Direct Current (DC) motors almost always rotate too quickly to be connected directly to wheels and other loads. Some sort of gear train is necessary to lower the speed, which conveniently increases the torque. Both the NXT and RCX motors have built-in gear reduction, as do the newer LEGO Power Functions motors. You might run across several other LEGO motors, but these are the only ones that can be ordered as accessories for the NXT.

The NXT motor is an impressive combination of gear reduction and feedback sensing (see Figure 1-28). The gear reduction alone involves eight different gears, and because the Rotation Sensor is way back by the motor end, it has one degree of revolution on the output shaft.

Figure 1-28. *NXT motor*

You can see the gears and Rotation Sensor in the breakdown shown in Figure 1-29.

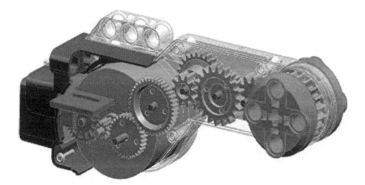

Figure 1-29. *Motor breakdown*

The NXT Rotation Sensor works on the same principle as the RCX Rotation Sensor, only on a smaller scale, as seen in the close-up photo in Figure 1-30.

Figure 1-30. *Close up of Rotation Sensor*

CHAPTER 2

■■■

Extreme Software

The programming language you choose is often a matter of personal preference. This book is mostly about building electronic hardware, but software is always an essential ingredient of any robotic project. Before tackling the projects in this book, you should be comfortable programming the NXT using just the software that comes with the MINDSTORMS kit known as NXT-G. We provide a brief survey of the major languages available to program the NXT in this chapter. Because this book relies exclusively on the NXT-G and an alternative language called NXC for its programming, we will only discuss them in detail.

NXT-G

NXT-G is the programming language that comes with the NXT. Its integrated development environment (IDE) window looks like Figure 2-1. The language is highly graphical, consisting of blocks that perform operations such as input, output, computation, and execution flow. You can download your NXT-G program to the NXT and perform other maintenance functions from the same environment.

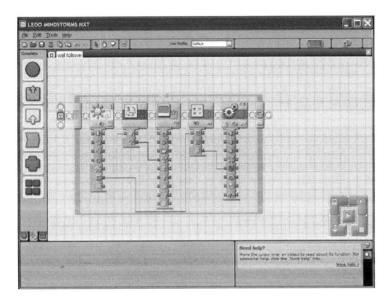

Figure 2-1. *NXT-G programming environment*

Data is passed from block to block on "data wires." For example, the first block in the program shown in Figure 2-2 is a Light Sensor. The light level as a percent number (0 to 100) is being passed to the Number block, to the Text block, and also to a Math block. The part of the block that sticks down from the icon is called the *data hub*. You can minimize the blocks to show only the inputs and outputs that are being used by clicking the top of the data hub.

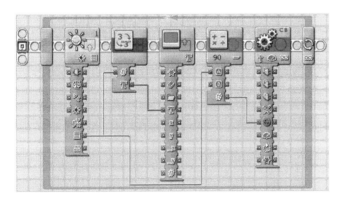

Figure 2-2. *NXT-G program with expanded blocks*

Figure 2-3 shows the neater and more compact version of the same program. You can add comments, such as the number 90 on the Math block, to make it easier to read the program.

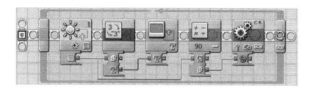

Figure 2-3. *NXT-G program with blocks minimized*

There are many ways to learn NXT-G. The documentation and tutorials that come with the NXT should be more than sufficient to get started. Beyond that, James Floyd Kelly has authored an entire book on NXT-G programming (*LEGO MINDSTORMS NXT-G Programming Guide*, Apress). However, there are a couple of advanced features of NXT-G that seem to have gone relatively undocumented. These features are critical to some of the projects in this book, so we will explore them now.

My Blocks

Subroutines are an important part of every computer language. They simplify the appearance of programs, making them easier to understand. They also make programming more efficient by allowing the reuse of common tasks. In NXT-G, subroutines are called *My Blocks*, and we'll explain how to use My Blocks through an example.

A common task in a NXT program is to show the value of a variable on the display. However, the basic Display Action block doesn't have the option to display Numbers, only Text. So every time you want to display the value of a variable you must convert it to Text first. Another shortcoming of the Display block is that you only have the choice of clearing the entire display. Finally, the block has some unfortunate defaults that force you to almost always reconfigure it.

A nice addition to the NXT-G block set would be a Display Number block that would simply write a number on a given row of the display. It would also be desirable if the block erased only the previous number's value from the screen without disturbing the whole display. Figure 2-4 shows the starting point for a My Block that will do just that.

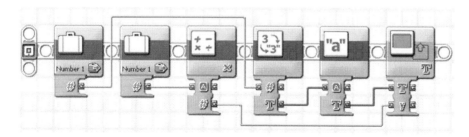

Figure 2-4. *Display Number My Block starting point*

The best way to start building a My Block is to use Variable blocks for any inputs or outputs of the block. In this case, we need two input blocks to represent the variable Number and another to represent the Row on the display. The Variable block can be configured to produce any of the three types of NXT-G variables; Logic, Number, or Text. Figure 2-5 shows the configuration widow for both of these blocks. The actual variable Name and its Value are not relevant at this point, only that its type is Number.

Figure 2-5. *Variable block configuration window*

Characters on the NXT display are 8 pixels high. For simplicity we will make the Row input to the Display Number block the row on the display, starting with row 0 on the bottom. That means we only need to multiply the value of Row by 8 to get the Y coordinate for the Display block. Figure 2-6 shows the Math block configuration widow where the Multiplication function is selected, and 8 is entered in the B field.

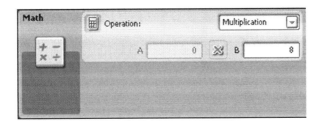

Figure 2-6. *Math block configuration window*

The Number to Text block converts the value to Text. This block creates the shortest possible string of characters to represent the value. The problem with that is if you display a large number with many digits and then immediately display a small number, some of the digits from the large number will be confusingly left on the screen. To prevent this, we tack 16 empty spaces onto the end of the converted value with a Text block, and that will be more than enough to erase any remaining characters. Although you can't see the 16 spaces, they have been typed in the B field of the Text block configuration window shown in Figure 2-7.

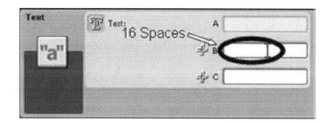

Figure 2-7. *Text block configuration window*

Finally, the Display block is configured to display Text, not to clear the screen, and to put the text with X equal to 0. Figure 2-8 shows the configuration of the block with the appropriate entries circled. The Y and Text values are not important because we will provide them as inputs to the block.

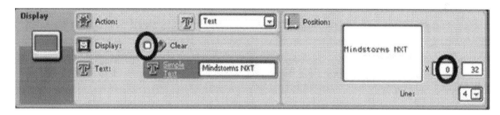

Figure 2-8. *Display block configuration window*

Now we are ready to actually create the My Block. First, select the four leftmost blocks by dragging across them as shown in Figure 2-9.

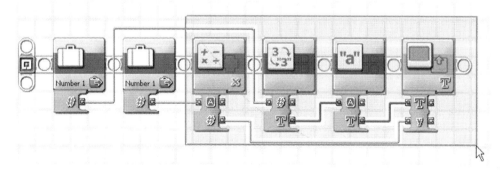

Figure 2-9. *Selecting blocks for the My Block*

The blocks will remain selected while you go to the Edit pull-down menu to select Make A New My Block, as shown in Figure 2-10.

Figure 2-10. *Select Make New My Block*

The My Block Builder will appear as shown in Figure 2-11. Notice that the wires that were connected to the Variable blocks are now little stubs on the right. Enter **Display Number** in the Block Name field. You can also enter a short description of the block before clicking the Next button.

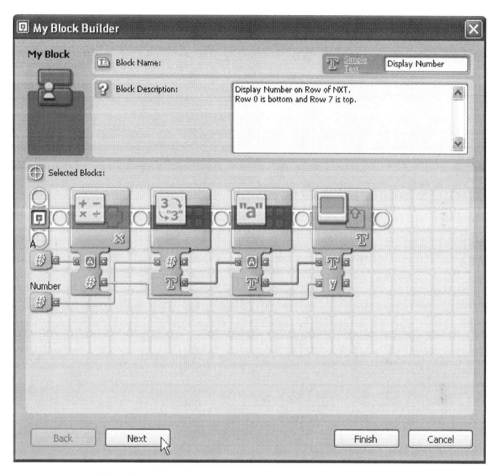

Figure 2-11. *My Block Builder window*

Now you create an icon for your block with the Icon Builder. You can only select from a palette of predefined symbols shown in Figure 2-12. However, you can select multiple symbols and build a more appropriate icon for your My Block. In this case we overlapped a symbol with the number 3 and some arrows with the NXT display to give the idea that the block displays numbers. When you are done, just click Finish.

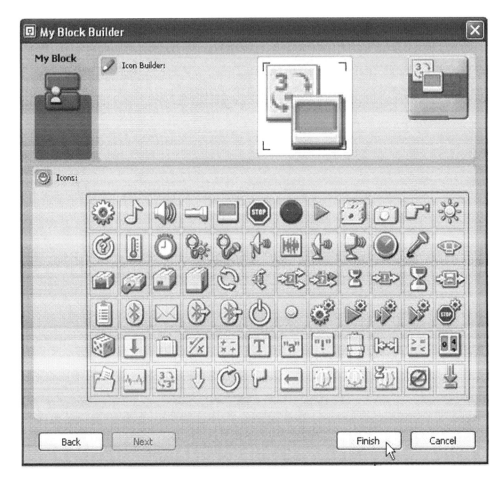

Figure 2-12. *Icon Builder*

The program will now show the new Display Number My Block where the four blocks were before. Double-click the My Block, and a new tab with the Display Number block program will automatically appear. Notice that the Row input is initially labeled "a" because that was the name of the input from the Math block. Click the "a" and change the name to **Row** as shown in Figure 2-13. Now save and close the Display Number window. The original starting point program is no longer needed and can be closed without saving.

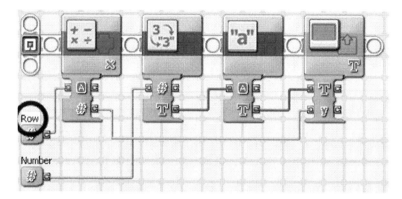

Figure 2-13. *Changing the input label to Row*

Now we will test the My Block by writing a little program. Start a new program and go to the Custom palette (See Figure 2-14) to get a copy of the Display Number My Block.

Figure 2-14. *Getting a Display Number block from the Custom palette*

Complete the rest of the program shown in Figure 2-15. The program first fills the screen with the Smile01 image and then keeps displaying the value of a random number that changes every second on Row 3.

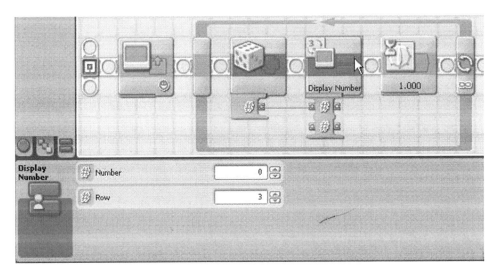

Figure 2-15. *Display Number test program*

When you run the test program, the NXT screen should look something like Figure 2-16. Notice that the program erases the entire row every time without disturbing the rest of the display. No matter how large the value might have been, no part of it will remain from one time to the next.

Figure 2-16. *Screen for Display Number test*

We made Display Number simple to illustrate how to create My Blocks. A more useful block would also allow you to write an identifying label before the number. Also you might want to erase the entire screen at some point. The content of a My Block called Display Value has these added features and is shown in Figure 2-17. The details of how to create this block will be left as an exercise.

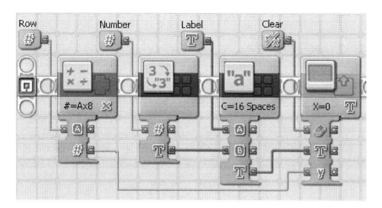

Figure 2-17. *Display Value My Block*

Figure 2-18 shows the Display Value block in a test program. The configuration window for the block shows how the Label can be entered, and checking the box in the Clear field will cause the NXT to clear the entire screen before writing the new value.

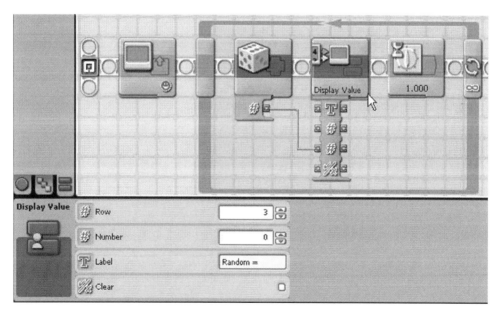

Figure 2-18. *Display Value My Block*

The screen output of this program is shown in Figure 2-19.

Figure 2-19. *Display Value output*

One last thing you need to understand about My Blocks is where they are kept on your computer. They aren't stored in the same directory as your NXT-G programs (…/LEGO Creations/MINDSTORMS Projects/Profiles/Default). You find them in a further subdirectory (/Blocks/My Blocks). If someone gives you a NXT-G program that contains My Blocks, they must be stored in that directory for everything to work.

With first–generation NXT-G software, this has to be done by hand. Second-generation NXT-G included a Create Pack and Go tool that made a single distribution (.rbtx) file that contains all the files needed for the program to run. That includes any My Blocks, image files, and sound files. The software also knows how to unpack these distributions and put all the files in the right place.

Importing Blocks

My Blocks are great for creating subroutines, but at some point you will need to add something so complex that it requires a whole new NXT-G block. Sensors, for example, require low-level NXT control that you just can't get in a My Block. Fortunately, you can easily import new blocks to NXT-G using the Block Import Wizard. We will illustrate the process by importing a couple of blocks essential to building projects in this book.

The original MINDSTORMS RCX had a couple of unique sensor types (Temperature and Rotation, for example) that are also supported by the NXT. The NXT software doesn't include these sensors by default because it is not very likely that someone buying a new NXT kit would own them. However, they are very useful for building homebrew sensors. Fortunately, LEGO provides a library of these Legacy Blocks on their MINDSTORMS Support page shown in Figure 2-20.

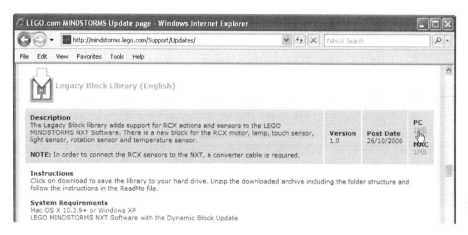

Figure 2-20. *Legacy Block Support download*

You need to download the library and unzip its contents to a folder on your computer. It doesn't really matter where the files are unzipped as long as you know where they are. The contents of the library can be seen in Figure 2-21. It is the Old Light Sensor and Temp Sensor that we will import. They are known as the Light* and Temperature* Sensors, where the * signifies legacy.

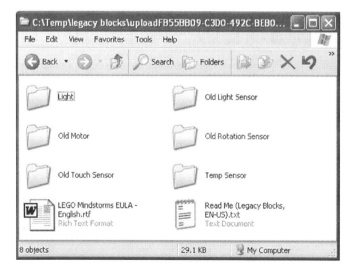

Figure 2-21. *Files in the Legacy Block library*

33

In the Tools pull-down menu, select Block Import and Export Wizard, as shown in Figure 2-22.

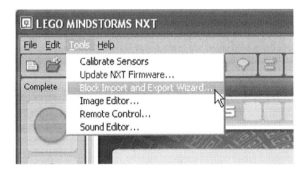

Figure 2-22. *Selecting the Block Import and Export Wizard tool*

A Wizard window will appear (see Figure 2-23).

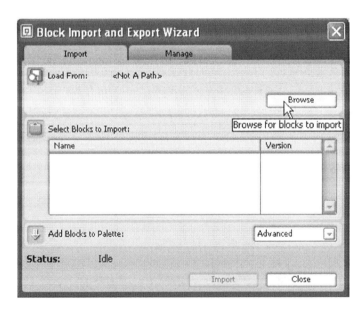

Figure 2-23. *Block Import and Export Wizard window*

Browse to the folder that contains the Legacy Blocks, and the window will look like Figure 2-24. You should stop at this level, but you could also navigate to the individual blocks as well.

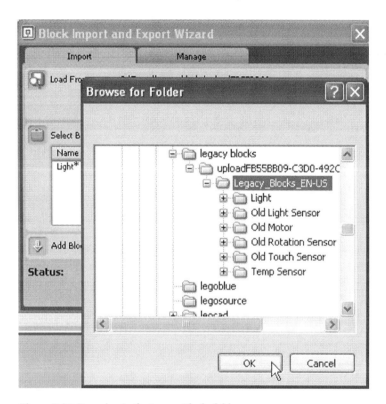

Figure 2-24. *Browsing to the Legacy Blocks folder*

You can select multiple blocks or just import one block at a time. Figure 2-25 shows both Light* and Temperature* Sensors selected. By default, new blocks go into the Advanced palette. Because both of these blocks are sensors, it makes more sense to add them to the Sensor palette. You select that from the palette list. After selecting the blocks and the palette, click Import.

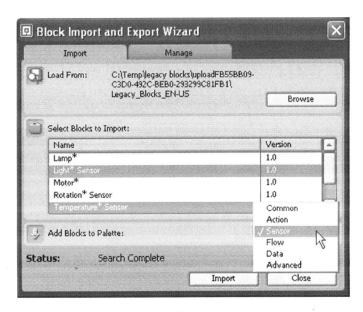

Figure 2-25. Selecting the Light* and Temperature* Sensor blocks

When you open the Sensor palette in the programming environment, you will now see the new Light* and Temperature* sensors. Figure 2-26 shows the Sensor palette for a second–generation NXT-G environment that also contains the Color sensor. You use these imported blocks exactly like the ones that came with the original software.

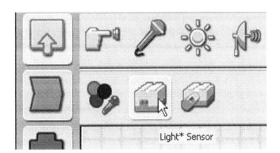

Figure 2-26. Appearance of the Sensor blocks palette after import

The nxtasy.org web site maintains the repository of non–LEGO NXT-G blocks that individuals have contributed (`http://nxtasy.org/repository/nxt-g-blocks/`). There are custom blocks for specialized input, output, and data operations. These blocks extend NXT-G and fill in missing functions to make it a more complete language

Not eXactly C and Bricx Command Center

NXT-G is a graphical language, as opposed to more traditional text-based computer languages such as C or Java. It is generally thought that graphical languages are easier to learn and use because they eliminate much of the tedious syntax required in text-based languages. The curious name Not eXactly C is derived from a C-like language called Not Quite C (NQC) developed by Dave Baum for the original RCX and the name NXT. Bricx Command Center (BricxCC) is the integrated development environment (IDE) for NXC and several other languages (see Figure 2-27). It is a powerful tool that not only facilitates general program development but also includes a suite of useful direct controls of the NXT.

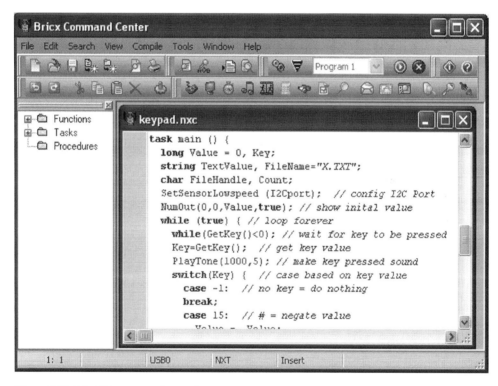

Figure 2-27. BricxCC programming environment

One of the greatest attractions for NXC and BricxCC is that they are freeware. The primary developer, John Hansen, provides them through a web site called Source Forge. He has published an entire book, *NXT Power Programming* (Variant Press, 2007) that is very helpful if you intend to develop a lot of programs in NXC.

We will not duplicate the vast amount of information and tutorials already available online for NXC. However, we will provide a quick start guide because several of the example programs in this book depend on using it. The place to start is Source Forge (`http://sourceforge.net/projects/bricxcc/`). Download the files as shown in Figure 2-28 (the exact appearance of these pages might change along with versions and dates).

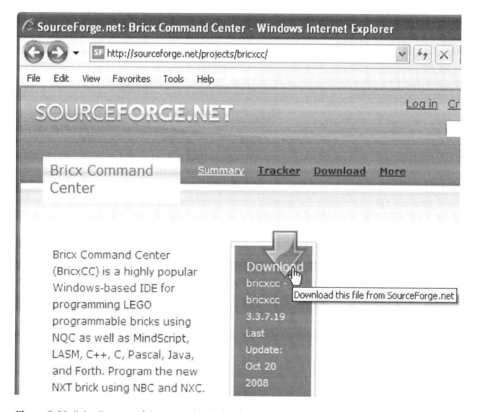

Figure 2-28. Bricx Command Center on SOURCEFORGE.NET

This should take you to the Download screen shown in Figure 2-29. There are several packages you can download, but you only want to select to BricxCC. NXC is automatically included in the BricxCC release, and I doubt you want to see the source code used to program the environment.

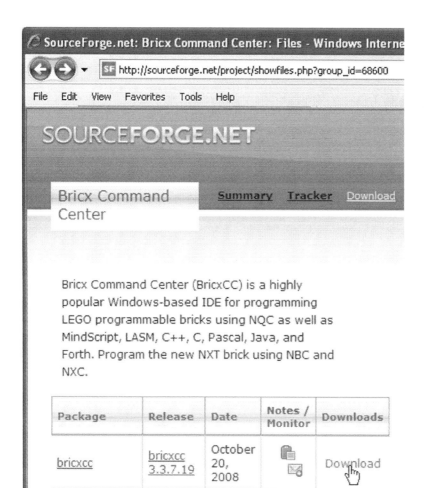

Figure 2-29. Downloading BricxCC

Select the file bricxcc_setup.exe (see Figure 2-30) because it will install everything you need to your computer in one step.

Figure 2-30. *Download Setup executable*

Just clicking the name will bring up the window shown in Figure 2-31, in which you click Run. You can also just save the file and run it later if you want.

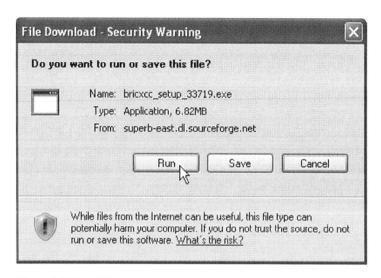

Figure 2-31. *Installing*

The BricxCC icon looks like Figure 2-32, and clicking it will bring up the BricxCC environment. The first thing it tries to do is establish a connection to a NXT.

Figure 2-32. *BricxCC Icon*

The Find Brick window (see Figure 2-33) has several options for communications port, type of brick, and Firmware. You will want USB, NXT, and Standard for your work in this book.

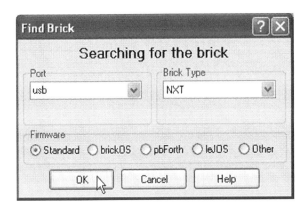

Figure 2-33. *Find Brick Window*

When you first install BricxCC, the assumed file type is NBC. Select Preferences from the Edit pull-down menu, as shown in Figure 2-34.

Figure 2-34. *Setting preferences*

In the Compiler tab of the Preferences window, select the NXC language radio button (the window can be seen in Figure 2-35). Click OK when you're done making the change. From now on, BricxCC will create NXC type files by default.

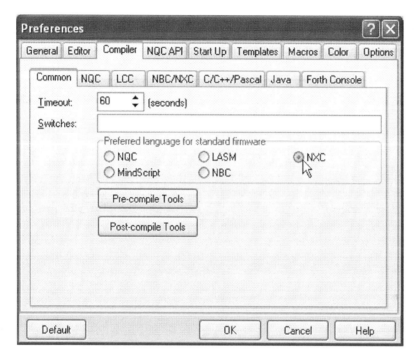

Figure 2-35. *Selecting NXC language default*

Create a new file and type in the tiny program shown in Figure 2-36. All the program does is play a 1,000Hz tone for 1,000ms (1 second) and then waits forever. It is about the simplest program you can write that still does something recognizable.

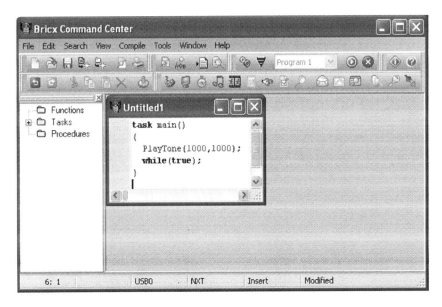

Figure 2-36. *Simple NXC test program*

When you finish entering the program, go to the Compile pull-down menu and select Download and Run (see Figure 2-37). Alternatively, you can press the Ctrl and F5 keys at the same time. In a few seconds the NXT will beep to confirm the download and then play the one second tone. You will have to press the dark grey button on the NXT to stop the program.

Figure 2-37. *Compile Download and Run*

Other Alternative Languages

There are many alternative languages you can use to program the NXT, and we assume that even more will become available over time. Often the choice of language is a matter of "using what you know" instead of any rational differences. Because you won't need any of these for the projects in this book, we will only briefly discuss them. More information about all of them can be found online.

RobotC

RobotC is a purchased C-based programming language for the NXT that includes an IDE much like NXC and BricxCC. Presumably, the documentation and support of purchased software like this makes it more suitable for education and training purposes. A wide range of books and packaged curricula are available that support using RobotC in the classroom.

However, there is another important reason you might choose this particular alternative language. Because it uses its own custom firmware, it achieves many times the program execution speed of NXT-G or NXC. This can be critical for high-speed control applications. Unfortunately, it also means the same NXT can't be used simultaneously with both NXT-G and RobotC.

LabVIEW

NXT-G is actually a simplified version of the graphical programming language called LabVIEW from National Instruments. NXT-G users should be able to quickly transition to it because of the similarities in program structure. The primary advantage of the LabVIEW IDE is that programs can be written to run on either the NXT or the PC. It uses the same firmware as NXT-G and NXC, so all three can be developed on the same NXT at the same time.

At the time this book was published, the LabVIEW NXT toolkit was available free of charge along with an older version of LabVIEW. The most significant documentation for the toolkit is the book *LabVIEW for LEGO MINDSTORMS NXT*, by Michael Gasperi (National Technology and Science Press, 2008). With added support and documentation, it too may become purchased software.

Java

In recent years, Java has become a very popular programming language especially for web development. NXJ is a reduced version of Java designed to run on the NXT, but also requires substitution of the firmware. It doesn't really include an IDE, but some generic ones can be used with it. The least mature of the alternative NXT languages, it requires more patience to get the environment and NXJ programs up and running than the alternatives. However, if you are proficient in Java, it might be the language you are most comfortable with when programming the NXT.

CHAPTER 3

■ ■ ■

Making a Connection

Before you can start homebrewing sensors and extending the outputs, you need to understand how to physically connect them to the NXT. In this chapter, we'll describe the unusual connector used on the NXT and describe the electrical signals found on the ports. We'll even show you some simple ways to make connections.

NXT Ports

The four sensor input ports are on the bottom of the NXT, and they're numbered from 1 to 4. The three motor output ports are on the top of the NXT, and they're labeled A, B, and C. If you look through the clear plug on the end of an NXT cable, you can see the six pins and wires that make up the interface. The wires are color coded: white, black, red, green, yellow, and blue. The function of each wire depends on whether it's connected to a sensor input or a motor output. It can also change depending on what type of sensor is used.

Sensor Input Pinout and Signal Description

Table 3-1 summarizes pin numbers, wire colors, and functions of input pins.

Table 3-1. *Colors and Names of Input Pins*

Pin Number	Color	Name
1	White	AN
2	Black	GND
3	Red	GND
4	Green	4.3V Power
5	Yellow	DIGI0
6	Blue	DIGI1

Pin 1—White—AN

You can use the first pin for two purposes: either as an analog input or as a 9V power supply used for compatibility with the old RCX sensors.

When you use the pin as an analog input, the signal is connected to a 10-bit analog-to-digital converter. The input signal can range from 0 to 5V, and is translated into a raw digital value between 0 and 1023. The value is sampled every 3 milliseconds. The pin is permanently connected to 5V through a 10KΩ pull-up resistor, and in the next few chapters you'll see how that simplifies many sensor designs.

You can also use the first pin as a power supply (Chapter 9 is totally devoted to sensors that use this supply). The voltage is actually that of the batteries. If you use NiMH batteries, you'll only be able to get about 7.2V from this output. You can use this power supply to power sensors that need higher voltages. For example, the RCX Light Sensor uses it, and the NXT Ultrasonic Sensor also uses the supply to get more power for its transmitter.

For these sensors, the NXT powers the sensor for 3 milliseconds and reads the value for 0.1 milliseconds. The sensor needs a capacitor to store power during the read interval. There is a current limit of approximately 14 mA per input port. If the current is greater than this value, the voltage rapidly drops.

The second and third pins are ground pins. These two pins are connected together in the NXT and in LEGO sensors. All signals are measured referring to these ground pins. Your sensor can use either pin, or both.

Pin 4—Green—4.3V Power

This is the main power supply for NXT sensors. It is not a good power supply for integrated circuits using 5V logic, but newer technology digital-logic parts can be powered from it. As opposed to the 9V power supply, it has a total current limit of 180 mA for all 7 input and output ports. Every port can use 25 mA on average, but it's also possible to consume more current on one port if another consumes less. For example, the currents for the NXT standard sensors and motor encoders are presented in Table 3-2.

Table 3-2. *Current Consumption of the NXT Sensors and Motors Encoders*

Device	Measured
Touch	0
Sound	1.7 mA
Light Sensor (light off)	2.6 to 3 mA (depends on light)
Light Sensor (light on)	16.3 mA
Ultrasonic Sensor	4 mA
Motor position encoders	9 to 12 mA (depends on encoder position)
All RCX sensors and motors (via cable adapter)	0

Pins 5 and 6—Yellow and Blue—DIGI0 and DIGI1

These pins are 3.3V digital signals and are directly connected to the NXT's microprocessor. They are primarily used for I²C communications, which we'll discuss in Chapter 13. When the pins are used as outputs, you need to be aware of the 3.3V limit. When they're used as input, the NXT has protection circuitry to prevent higher voltages from damaging anything. This circuit includes a 4.7kΩ resistor connected in series with the port. That way, even if the voltage of the sensor is too high, the corresponding current will be low so that the electronics aren't damaged.

In addition to I²C communications, DIGI0 is used for the NXT Light Sensor to command the state of the light emitting diode: on (reflection mode) or off (ambient light). (You'll see how to make use of this in Chapter 10.) It's also used in the Sound Sensor to switch between the DB mode (raw sound level) and the DBA mode (filtered sound level with similar sound sensitivity to the human ear).

Motor Output Pinout

Table 3-3 summarizes pin numbers, wire colors, and functions of output pins.

Table 3-3. *Colors and Names of the Output Pins*

Pin Number	Color	Name
1	White	M1
2	Black	M2
3	Red	GND
4	Green	4.3V POWER
5	Yellow	TACHO0
6	Blue	TACHO1

Pin 1 and 2—White and Black—M1 and M2

These pins provide power to the motor. The maximum voltage is the voltage of the batteries (9V for standard batteries and 7.2V for NiMH batteries). The motor is controlled by a circuit called an *H-bridge* (IC drivers LB1836M and LB1930M). An H-bridge is made from four transistors, and in the following figures the transistors are labeled 1 through 4.

The control circuit is designed so that transistors 1 and 2 on one side and 3 and 4 on the other side are not simultaneously conducting, to avoid shorting supply. Figure 3-1 shows the state of the transistors for going forward, with transistors 1 and 4 on. Figure 3-2 shows reverse with 2 and 3 on. Figures 3-3 and 3-4 illustrate the current flow for the brake and floating states.

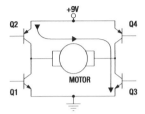

Figure 3-1. *Forward state*

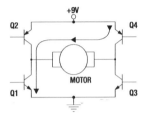

Figure 3-2. *Back state*

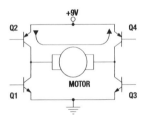

Figure 3-3. *Brake state*

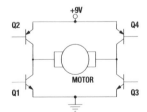

Figure 3-4. *Floating state*

The speed of the motor is controlled by pulse width modulation (PWM), as shown in the diagram in Figure 3-5. The motor power is rapidly turned on and off over a time interval. The speed of a motor depends on the average voltage applied to it, and the PWM method is a way of controlling this average voltage. It is energy efficient because the transistors are either completely off or on.

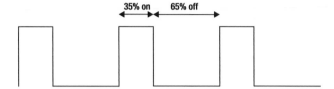

Figure 3-5. *PWM for motor at power level of 35%*

With the standard firmware, the length of the whole cycle is 128µs. This corresponds to 7,800Hz, which is an audible frequency that can sometimes be heard as a high-pitched whistling sound coming from the motor. For the NXT, the relationship between the motor speed and the applied voltage is linear. We'll describe all that in more detail in Chapter 12. The available current on the output ports is approximately 800mA for port A and 500mA for B and C. The output driver is equipped with thermal protection that limits the current if it is overheating.

Pin 3—Red—GND

This is the ground pin. Usually pins 2 and 3 are connected together in sensors, but not in motors. If a sensor is accidentally connected to an output port, the driver will be partially short-circuited. Fortunately, the driver is well protected, but it is a good idea to avoid this situation.

Pin 4—Green—4.3V POWER

This pin is connected to the 4.3V power supply that's shared between all the ports of the NXT.

Pin 5 and 6—Yellow and Blue—TACHO0 and TACHO1

The two inputs are used for the optical encoder built into the NXT motors. The encoder generates signals in quadrature, which allows the NXT to determine the direction and speed of the motor. The two signals are shifted rectangular pulses, and the shift represents one quarter of a cycle (hence the term *quadrature*). Figure 3-6 illustrates the signals for a motor turning forward, and Figure 3-7 is for reverse. The frequency of the signal gives the rotational speed of the motor. One-half cycle of the signal corresponds to one degree of rotation of the motor.

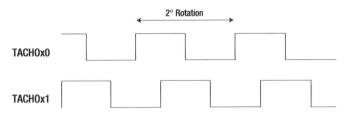

Figure 3-6. *Quadrature signals for motor running forward*

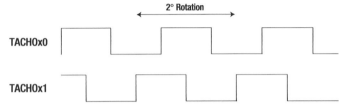

Figure 3-7. *Quadrature signals for motor running backward*

Physically Connecting to the NXT

The NXT port plugs are similar to RJ-12 modular telephone connectors with six contacts. However, the lock of the cable is on the side of the connector, instead of the middle, for a standard RJ-12 connector. Note that there are connectors, known as *DEC connectors*, that also have a side lock, but on the wrong side. Figure 3-8 illustrates an NXT cable and a standard RJ-12 connector.

Figure 3-8. *NXT cable on the left and standard RJ-12 cable on the right*

Buying Connectors

NXT plugs (see Figure 3-9) can be purchased from http://mindsensors.com. An RJ-12 crimping tool (shown in Figure 3-10) must be modified to crimp the plugs. You will find detailed instructions for doing this on Philo's web site: http://www.philohome.com/crimp/crimp.htm. You will also need flat 6 conductor wire, designed for telephone use. Fortunately, the color and order of the wires exactly matches those of the NXT cable.

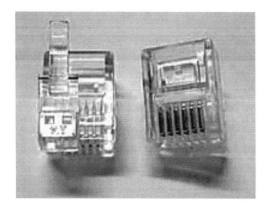

Figure 3-9. *NXT Plugs*

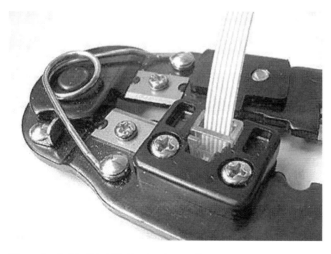

Figure 3-10. *Modified RJ-12 crimping tool*

Making Your Own Connectors

If the LEGO connectors aren't available or if you want to make your own, you can modify a telephone RJ-12 plug as explained in the following sections. However, be careful when choosing the cables to modify. The RJ-12 cables have six conductors on six positions, while RJ-11 cables (standard telephone cables) have four conductors on six positions, RJ-9 cables have four conductors on four positions, and RJ-45 (standard network cables) have eight conductors on eight positions (see Figure 3-11). There's no need to buy already-made RJ-12 cables. You can also buy cable and connectors, and crimp them yourself using a low-cost tool.

Figure 3-11. *These connectors are not suitable for NXT modification*

Taped Telephone Plug Method

For this method, remove the latch from a standard RJ-12 and its support by filing, as shown in Figures 3-12 and 3-13. Then wrap the plug with some cellophane tape so that it fits snugly in the NXT connector. This operation is illustrated in Figure 3-14. The sides and the top must be covered, but obviously not the bottom that contains the contacts. The method is simple, but not very reliable because there is no lock and it can be easily pulled out.

Figure 3-12. Filing off the latch

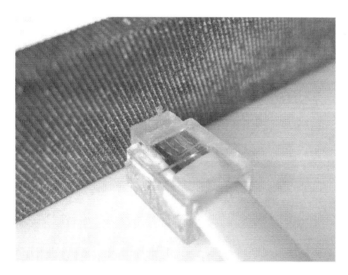

Figure 3-13. Filing off the front support

Figure 3-14. The connector is thickened with tape

Modified Telephone Plug Method

Philo pioneered the RJ-12 surgery method. The latch is cut, trimmed, and glued back on at the right place. The sliced RJ-12 connector is shown in Figure 3-15. This method is more delicate, but the connectors are more reliable. You can find a complete how-to on Philo's web site: http://philohome.com/nxtplug/nxtplug.htm.

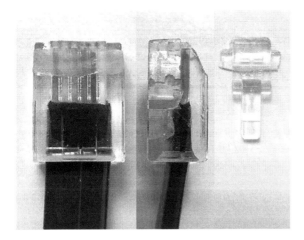

Figure 3-15. Sliced RJ-12 connector

Cut Cable Method

By far the easiest way to connect to the NXT is to order extra cables and just cut them in half. That gives you the plugs you need for two homebrew projects with wires already connected. The cable jacket is rather tough and must be cut with care so that you don't cut the insulation on the wires inside. Here are the step-by-step instructions:

1. Strip 2 inches (5cm) of the black jacket with a sharp knife, as illustrated in Figure 3-16. Be very careful not to hurt yourself or damage the underlying wires. Once stripped, the NXT cable contains six colored wires; in the photo in Figure 3-17, from left to right, they are blue, yellow, green, red, black, and white.

Figure 3-16. *Cut cable method step 1: cut the jacket*

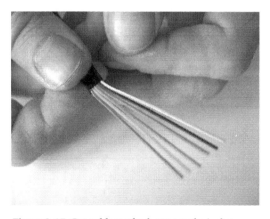

Figure 3-17. *Cut cable method: remove the jacket*

2. Strip all the wires—or only the ones you need if your sensor just uses a few of them. This operation is illustrated in Figure 3-18.

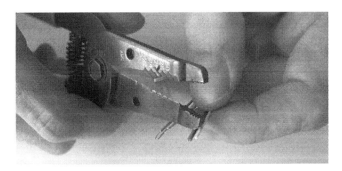

Figure 3-18. *Cut cable method step 2: strip the individual wires*

3. If you want to terminate the cable with a terminal block, fold down the color wire ends (see Figure 3-19). This is a good idea because inserting some insulator along with copper under the terminal screw provides some strain relief as the wire twists around and avoids wire breakage.

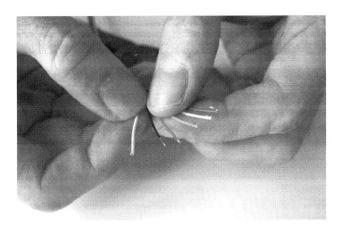

Figure 3-19. *Cut cable method step 3: fold wire back on insulation*

4. Screw the wires in the screw terminal, as shown in Figure 3-20. The first part of the cable should look like Figure 3-21.

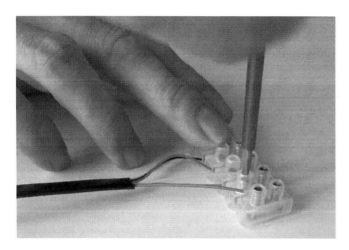

Figure 3-20. *Cut cable method step 4: screw the cable*

Figure 3-21. *Cut cable method step 5: all wires are screwed in the terminal block*

5. Now you can connect any type of wire you need (see Figure 3-22) to extend the cable or connect it to a homebrew sensor. You should use solid wire to connect the cable to a solderless breadboard for projects described in later chapters. Appendix A describes the details for this construction method.

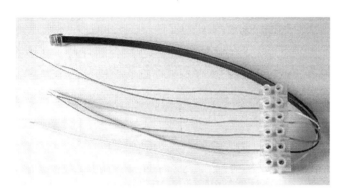

Figure 3-22. *The finished screw terminal breakout box*

Screw Terminal for Passive Sensors

This is a simplified version to be used for building sensors that need only a few of the pins. For example, only pins 1 and 2 (white and black wires) are used for sensors in Chapters 4 through 7. You can use a three-contact screw terminal to get a spare connection point, as illustrated in Figure 3-23.

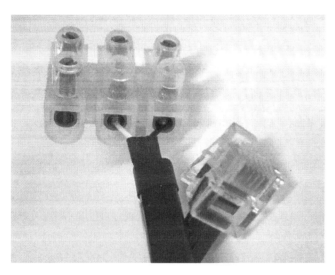

Figure 3-23. *Screw terminal cable for passive sensor prototyping*

The use of the spare connection point can be seen in this Temperature Sensor (described in Chapter 5) shown in Figure 3-24.

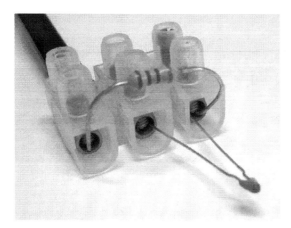

Figure 3-24. *Prototype of Temperature Sensor*

CHAPTER 4

■■■

Contact Sensors

Contact sensors are the simplest NXT sensors because they're only on or off. The LEGO Touch Sensor is a good example of a contact sensor. Homebrew contact sensors use the same NXT-G Touch Sensor block shown in Figure 4-1 as the LEGO ones. You probably already have everything you need to homebrew one. Even if you don't, the parts are readily available from electronic stores such as Radio Shack, and even from hardware stores.

Figure 4-1. *NXT-G Touch Sensor block*

We've already covered many methods for connecting to the NXT sensor inputs in Chapter 3. For contact sensors, we're interested in only two of the six possible connections. On the NXT plug, they're pins 1 and 2, and in the cable they're the black and white wires. For now, it doesn't even matter which is which. In the examples that follow, we'll show only some 18 gauge (0.8mm²) speaker wires, and you can presume they're attached to these two NXT connections.

Touching Wires

Bring up the View menu on the NXT and select the Touch Sensor on Port 1 using this sequence: NXT Menu ➤ View ➤ Touch ➤ Port 1. It should display the value 0, as in Figure 4-2. Now touch the ends of the wires together. Somehow the NXT knows you're doing that, and it changes the display to a 1, as in Figure 4-3. We know it isn't rocket science, but we can make a little game out of this.

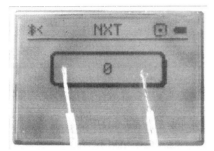

Figure 4-2. *Wires not touching reads 0*

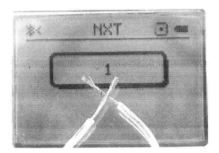

Figure 4-3. *Touching wires reads 1*

Electronic Surfboard

Over the years this game has been called many things. "Electronic Surfboard' is the most imaginative, but "The Steady Hand Game" seems a little mundane. It's a dexterity game in which you try to pass a small loop of wire over a second wire from one end to the other without touching it. To make things challenging, the second wire is bent randomly around like waves, hence the surfing theme. If the game is too easy, simply make the loop smaller.

Construction

Construction of the game is simple enough to figure out using only the photograph in Figure 4-4. We used heavy 12-gauge (3mm^2) house wire for the loop and waves, but you could use much lighter single-strand hook-up wire if you wanted to.

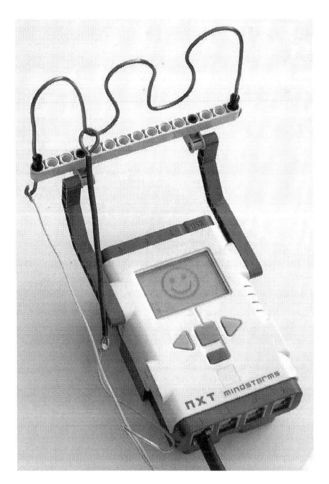

Figure 4-4. *Electronic Surfboard game*

Programming

In the elementary school version of the game, touching the wires together completes a circuit that has a buzzer in series with a battery. Our wires are connected to a 32-bit computer, so you might expect a little more than a buzz. Referring to the NXT-G program in Figure 4-5, the number of times the wires touch is counted up to a maximum limit. The display is animated, and a dramatic "Ouch" is played whenever there is a touch. Finally, if the limit of touches is reached, the "Game Over" phrase is uttered.

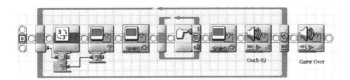

Figure 4-5. *NXT-G Surfboard game*

Switches

Switches are the workhorses of the input world. Figure 4-6 shows just a few examples of what switches look like. People turn switches on all the time to make things happen. If a room is too dark, you turn on a light with a switch. The vast majority of automated electrical control is also done with switches that change state with temperature, pressure, humidity, weight, liquid level, position, or practically anything else you can imagine. If the temperature is too cold, turn on the heat with a thermostatic switch.

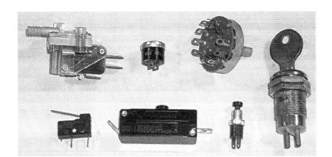

Figure 4-6. *Examples of switches: pressure, temperature, rotary, 2 micro, push button, and key*

The humble wall switch like the one in Figure 4-7 is the easiest place to start. Sure, it's overkill to use a switch capable of controlling about a thousand times the current of an NXT, but they are dirt cheap and simple to hook up. The nice thing about this type of toggle switch is that, unlike the LEGO Touch Sensor, it stays however you set it. Just connect one wire to each screw and you're ready to go.

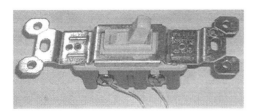

Figure 4-7. *Wall switch*

Parallel and Series

Sometimes you need more than four contact sensors for a project, but the NXT only has four inputs. In Chapter 13, we'll cover ways to expand the number of NXT sensor inputs, but for now let's look at some simple ways to connect multiple switches to the same input.

If you connect more than one switch to the same input by connecting them in parallel as shown in Figure 4-8, then when any switch is turned on the NXT input is considered to be on. You can use this for a vehicle with bumper switches located on all four sides. Touching any one of the bumpers triggers the same avoidance reaction. You could easily make this type of connection with the old RCX by just plugging multiple switches onto the same input. The NXT connectors don't allow this, so you have to do it with wire.

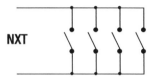

Figure 4-8. Parallel switches on one input

If the switches are connected in a series, as shown in Figure 4-9, then they must all be on to make the NXT input on. Typically this kind of circuit is used for applications in which a unanimous vote from multiple inputs is needed to cause some important thing to happen. For example, a switch located on the bottom of each foot of a robot dog is used to make sure it has all its feet firmly planted on the ground.

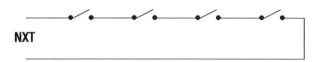

Figure 4-9. Series switches on one input

Antenna Sensor

You can build an antenna sensor or feeler using the same principle as the Electronic Surfboard game. The antenna or whisker is made from an electric guitar D string. This type of string is a thin wire that has another steel wire wound around it to make it heaver. The A and E strings also work, but their wire is thicker and stiffer, which makes a slightly less-sensitive feeler. You can purchase a whole set of inexpensive guitar strings at music stores and even discount stores. One guitar string is long enough to make about five sensors. Figure 4-10 shows the NXT Quick Start Vehicle outfitted with two antenna sensors.

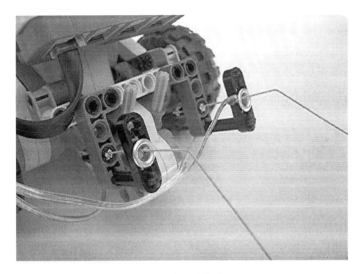

Figure 4-10. *NXT Quick Start Vehicle with feelers*

The contact ring support is a type of Technic lift arm beam that isn't included with the NXT kit. You can get this part as the Technic Lever 3M, part number LFH101, from the online LEGO Shop. The ring is a 3/16-inch (4.76mm) brass eyelet shown in Figure 4-11. Normally they are used to reinforce a material such as fabric or leather, in which a lace or screw has to pass through it. You should be able to find them at hardware or craft supply stores.

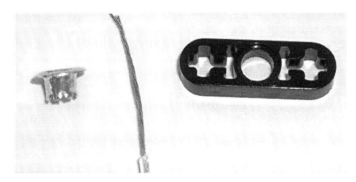

Figure 4-11. *Contact ring: step 1*

Using 18-gauge speaker wire, loop it through the hole twice, as shown in Figure 4-12, and twist it on itself. This decreases the hole diameter a little and makes the eyelet fit tightly without any glue. After you press the eyelet into the hole, it will look like Figure 4-13.

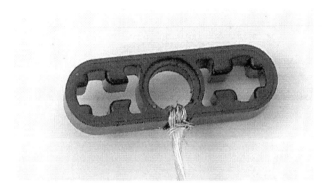

Figure 4-12. *Contact ring: step 2*

Figure 4-13. *Contact ring: step 3*

Use about 7 inches (18cm) of guitar wire for the antenna. Don't cut the guitar wire with your good electronic cutters; it is very hard and will probably wreck them. Use heavy-duty diagonal cutters or pliers to cut it instead. Bend one end of the wire into the T shape shown in Figure 4-14. The base of the antenna is made from a Technic friction pin and a little aluminum foil.

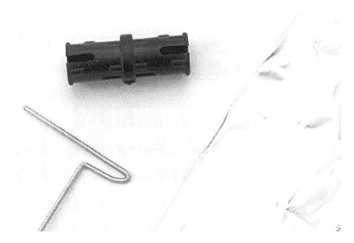

Figure 4-14. *Antenna base: step 1*

Feed the antenna through one of the little slots in the side of the pin (see Figure 4-15). Work the T end so that it bridges through the slot on the other side of the pin. You can now connect the other speaker wire to the antenna through the loop in the T.

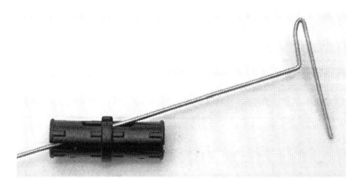

Figure 4-15. *Antenna base step 2*

Twist some aluminum foil into a thin roll and pack it all around the wire to center it inside the pin. This also keeps it from pulling out of the pin. Your finished antenna base should look like Figure 4-16.

Figure 4-16. *Antenna base: step 3*

Combine the antenna and contact ring using the Technic right-angle beam and an axle assembled like Figure 4-17. The distance from the pin to the contact ring adjusts the sensitivity of the feeler. The closer the ring is to the pin, the less sensitive the feeler becomes. If you're making more than one, it's a good idea to reverse the direction of the right-angle beam so you end up with two symmetrical sensors.

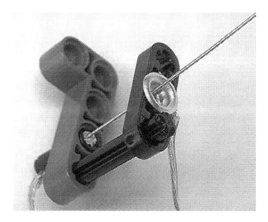

Figure 4-17. *Finished antenna sensor*

After you've mounted the antenna sensors on the vehicle, bend the antennas so they point slightly down and outward. You'll probably need to modify the construction to make them work with other robot designs. The antennas might also need to be periodically adjusted because they get bent from use.

The sensors are connected in parallel, as shown in Figure 4-18, and use only one input for the avoidance reaction. The NXT-G program is shown in Figure 4-19. The robot goes forward until one of the feelers touches something. Then the robot quickly reverses and turns about 90 degrees. After that it continues to go forward until it hits something again.

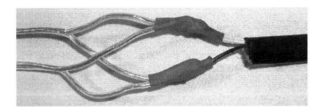

Figure 4-18. *Parallel connection of two antenna sensors*

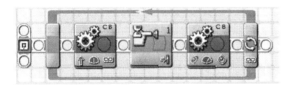

Figure 4-19. *Quick Start Vehicle with feeler program*

Going Further

In this book we try to emphasize designs that involve all new components so that you can reproduce the projects exactly as presented. However, switches are everywhere. There are two nice ones in that discarded computer mouse over there in your junk box. Recycling switches is a practical and economical way to expand your NXT's sensor inputs.

CHAPTER 5

■ ■ ■

Resistive Sensors

Resistive sensors are an example of a NXT passive-type sensor. The term *passive sensor* sounds like it could be an oxymoron. After all, how could anything that senses also be passive? The term is a carryover from the old RCX days when there were only two types of sensors: those that required a power supply and those that didn't. You probably figured out that passive sensors were the type that didn't. The contact sensors you learned about in Chapter 4 were also passive sensors.

Connecting a resistive sensor to the NXT is just like the contact sensor. You use only two of the six sensor input connections. On the NXT plug, they're pins 1 and 2; in the cable, they're the black and white wires. It still doesn't matter which is which. In the examples that follow, we'll show you 18 gauge (0.8mm²) speaker wires, and you can presume that they're attached to these two NXT connections.

Analog-to-Digital Conversion

There's a lot more going on inside your NXT than just what's needed to decide whether a switch is on or off. The NXT uses an analog-to-digital converter to change the analog voltage between the two wires into a digital number, from 0 for 0V to 1,023 for 5V. Right about now you're probably wondering, "A switch doesn't make voltage, so how is the NXT going to convert anything?" Inside the NXT, a 10kΩ resistor is permanently connected from pin 1 (or the white wire in the cable) to 5V. Pin 2 (or the black wire in the cable) is permanently connected to ground or 0V. Figure 5-1 is a diagram of the internal circuitry.

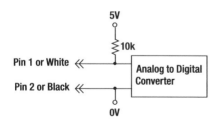

Figure 5-1. NXT sensor input

If all you have is a switch hooked up to the input as in Figure 5-2, the input is either pulled up to 5V when the switch is off or 0V when it is on. Those are the extremes, but if the connection is somewhere between open and shorted, you get a voltage somewhere between 0V and 5V, and a converter value between 0 and 1,023. This is what happens when you connect a resistor to the input, as in Figure 5-3.

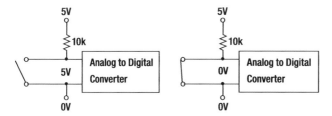

Figure 5-2. *Open and closed switch input*

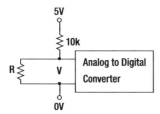

Figure 5-3. *Resistor input*

A circuit with two resistors in series is called a *voltage divider* because the voltage across both of them is divided in the middle. How much the voltage is divided depends on the values of the resistors. This equation describes the voltage across the external resistor R, where the 10,000 comes from the 10kΩ resistor inside the NXT, and the 5 is from the 5V supply:

$$V = \frac{R}{10,000 + R} 5$$

The NXT analog-to-digital converter scales the voltage to what are called Raw units. The 1,023 comes from the fact that the converter has 10 bits of accuracy, and 1,023 is the biggest number you can express with 10 bits:

$$Raw = \frac{1023}{5} V$$

When the NXT thinks it's connected to a switch, it compares the Raw value to 460. If the input value is greater, it takes the input to be open; if it's less, it is closed. The Raw value is available in NXT-G by using the expanded Touch Sensor block shown in Figure 5-4. The lowest terminal with the 10101010 next to it outputs the Raw value.

Figure 5-4. *Expanded Touch Sensor block*

Ohmmeter

Although you can buy a good digital Ohmmeter for a fraction of the cost of a NXT, sometimes it's handy to know the resistance of whatever you have connected to the input. With a little algebra, you can write an equation that converts Raw values into the value of the external resistor R:

$$R = \frac{10,000 \text{ Raw}}{1023 - \text{Raw}}$$

Ohmmeter Program

Creating a NXT-G program to display the resistance is straightforward. All you need to do is read the input and run the Raw value through the equation, as illustrated in Figure 5-5. The smallest resistance value displayed greater than 0 is 9Ω, and the biggest value is 1,022,000Ω. That's a pretty wide range.

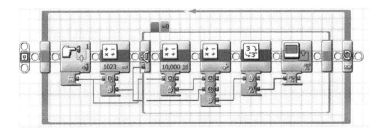

Figure 5-5. Ohmmeter program

One little problem occurs when the input isn't connected to anything, and the Raw value becomes 1,023. That results in a division by 0, which is correctly infinity, but the NXT doesn't do infinity. It just gives up and outputs a value of 0. For that single case, Figure 5-6 shows how the NXT-G program displays the word *Infinity*.

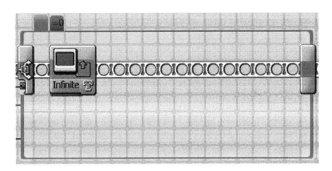

Figure 5-6. Ohmmeter program special open-circuit case

Measuring Salinity

As long as you've made an Ohmmeter, you might as well use it for something scientific. *Salinity* is an important water-quality measurement because plants and animals can't tolerate a lot of salt in their water. The more salt dissolved in water, the more conductive or less resistive it becomes. It's remarkable how little salt it takes to drop the resistance in half.

Stick the two bare ends of the wires into a flask of clean water, as shown in Figure 5-7, and note the resistance. Ideally, pure water will have infinite resistance, but tap water will probably show some resistance. Carefully, without moving the distance between the wires, add a few grains of salt. Wait for it to dissolve entirely and note the resistance.

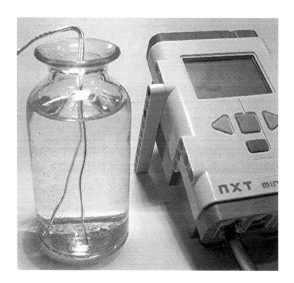

Figure 5-7. Measuring the salinity of water

Repeat this process till you have a plot of resistance and concentration, as shown in Figure 5-8. Then you can use the plot backward to determine the salinity given the resistance of an unknown sample.

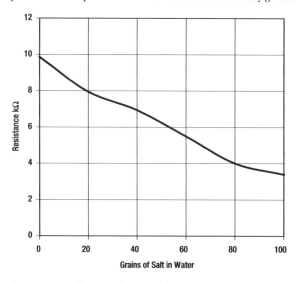

Figure 5-8. Resistance of water with varying amounts of salt

Legacy Temperature Sensor

Temperature is one of the most useful measurements you can make with your NXT. You can use the NXT as a digital thermometer to monitor the temperature of an experiment continuously, or you can log the temperature into a file to see how the value has changed over a long time period. You can even use the value in a control loop that regulates temperature.

LEGO makes a Temperature Sensor, as pictured in Figure 5-9 (9V Temperature Sensor PN#W979889). It is a legacy sensor from the RCX and requires the NXT conversion cable (PN#770323) or one you make yourself with instructions in Chapter 11.

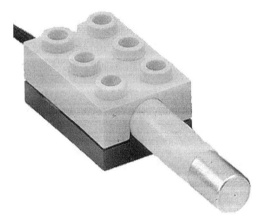

Figure 5-9. *LEGO Legacy Temperature Sensor*

It's a little expensive, considering that you can build your own for a fraction of the price. The LEGO sensor isn't suitable for every sensing application anyway. For example, I wouldn't use it to monitor the temperature inside a hamster cage—the hamster might mistake it for a chew toy.

The temperature-measuring range of the NXT is from –4°F to 158°F (–20°C to 70°C). LEGO probably didn't want you to boil your temperature probe. Although limited, it still represents a decent range of temperatures that you're likely to encounter.

Using the sensor in a NXT-G program requires importing the Legacy Temperature block shown in Figure 5-10. (We covered importing NXT-G blocks like this back in Chapter 2.)

Figure 5-10. *Legacy Temperature block*

The configuration window for the block, in which you decide whether the reading is in Celsius or Fahrenheit, is shown in Figure 5-11. An important thing to know about the block is that the temperature output is ten times the actual temperature. That allowed you to have 1/10 degree accuracy with only the integer arithmetic of the original NXT software.

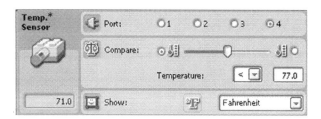

Figure 5-11. *Configuration window*

Thermistors

The LEGO Legacy Temperature Sensor is based on an electronic component called a thermistor, like those illustrated in Figure 5-12. A thermistor is an unusual resistor that changes resistance value with temperature. (The name *thermistor* is just the combination of the two words *thermal* and *resistor*.) The particular thermistor used with the NXT decreases in resistance with an increase in temperature. Because the slope of the relationship between temperature and resistance is negative, the type is known as a Negative Temperature Coefficient (NTC) thermistor.

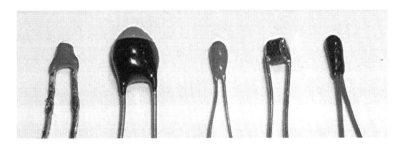

Figure 5-12. *Examples of thermistors, with the GE RL0503-5820-97-MS on the right*

A thermistor is manufactured by attaching two wires to a tiny pellet of semiconducting material, which is usually a metallic oxide (see Figure 5-13). When the temperature of the pellet increases, more electrons in the semiconductor are made available to conduct electricity, so the resistance goes down. Usually the whole thing is coated with epoxy to seal it from moisture and other contamination. Variations in the room temperature resistance and the amount that the resistance changes with temperature create hundreds of different thermistors to choose from. Additionally, size, packaging, and accuracy take the selection well into the thousands.

Figure 5-13. *Semiconducting pellet inside a thermistor*

Reverse Engineering the NXT

How do we find a thermistor compatible with the NXT? We start by reverse engineering the NXT Raw-to-temperature-conversion equation. The plot in Figure 5-14 was made by recording both the temperature and Raw values simultaneously. As you can see, the NXT conversion equation isn't a simple offset or multiplier.

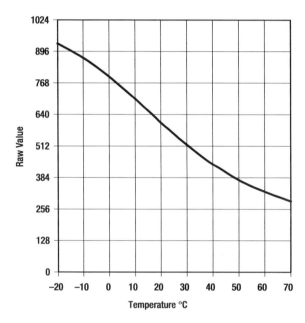

Figure 5-14. *Plot of temperature and Raw value*

You already know how to convert a Raw value into a resistance measurement from the NXT Ohmmeter project. Feeding Raw values into the equation and calculating R values allows you to make a plot of temperature and sensor resistance, as in Figure 5-15. You must match this plot for a NXT-compatible Temperature Sensor.

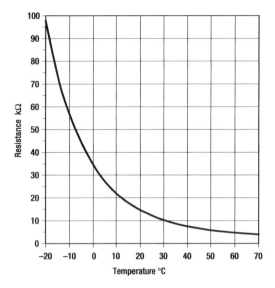

Figure 5-15. *NXT Temperature Sensor resistance plot*

You can compute the resistance value of any thermistor by a rather complex equation, where β is related to the shape of the curve and R_{25} is the resistance at 25°C. The two parameters, β and R_{25}, are all that's needed to thermoelectrically define a thermistor:

$$R = R_{25}\exp\left[\frac{\beta(25-T)}{(T+273.15)(298.15)}\right]$$

The value for R_{25} from the NXT Temperature Sensor plot is 12.2kΩ. This is a big problem because no commercially available thermistor has an R_{25} of 12.2kΩ. The closest value is 10kΩ. So LEGO must have put a 2.2kΩ resistor in series with the thermistor for some reason. We'll spare you the painful details, but the β value can be determined by a least squares regression between the equation and the NXT plot. The value turns out to be 3,750, or a temperature coefficient of –4.22%/°C @25°C.

The good news is that you can buy a thermistor just like this with an R_{25} of 10kΩ and a β of 3,750. It's the GE Infrastructure Sensing type NHQM103B375T10. The bad news is that it's a tiny surface-mount chip to which you can't easily make connections. There are a lot of thermistors with an R_{25} of 10kΩ, but their β values are a little different.

Probably just to make life interesting, not all supply catalogs print values for β. Instead they give an equivalent temperature coefficient expressed as %/°C @25°C, which is usually a negative number around 5. You can just multiply the temperature coefficient by –888 to convert it to β. Occasionally you'll see a Resistance Ratio, which is the resistance at 0°C divided by the resistance at 50°C. You can convert this to a β, too, with an equation where *ln* is the natural log function. If you work the equation backward, it turns out that the NXT thermistor Ratio should be 8.37.

$$\beta = \frac{\ln(Ratio)}{.0005665}$$

A thermistor with a β of 3,907 or temperature coefficient of –4.4%/°C would have less than 1/2°C error over most of the temperature range you're likely to be measuring, and barely a degree at the extremes, as shown in Figure 5-16. That thermistor is a GE Infrastructure Sensing type RL0503-5820-97MS, which can be purchased from Digi-Key (PN# KC003T-ND.) It features good accuracy, insulated leads, and is reasonably priced.

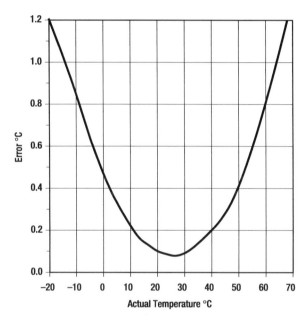

Figure 5-16. *Temperature error using a thermistor with b = 3907*

Homebrew Legacy Temperature Sensor

You can make the thermistor into an NXT Legacy Temperature Sensor using the screw terminal method described in Chapter 3 or with a little solder and heat shrink tubing to make it more compact. We need to put a 2.2kΩ resistor in series with the thermistor to make it look just like the LEGO Sensor to the NXT. In addition to different values of resistance, resistors come in different sizes to accommodate heat generated by the part. Quarter- and half-watt values are the most common for leaded parts. The power levels are insignificant in this case, so we'll use the quarter-watt size. Resistors also come with different accuracies, with 1% and 5% most common. A 5% accuracy will do just fine, so the color-coded bands on the resistor should read red-red-red-gold. Figure 5-17 shows all the components you need except the heat shrink tubing.

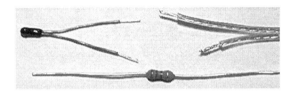

Figure 5-17. Homebrew Temperature Sensor step 1

After cutting the leads of the resistor and stripping the wire to about 3/16" (4mm) as shown in Figure 5-18, solder the thermocouple, resistor, and wire as shown. Don't forget to slide the heat shrink tubing on first! Watch that you don't heat the tubing up with the soldering iron and shrink it before you want to.

Figure 5-18. Homebrew Temperature Sensor step 2

After soldering, slide the heat shrink tubing over the joints and shrink by using a hair dryer. You should end up with something like Figure 5-19.

Figure 5-19. Homebrew Temperature Sensor step 3

Shrinking a large piece of tubing over the whole assembly, as in Figure 5-20, protects it and gives it a more "finished" look.

Figure 5-20. Finished homebrew Temperature Sensor

Depending on how you intend to use your Temperature Sensor, you might need to package it further. An easy way to waterproof the sensor is to slip it into one of those long skinny balloons that clowns twist up to make animals (see Figure 5-21). You also could put it into a metal tube to guard it from hamster teeth.

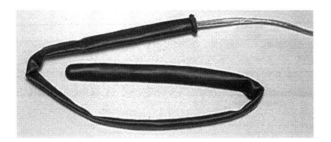

Figure 5-21. Waterproofed Temperature Sensor

NXT Digital Thermometer

The easiest way to use your Temperature Sensor is with the NXT-G program shown in Figure 5-22. This turns the NXT into a digital thermometer. The thermistor has very little mass, and you'll be amazed how fast the temperature changes by just pinching the Temperature Sensor between your fingers. The temperature displayed will be ten times larger than the actual temperature. For example, 40 degrees will be displayed as 400.

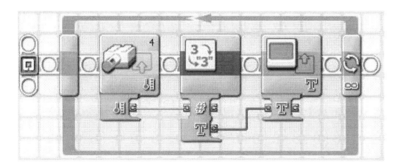

Figure 5-22. NXT digital thermometer program

A quick way to check the calibration of your new Temperature Sensor is to submerge it in a mixture of crushed ice and a little water. You definitely need to use a balloon to waterproof the sensor, as illustrated in Figure 5-23. Poke a channel through the ice with something like a pencil, and insert the sensor into the middle. After a few minutes, the NXT should read a temperature just a little above freezing, such as 0.5°C.

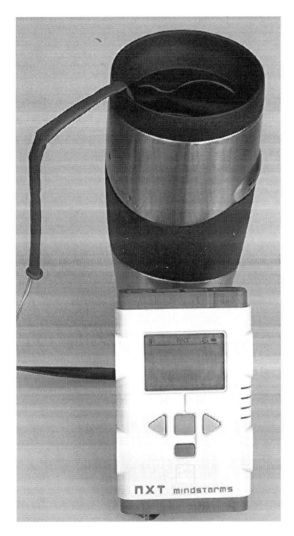

Figure 5-23. *Measuring the temperature of ice water*

Adding some salt to the ice water mixture forces some of the ice to melt. As it does, it absorbs heat, and the temperature of the water drops. We put in only a tablespoon of salt, and the temperature dropped more than 8°C. You can approach a temperature of –20°C this way.

Relative Humidity Sensor

Relative humidity is a measure of how much moisture is in the air. One hundred percent means you can't get more water into the air, so it must be a very damp place. Zero percent is totally dry, so it must be in a desert somewhere. People are comfortable within only a limited range of temperature and humidity. The plot in Figure 5-24 shows the comfort zone for an average person in both the winter and summer. In the summer you can see that the humidity must only be 50% to be comfortable at 27°C (81°F).

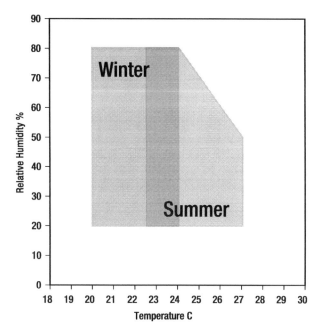

Figure 5-24. *The comfort zone*

One way to measure the relative humidity is to make two temperature measurements. One that directly measures the air is called the *dry bulb temperature (Tdry)*, and the other temperature is of a wet object—the *wet bulb temperature (Twet)*. You can then use the dry bulb temperature and the difference between it and the *wet bulb temperature (DeltaT)* to look up the relative humidity in a table or calculate it from a formula.

$$H = 100 - \frac{244\,(\text{Tdry} - \text{Twet})}{(\text{Tdry} + 120)}$$

Figure 5-25 shows how to measure the wet bulb temperature. The Temperature Sensor extends only to about the lip of the jar. The rest of the absorbent material wrapped around it supplies water from the vial to keep the sensor wet. Don't submerge the sensor into the water, or else you'll read a temperature that's warmer than the wet bulb.

Figure 5-25. Wet bulb Temperature Sensor

The humidity calculation is related to the ratio of vapor pressures of water at the two temperatures, plus other factors such as air pressure. They're rather complex, and the NXT doesn't have the math capability to implement them. Instead, you can use a simplified equation that won't have more than 5% error over the range you're likely to be measuring. The equation expects the temperatures to be in Celsius.

The NXT-G program in Figure 5-26 shows the equation converted to code. The original NXT used only integer arithmetic, so the multiplication by 244 needed to be done before the divide. You don't need to worry about the order with second–generation NXT software because it uses floating-point arithmetic. Remember to set the Legacy Temperature blocks for Celsius.

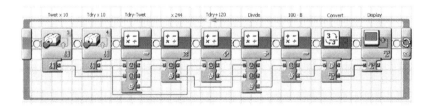

Figure 5-26. Relative humidity program

Light Sensor

You're probably saying, "I already have a perfectly good Light Sensor." Is your sensor's sensitivity to wavelength the same as the human eye? Is it smaller than a pencil eraser? Does it have an extremely broad operating range, and can it be purchased for less than $2? Not if you're talking about the NXT Light Sensor. Also, what if your project needs more than one Light Sensor? The Cadmium Sulfide (CdS) photocell or Light Dependent Resistor (LDR) is a good alternative to the NXT Light Sensor.

LDRs vary in resistance over a wide range of values, from about 1,000 ohms in bright daylight to millions of ohms in total darkness. They are made from a ceramic disk with two electrodes plated on the face that have a thin gap between them. The gap between the electrodes is maximized in length by making it into a serpentine shape that can be seen through the layer of photoresistive—in this case CdS—material painted on the surface.

A large variety of CdS LDRs are commercially available, such as those in Figure 5-27. They differ primarily in the operating resistance range and package size. They all work with the NXT to some extent, but when buying individual devices, look for a bright light resistance such as 3kΩ. This maximizes the range of values the NXT can convert given the internal 10kΩ pull-up resistor. Don't worry about characteristics such as voltage or wattage. Also, don't confuse photocells with solar cells, which actually generate voltage from light.

Figure 5-27. *Examples of CdS photoresistors or Light Dependent Resistors (LDRs)*

Building the Light Sensor

The easiest way to build your own Light Sensor is to purchase an assortment of five LDRs from Radio Shack (276-1657). If there are several packages in the store to pick from, get an assortment that has at least two that look exactly the same. This pair will come in handy for projects that need equally matched sensors. The other approach is to buy some specific LDRs; then you know exactly what you're going to get.

The Selco Products' plastic-coated type 8P LDRs are ideal LDRs for the NXT, in particular the model 8001 (Digi-Key PDV-P8001-ND). These LDRs have a low cell resistance in bright light, and the 5.08mm diameter is also compatible with the Technic hole size for easy mounting.

Start by stripping the connecting wires and clipping the leads of the LDR to about 3/16 inch (4mm). Make sure that you slide some heat shrink tubing over the wires before you solder the connections, as shown in Figure 5-28.

Figure 5-28. *Homebrew Light Sensor step 1*

Twist the wires around the LDR leads and solder them to look like Figure 5-29.

Figure 5-29. *Homebrew Light Sensor step 2*

Push the tubing tight to the LDR and shrink it with a hair dryer. Your sensor should look like Figure 5-30.

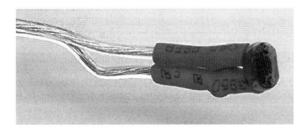

Figure 5-30. *Homebrew Light Sensor step 3*

Slide an additional piece of heat shrink tubing over both wires to additionally strain-relief the connections. Now your sensor should look like Figure 5-31.

Figure 5-31. Homebrew Light Sensor step 4

Run the connecting wires through the hole in the Technic right-angle beam, as shown in Figure 5-32. Using a friction pin and a blue axle pin, sandwich the photocell with a three-hole beam. This beam holds the LDR in place and makes the light sensitivity of the sensor more directional.

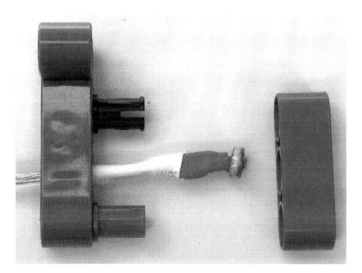

Figure 5-32. Homebrew Light Sensor assembly

Your finished Light Sensor should look like Figure 5-33. When you're making more than one of these, it's a good idea to reverse the direction of the right-angle beam. That way you end up with two symmetrical sensors.

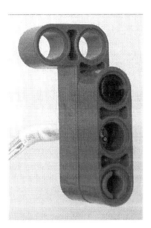

Figure 5-33. *Finished homebrew Light Sensor*

Comparison of LEGO and CdS Light Sensor

The resistance of a CdS LDR drops with light level, just like the NTC thermistor resistance changes with temperature, and for the same reason. Probably not all LDRs work this way, but you can model the resistance of the type 8P sensors with a simple equation. For the 8001, the value of K is 10,000:

$$R = \frac{K}{\sqrt{Lux}}$$

Humans experience light levels over a huge range in the course of a day. Table 5-1 shows that light variation from starlight to sunlight is a variation from 0.001 to 100,000 lux.

Table 5-1. *Typical Light Levels*

Light	Lux
Daylight	50,000–100,000
Hazy	25,000–50,000
Cloudy bright	10,000–25,000
Store windows	1,000–5,000

Table 5-1. *Typical Light Levels (continued)*

Light	Lux
Office	200–500
Living room	50–200
Hallway	50–100
Street lights	1–20
Full moon	0.01–0.2
Starlight	0.001

The resistance of the CdS sensor over a somewhat more limited range is shown in the plot in Figure 5-34. The light level axis has to be plotted with a logarithmic scale to allow for the wide range of values.

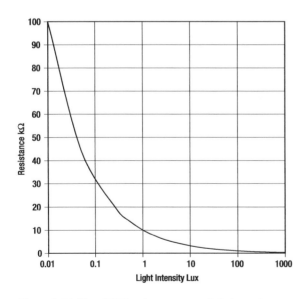

Figure 5-34. *Plot of LDR resistance versus light intensity*

Using the resistance equation for the 8001 LDR, a Raw value can be predicted for the sensor at various light levels and plotted in Figure 5-35. Unlike the NXT Light Sensor, the Raw value decreases with increasing light. The Raw values vary over a range from almost 0 to more than 900. The CdS sensor also varies more at low light level than the NXT, and continues to vary after the NXT sensor hits 100 in bright light. The biggest disadvantage of the CdS sensor over the NXT sensor is that it changes value much more slowly.

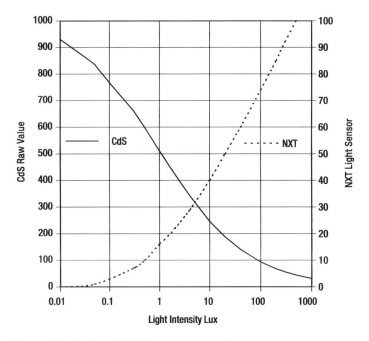

Figure 5-35. *CdS and NXT Light Sensor comparison*

Theremin

The *theremin* was named after Léon Theremin, who invented it in 1919. It was probably the first all-electronic musical instrument, and Figure 5-36 shows Léon playing it. It was played by a musician merely waving his hands around the instrument without ever touching it. The distance of the right hand to a vertical antenna controlled the pitch or frequency of the note, while the distance of the left hand to a loop antenna controlled the volume. It produces an eerie monotone that was popular in 1950s science fiction films.

Figure 5-36. *Inventor Léon Theremin playing his theremin*

The original theremin used radio waves to detect the placement of the musician's hands. The NXT theremin uses the amount of light falling on two homebrew Light Sensors. The sensors are mounted on arms extending from the sides of the NXT, as shown in Figure 5-37. While playing, you need to arrange the light so your hands cast shadows onto the sensors. The closer you hold your hand to the sensor, the darker the shadow.

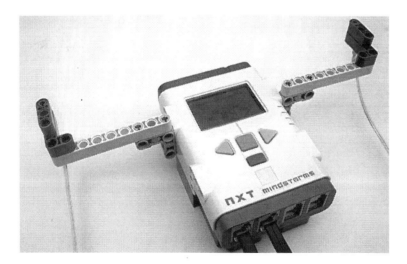

Figure 5-37. *NXT theremin*

The NXT-G program shown in Figure 5-38 couldn't be much simpler. The Raw value from the volume sensor is read in on port 1. To make sure that the value reaches 0 or less, the first math block subtracts 400 from the Raw value. The next Math block scales the value to the range of the volume input on the Sound block. You might need to adjust these values for your particular sensors and lighting conditions. The Sound block volume input range is 0 to 100, but it actually has only 5 volume levels: 100, 75, 50, 25, and 0 for mute. Unfortunately, this coarse volume control limits the vibrato effects the original theremin is famous for. The tone or pitch is read in on port 2, and can be fed directly to the tone input of the Sound block.

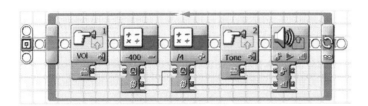

Figure 5-38. *NXT-G theremin program*

Moving your hand toward the volume Light Sensor increases the volume, while moving your other hand toward the tone Light Sensor increases the frequency of the note. A unique feature of a theremin is that it can hold a note indefinitely if you don't move either hand.

Braitenberg Vehicle 2

In the book *Vehicles: Experiments in Synthetic Psychology* (The MIT Press, 1986), Valentino Braitenberg wrote about the dynamic behavior of several minimalistic vehicles. Despite their simple design and control, their behavior was often complex and unexpected. Figure 5-39 shows his vehicle number 2. It has two photo sensors in the front that point forward, and two motor-driven wheels in the rear. Model 2a's control is arranged so that the brighter the light shining on a photo sensor, the faster the motor turns on the same side. Model 2b has the control signals crossed.

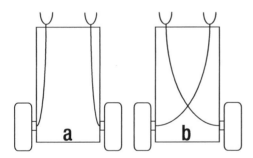

Figure 5-39. *Braitenberg vehicles number 2a and 2b*

Vehicle number 2 is easy to reproduce with the NXT Quick Start Vehicle and two homebrew Light Sensors. The original NXT wheeled version is pictured in Figure 5-40, but you could also use the NXT2 Shooterbot. They can just hang down from the horizontal beam in the front, much like the feelers from Chapter 4.

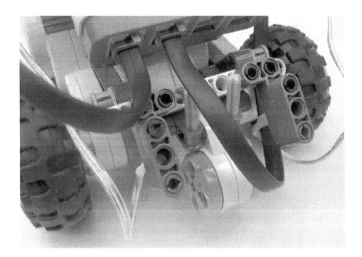

Figure 5-40. NXT Quick Start robot with Light Sensors

The NXT-G program in Figure 5-41 is an endless loop that reads the two Light Sensors and adjusts the power to the two motors. Because the homebrew Light Sensor's Raw value decreases with increasing light level, the first Math block subtracts the Raw value from 1,000. This makes a value that's larger with brighter light. The second Math block divides the number by 10 to scale it into the 0-to-100 range used for the power input to the Motor block. All you need to change between the 2a and 2b vehicles' programs is the motor designator letters B and C.

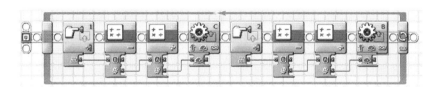

Figure 5-41. Vehicle 2b NXT-G program

Suppose that model 2a is in a dark room, and a bright light that's in front and to the right of the vehicle is turned on, as in Figure 5-42. The right photo sensor receives more light than the left, and therefore the right motor turns faster than the left. This causes the vehicle to go forward but turn to the left, avoiding the light source. The vehicle behaves as if it "hates" light.

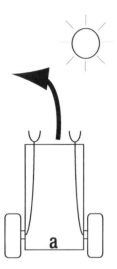

Figure 5-42. *Vehicle 2a's "hate light" behavior*

Now suppose that model 2b is exposed to the same bright light, as in Figure 5-43. Again the right photo sensor receives more light than the left, but this time the left motor turns faster. This causes the vehicle to move forward but turn to the right, seeking the light source. The vehicle behaves as if it "loves" the light.

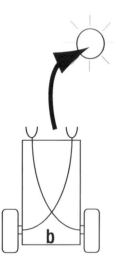

Figure 5-43. *Vehicle 2b's "love light" behavior*

Two-Switch Input

One problem with the parallel and series methods already covered is that you can't tell which switch is being operated. An easy way to make the switches identifiable is to put a unique resistor in series with them. Figure 5-44 shows the schematic diagram of the concept.

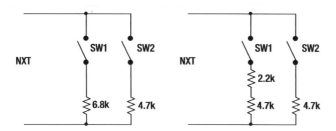

Figure 5-44. *Two versions of the two-switch multiplexer*

Figure 5-45 shows the Raw values for all four possible switch combinations. If neither switch is closed, the NXT reads a Raw value of 1,023. If only switch one (SW1) is closed, the voltage divider is the 10k of the NXT and the 6.8k resistor. The NXT will read this as a Raw value of 414. If only switch two (SW2) is closed, the voltage divider has a 4.7k in place of the 6.8k, and this will be read as a Raw value of 327. Finally, if both switches are closed, then the voltage divider has the parallel combination of the 4.7k and 6.8k, which is 2.8k. This will be read as a Raw value of 222.

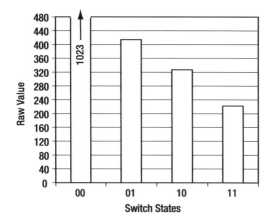

Figure 5-45. *Values for the different combinations of switches*

In theory, you could extend this concept to even more switches and resistors. However, the decoding process gets more complex, and the tolerance for variations in the resistors gets smaller. Besides, in Chapter 13 we'll really show you ways to expand the inputs.

The values of the two resistors are important. If you use resistors that are too different, the Raw values won't end up in the right place for the decoding process to work. The 4.7k resistor is easy to get at Radio Shack in a package of five or in a big assortment kit. The 5% color code is yellow-blue-red-gold. The 6.8k (5% color code: green-violet-red-gold) resistor is harder to find. However, you can use another 4.7k and a 2.2k (5% color code: red-red-red-gold) in series to create a 6.9k resistor, and this will still work without any adjustments to the program.

Building a Two-Switch Input

Building the two-switch input is easy. In step 1, shown in Figure 5-46, solder the resistors to the switch and interconnect wires. Remember to have a short piece of shrink tubing to slide over the terminal without a resistor. Shrink the short piece of tubing and then slide a long piece of tubing over the wire to cover all the connections. Naturally your switches don't have to be right next to each other like the ones in the photograph. They could be on the front and back of a robot to detect that it has driven or backed into something.

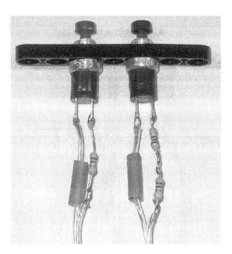

Figure 5-46. *Two-switch step 1*

After soldering, slide the heat shrink tubing up to the switch and shrink it with a hair dryer. It should look like Figure 5-47.

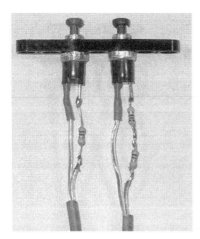

Figure 5-47. *Two-switch step 2*

Finally, shrink a piece of tubing over all the connections and resistors. Your finished two-switch input will look like Figure 5-48.

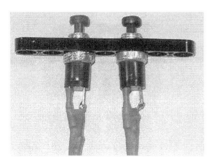

Figure 5-48. *Two-switch step 3*

Programming a Two-Switch Input

A NXT-G My Block (shown in Figure 5-49) sorts out the four switch combinations by comparing the incoming Raw value with levels that are in between the switch states. The state of SW2 is easy to decode because it must be on if the Raw value is less than 371. Switch 1 requires checking to see if the Raw value is in the range between 460 and 371, where it is on by itself; it can also be on with SW2, which makes the Raw value less than 275.

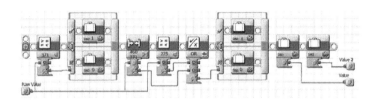

Figure 5-49. *Two-switch decode My Block*

It's a good idea to run the test program shown in Figure 5-50 with your two-switch input to make sure that the values you're getting decode properly. The program displays the Raw value and the decoded state of the two switches. You might need to adjust the threshold levels to compensate for the particular resistor values you used.

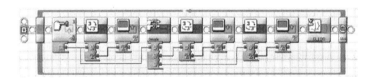

Figure 5-50. *Two-switch test program*

■ ■ ■

CHAPTER 6

Potentiometer Sensors

A *potentiometer*, or *pot* for short, doesn't change in resistance with temperature like a thermistor, or light level like a CdS light-dependent resistor. It changes with the rotation of a mechanical shaft. You're probably already familiar with the device because it's commonly used as the volume control on audio equipment. Rotating the shaft changes the resistance between the center and outer two terminals. It's a kind of self-contained voltage divider. Usually the shaft can rotate only 270 degrees, but multiturn versions are available. Figure 6-1 shows several examples of potentiometers.

Figure 6-1. *Examples of potentiometers*

Connecting to the Pot

A potentiometer is also a passive-type sensor, and is connected to the NXT using the same two connections you used for the contact and resistive sensors from Chapters 4 and 5. Connecting the NXT to the left and center terminals creates an angle sensor that increases in resistance with clockwise rotation, as shown in Figure 6-2. Connecting to the center and right terminals makes a counterclockwise sensor. In either case, it's a good idea to connect the remaining outer terminal to the center terminal.

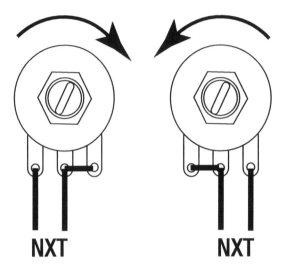

Figure 6-2. *Connections for clockwise and counterclockwise rotation*

Resistance Selection

Potentiometers come in many different full-scale resistance values and tapers. *Linear taper* means the resistance changes evenly with angle, and that's what you're looking for. You can write an equation for the resistance, where A is the angle in degrees and R_{pot} is the full-scale resistance. Plugging that equation into the one you already have for Raw values leads to an equation that tells you what Raw value you'll get at any angle.

$$R = \frac{A}{270} R_{pot}$$

$$Raw = \frac{1023}{\left[\dfrac{2,700,000}{A \, R_{pot}}\right] + 1}$$

Not surprisingly, the Raw value doesn't change linearly with angle. The plot in Figure 6-3 shows the results you get for three R_{pot} values. Clearly the Raw value for the 50kΩ changes the most in the first 90 degrees of rotation, but after that it levels off. In the range from 90 to 180 degrees, the 20kΩ pot changes the most and is the best choice for applications with up to 180 degrees of rotation. For full 270-degree rotation, the 10kΩ is the best because it has the most change in the 180-to-270 degree range.

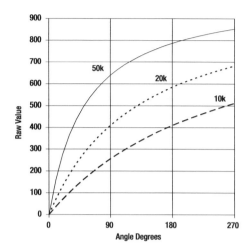

Figure 6-3. *Plot of Raw values versus shaft angle*

The pot resistance value you buy depends on how many degrees of rotation your application requires. The 10kΩ Raw values change almost linearly with angle, so if you were going to be marooned on a desert island, you'd pack the 10kΩ pot. However, picking the right resistance for your application greatly improves the angular resolution you'll get. The graph in Figure 6-4 shows the range of Raw values, given that you're only using the pots in their optimal range: 90 degrees for the 50kΩ, 180 degrees for the 20kΩ, and 270 degrees for the 10kΩ.

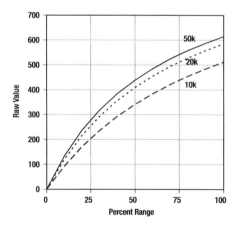

Figure 6-4. *Raw value over optimal operating range*

Angle Sensor Construction

The Bourns 3310C or 3310Y potentiometers make excellent angle sensors for the NXT. The 3310C in Figure 6-5 has three terminals on one side, whereas the 3310Y has them coming out the back in a triangle pattern. You should definitely solder your connections to these pots, or else the wires will pull off too easily. (Both these potentiometers can be purchased from Digi-Key in a variety of resistance values.)

Figure 6-5. *Bourns 3310C potentiometer*

Start by stripping the ends of the speaker wires about the same length as the terminals on the pot. Figure 6-6 shows all the components. Remember to have some heat shrink tubing slipped on the wires before you solder.

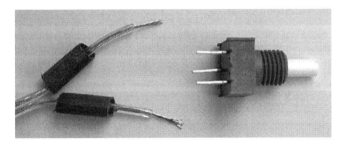

Figure 6-6. *Homebrew angle sensor step 1*

For the example shown in Figure 6-7, the angle sensor will increase in the counterclockwise direction. The connections might look backward, but remember that the terminals are on the back of the 3310Y. Although it will work either way, it's a good idea to tie the unused outer terminal to the center. After the wire has been wrapped around the terminals, solder the connection.

Figure 6-7. Homebrew angle sensor step 2

Slide the heat shrink over the connection and shrink with a hair dryer. Your sensor should look like Figure 6-8.

Figure 6-8. Homebrew angle sensor step 3

The mounting hole size for the pot is 1/4 inch (6.355mm), which is just a little bigger in diameter than a Technic hole. Enlarging the hole is easy because you can drill through LEGO plastic with only a drill bit held in your fingers or with pliers, as shown in Figure 6-9.

Figure 6-9. *Hand drilling triangle beam*

A Technic triangle beam is an excellent part to modify because it's thin enough to use the mounting nut included with the potentiometer to fasten it. Figure 6-10 shows the pot mounted to the triangle beam. The original NXT kit came with two of these triangles, but you can buy them from vendors listed in Appendix B (for example, you can buy 25 Technic triangles from LEGO Education by ordering part number W991332). I usually drill out only the center hole on the wide side of the triangle and leave the rest of the holes for mounting to the project.

Figure 6-10. *Mounted angle sensor*

The shaft of the pot fits nicely in the 16- and 40-tooth gear centers with only friction. However, you can make a more universal connector by gluing a blue axle peg to the shaft. This needs to be done with a little fixture to ensure the proper alignment and positioning.

Build up the fixture shown in Figure 6-11 and make sure that the little screwdriver slot in the end of the pot shaft is horizontal. Put a drop of gel-type, fast-setting glue into the hollow of the axle peg. Slowly slide the triangle/pot assembly down so the pot shaft fits inside the peg. While you're pushing, watch that the glue is not pumping out and getting into the moving parts of the pot. Also make sure you fully seat the assembly against the spacers, as shown in Figure 6-12. Let the whole thing sit long enough for the glue to set fully.

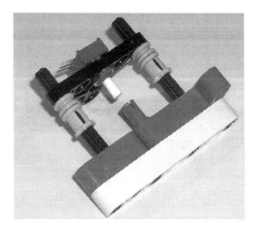

Figure 6-11. *Potentiometer blue axle peg mounting fixture*

Figure 6-12. *Fully seated*

109

NXT Protractor

Converting the measured Raw value into an angle only requires a little algebra. R_{pot} isn't a variable because it doesn't change once you pick the pot, so you can simplify the equation a little. This equation is coded in Figure 6-13 to make a NXT protractor that reads the pot angle and displays it on the screen.

$$A = \frac{2,700,000\ Raw}{R_{pot}(1023 - Raw)}$$

[degrees]
where G = 54 for the 50kΩ, 135 for the 20kΩ, and 270 for the 10kΩ

$$A = \frac{G\ Raw}{1023 - Raw}$$

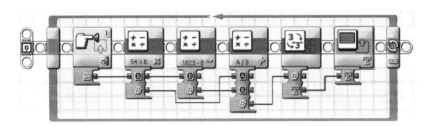

Figure 6-13. *NXT-G protractor program*

Pressure Sensor

Figure 6-14 shows how you can combine a potentiometer and a LEGO pneumatic cylinder to make a simple pressure sensor. The pneumatic cylinder tries to extend its piston when pressure is applied to the lower input, but two rubber bands resist the motion. The rubber bands exert a force that is linear with the amount they are stretched, so the extent the pneumatic cylinder moves is directly related to the pressure in the cylinder. As the piston is pushed outward, it rotates a connecting arm connected to the pot. Because the total rotation is only about 90 degrees, use the 50kΩ pot.

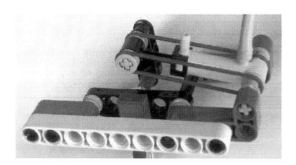

Figure 6-14. *Pressure sensor using pneumatic cylinder and 50kΩ pot*

LEGO rubber bands come in a variety of sizes and are color coded. Blue ones are large enough that they are barely stretched with the piston in the starting position. White ones are small enough that they are already stretched in the same position. You need to pick a color or combination of colors to set the range of pressures you want to measure. Figure 6-15 shows the pressure ranges we measured with two blue, one blue and one white, and two white rubber bands.

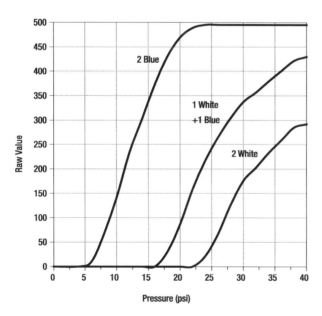

Figure 6-15. *Raw versus pressure for three different rubber band combinations*

Broom Balancer

You can probably balance a broom by the end of its handle on the open palm of your hand. It's not that hard because the broom's center of gravity is way up near the bristles, and it can't move as quickly as you can move the handle. Designing a machine that can balance a broom like this is not as easy as it might seem. People have earned PhDs in engineering studying this control problem. Although the example in Figure 6-16 works, it's just a starting point for further experimentation.

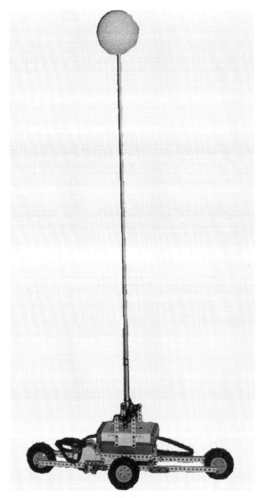

Figure 6-16. Broom and balancer cart

The 20kΩ pot is an excellent angle sensor for this application because it rotates with little friction, and only 180 degrees of motion is needed. The angle sensor is mounted so that the angle of the broom is directly measured. For simplicity, the Raw value is not converted to a true angle. You need to wire the pot for counterclockwise operation if it's mounted exactly as in Figure 6-17. You also need to adjust it so the 0Ω position is near the point where the broom is lying horizontally toward the bottom of the NXT.

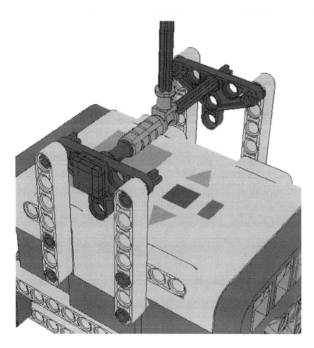

Figure 6-17. *Close-up of pivot mount for broom handle*

The NXT motors are internally geared down, and unfortunately their speed is a little slow for this application. You need the cart to move quickly to correct for the broom tilting even a little. The gear train shown in Figure 6-18 multiplies the motor speed by 3. The two gear trains are in parallel to increase the torque-handling capability.

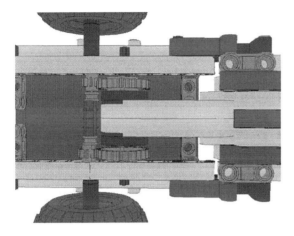

Figure 6-18. *Close-up of gear train for broom cart wheels*

The broom handle is made from a 3/16 inch (4.75mm) diameter, 25 inch (64cm) long wooden dowel rod. You can fasten it to the angle sensing axle in a variety of ways. Our favorite is to use two Technic socket joints, as shown in Figure 6-19. The dowel rod is pushed through the two holes on the sides of the joint sockets. A 2.5 inch (6.4cm) diameter Styrofoam ball tops the pole to make it act more like a broom.

Figure 6-19. *Example broom handle holder*

The main program for the broom balancer is illustrated in Figure 6-20 and has two parts. The broom must be initially vertical and in the balanced position when the program is started. This position is remembered as X. Then the program goes into the endless loop of updating the control and driving the motor.

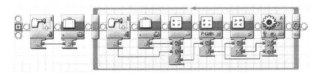

Figure 6-20. *Inverted pendulum main program*

The control loop reads the current pot value and subtracts the original value X from it. This creates an angle error, and the amount of power delivered to the motor is dependent on this error multiplied by a gain. The value of this gain depends on a lot of factors beyond the scope of this book, but you need to play with it to get good stability.

Joysticks

Joysticks are great for manual and remote-control applications. You can combine two angle sensors in a simple gimbal mount to make a joystick. This is a good application for the 50kΩ pot because its total angle of motion is only about 90 degrees.

Bottom Mounted Joystick

You can build a remote-control platform with the joystick on the bottom of the NXT, as shown in Figure 6-21. Building it on the bottom leaves the display and control buttons free for other things. For example, you can operate the joystick with one hand and push the buttons with the other. In Chapter 14 we'll show you how to use this joystick to remotely control another NXT using Bluetooth wireless communications.

Figure 6-21. Joystick built on the bottom of the NXT

The test program in Figure 6-22 allows you to check the operation of your joystick. You need to hold the NXT so you can see the display, but you're moving the joystick from behind. Moving the handle left and right should move the Aim image shown in Figure 6-23 back and forth on the display. Moving the handle up and down moves the image top to bottom on the display.

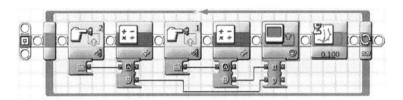

Figure 6-22. Joystick test program

Figure 6-23. Joystick test display

Top Mounted Joystick for a Robot Arm

The T-56 Robot Arm project included with the original NXT kit is limited to preprogrammed movements. Plans for the arm can be found at links given in Appendix B, but it does require some parts not included with second generation NXTs. Adding a joystick control (see Figure 6-24) lets you swing and elevate the arm to any position you want. You can also program the left and right NXT buttons to open and close the jaw on command.

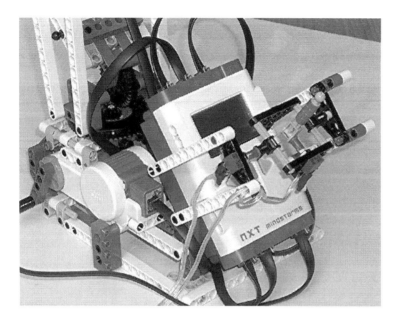

Figure 6-24. *Front mounted joystick for the T-56 robot arm*

The joystick gimbal for the front mount is the same as the back mount joystick. If it's mounted far enough above the NXT, the display and buttons are still accessible. Because the T-56 already makes use of input ports 1 and 3, the swing axis control has to be brought into port 2 and the elevation axis into port 4.

The idle position of the joystick is recorded when the program first starts. These raw values are saved in variables C0 and B0, as shown in Figure 6-25. Then the program goes into a long endless loop of moving the two axes and checking whether the jaw should open or close.

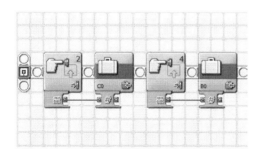

Figure 6-25. *T-56 program initialization*

The control is exactly the same for both axes, as seen in Figures 6-26 and 6-27. The current value of the pot is read and subtracted from the initial position to create a motor power command. The direction of the command is determined by comparing the value to zero. Fortunately, the Motor block doesn't care if the power command is positive or negative; it just uses the size of the number.

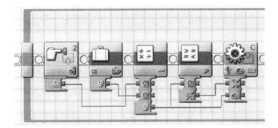

Figure 6-26. *First axis control*

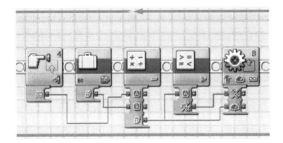

Figure 6-27. *Second axis control*

The jaw control part of the NXT-G program checks if the left or right NXT button has been pressed, as shown in Figure 6-28. A fixed 0.5s command is issued to the jaw motor that opens or closes it.

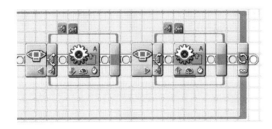

Figure 6-28. *Jaw control*

CHAPTER 7

■■■

Voltage Sensors

In Chapter 5, you learned that the NXT converts the voltage on a sensor input into a digital value. Until now, the only voltage being converted was the 5V supply inside the NXT or some part of it divided through an external resistor. It probably doesn't come as a big surprise that you can connect an external voltage to the input and have the NXT convert that instead.

■ **Caution** Never connect these voltage sensors to anything but low-voltage, battery-operated equipment. Connecting them to household electricity could be lethal both to you and the NXT.

Design of a –5V to +5V Sensor

Figure 7-1 shows a circuit diagram of the NXT input with a simple voltage sensor. The only component needed is a 10kΩ resistor. The external voltage you'll measure is labeled as E on the circuit. Some examples should help you to understand how it works.

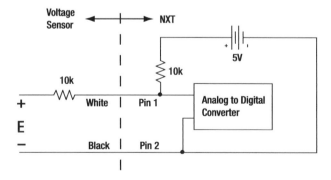

Figure 7-1. *–5V to +5V sensor circuit*

First, assume that the external voltage E is 0V. That's the same as connecting the external 10kΩ resistor across the input, as you've been doing for the last three chapters. The NXT's 5V will be evenly divided between two 10kΩ resistors. That means the voltage at the analog-to-digital converter will be 2.5V and it will be converted to a Raw value of about 512. This is the center point on Figure 7-2.

Next, assume that the external voltage E is 5V. Now the input is being pulled up to 5V through 10kΩ resistors both internally and externally. The input doesn't have any choice but to be 5V, which will be converted to a Raw value of 1,023. That is the top-right point in Figure 7-2.

Finally, assume that the external voltage is –5V. The internal 10kΩ resistor is pulling the input up to 5V, and the external 10kΩ resistor is pulling the input down to –5V. That evenly matched tug-of-war results in 0V, which converts to a Raw value of 0 and is plotted as the lower-left point on Figure 7-2.

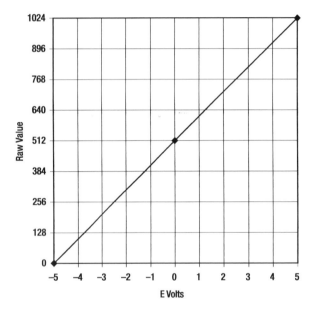

Figure 7-2. *Plot of external voltage and Raw value*

The following equation calculates the external voltage E knowing the measured Raw value:

$$E = \left[\frac{2\,Raw}{1023} - 1 \right] 5$$

The second-generation NXT software has floating-point arithmetic, but the integer arithmetic of the original NXT would really cause problems if you blindly tried to code this equation into a program.

Without a decimal point, the result of the first division would result in only 0, 1, or 2, which would be a very coarse measurement of voltage. The way around this problem is to scale up the numbers by 1,000 and make sure that you always multiply before you divide. After multiplying by 1,000, you end up with a smaller unit of voltage known as a millivolt, or mV:

$$E = \frac{10,000 \; Raw}{1023} - 5,000$$

The program shown in Figure 7-3 is really intended for first-generation NXT software. It reads the input and passes the Raw value through the parts of the equation. The voltage, scaled by 1,000, is then displayed on the screen. You could add some additional blocks to display a decimal point, but that detail is left to you. If nothing is connected to the input, the display will read 5000, which is just the 5V supply internal to the NXT. A NXT2 version of the program would multiply only by 10, subtract only 5, and automatically show the value with a decimal point.

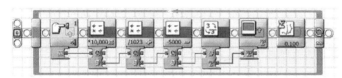

Figure 7-3. *NXT –5V to +5V voltmeter program*

Constructing the Voltage Sensor

Unlike the sensors in the previous chapters, you need to pay attention to which wire is connected to the black and which to the white. If you look carefully, one of the two 18-gauge (0.8mm²) speaker wires will have some kind of identification. For example, some speaker wire has a stripe painted on one side. Make the identified wire the one you connect to the black cable wire and it will become the – terminal of your voltage sensor. Naturally, the other wire will become the + terminal.

The best place to put the 10kΩ resistor is at the junction between the NXT cable and the speaker wire. You can attach it using a terminal block, but soldering is more compact and permanent. Cut the speaker wire so that the wire to be connected to the black cable wire is about 1/4 inch (10mm) longer to compensate for the length of the resistor. It makes the assembly look much neater. Figure 7-4 shows all the parts except the heat shrink.

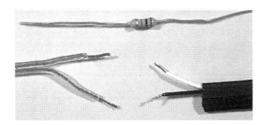

Figure 7-4. *Voltage sensor step 1*

Put a short piece of heat shrink tubing on the longer speaker wire and solder it to the black wire in the NXT cable. Slide the heat shrink down to cover the connection and shrink it with a hair dryer. Then solder the 10kΩ resistor (brown-black-orange-gold) to the white wire in the cable. Shrink some tubing over the end of the resistor and the connection. It should now look like Figure 7-5.

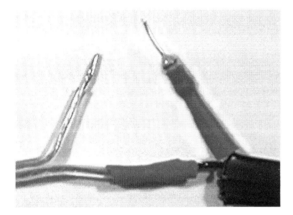

Figure 7-5. *Voltage sensor step 2*

Slip some heat shrink tubing over the resistor and solder the remaining connection. Then pull the tubing back over the resistor and shrink it so it looks like Figure 7-6.

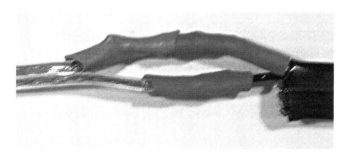

Figure 7-6. *Voltage sensor step 3*

Finally, shrink a large piece of tubing over the whole assembly, including a short length of the NXT cable. This provides strain relief and further protects the connections. The finished voltage sensor should look like Figure 7-7.

Figure 7-7. Voltage sensor step 4

NXT Battery Tester

Probably the most useful voltage to measure with the NXT voltmeter is an AA battery. It's always a good idea to check to see whether there is any life left before throwing batteries away. You can make the AA holder from just a few LEGO parts, as shown in Figure 7-8. Electrical connection is made by stripping about an inch (25mm) of insulation off the ends of the speaker wire and looping it through the holes at the end of the beams. The + wire should go to the rotating beam on the top and the – wire to the one on the bottom. Wrapping aluminum foil around the end of the beams makes getting a good connection easier.

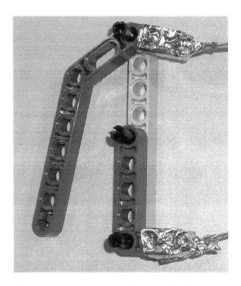

Figure 7-8. Partial assembly of AA holder

The AA battery is pinched much like a nut in a nutcracker between the ends of the beams, as shown in Figure 7-9. You should read the voltage using the NXT voltmeter program first to make sure everything works. If your meter reads a negative voltage, you mixed up the wires somehow and you need to exchange them.

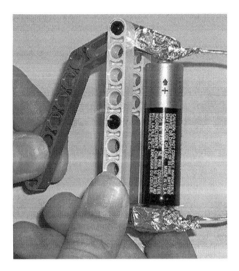

Figure 7-9. *Using the AA holder to measure battery voltage*

A simple battery tester program is shown in Figure 7-10. It classifies the battery quality into three bands. Above 1.45V, the battery is considered Fantastic; between 1.45V and 1.25V, it's Good; and below 1.25V, it's Low.

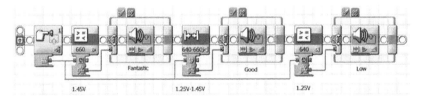

Figure 7-10. *Battery tester program*

A –15V to +15V Sensor

Five volts isn't always a wide enough measurement range. Laboratory instruments have an output signal for connecting to other instruments that's in the range of 0V to +10V. Industrial sensors are often –10V to +10V. Automotive electronics are around 12V, and 9V is common in portable electronics such as the NXT itself.

The voltage sensor design in Figure 7-11 allows the input signal to swing from –15V to +15V and needs only two resistors. You can get 15kΩ (5% color code: brown-green-orange-gold) resistors from Radio Shack in their assortment packs, but if you don't want to buy the 30kΩ (5% color code: orange-black-orange-gold) from another supplier, you need to make it from two 15kΩ resistors in series.

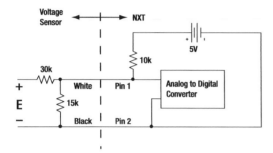

Figure 7-11. *–15V to +15V sensor circuit*

Figure 7-12 shows the plot of external voltage and Raw value. The program shown in Figure 7-13 is basically the same as the –5V to +5V program, except the numbers are scaled up by a factor of 3. A NXT2 version would multiply by 30, subtract only 15, and automatically show the value with a decimal point.

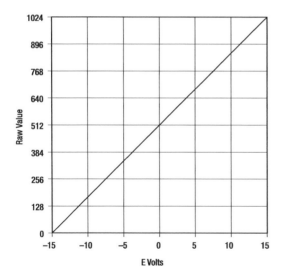

Figure 7-12. *Plot of input voltage and Raw value*

125

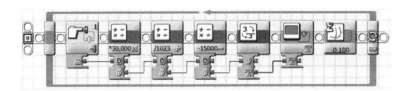

Figure 7-13. *–15V to +15V NXT voltmeter program*

CHAPTER 8

■■■

4.3V Powered Sensors

The NXT provides a DC voltage on the sensor input port for sensors that require a power supply. (The LEGO Light Sensors and Sound Sensors are examples of sensors powered this way.) It's defined as the 4.3V power supply, but the voltage actually varies about 7% with load. The plot in Figure 8-1 shows the voltage ranging from 4.6V, when the power supply is lightly loaded, to 4.0V when it's fully loaded. It is important to note that this plot is for the total current of all the ports put together.

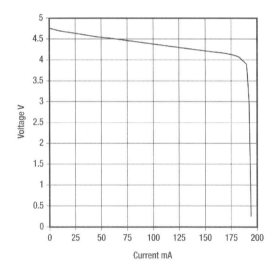

Figure 8-1. *4.3V supply voltage versus current*

Hall Effect Sensor

The Hall Effect Sensor describes a magnetic field phenomenon in semiconducting materials. Without getting overly technical, electrons moving in a semiconductor are deflected by a magnetic field. The amount of deflection depends on the strength and orientation of the field. The deflection becomes a voltage that can be processed and converted into a switch-like output. Panasonic makes the DN6849 switch-type Hall Effect Sensor (Digi-Key #DN6849SE-ND). The DN6848 is a similar but discontinued part.

Figure 8-2 shows the internal block diagram of the DN6849SE. The voltage generated by the Hall element is very small and requires an amplifier. Following the amplifier is a block of circuitry called a Schmitt Trigger, which determines whether the level is above a threshold and turns the switch on. It also prevents the output from rapidly toggling on and off when the level is equal to the threshold. Finally, the output is a transistor that's well-matched to the NXT sensor input.

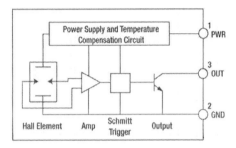

Figure 8-2. *DN6849SE Hall Effect Sensor block diagram*

Hall Sensor Construction

The DN6849SE is so simple it can be connected directly to the end of a cut NXT cable, and it's so small it can be used without extensive packaging. The outline and pin out of the device is shown in Figure 8-3.

Figure 8-3. *DN6849SE pin out*

The green wire in the NXT cable connects to the left, the black to the center, and the white to the right leg of the part. Figures 8-4 and 8-5 show the construction steps. Use heat shrink tubing to protect and insulate the connections.

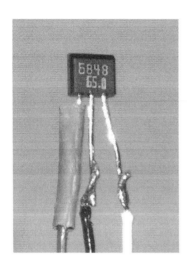

Figure 8-4. Hall Sensor construction step 1

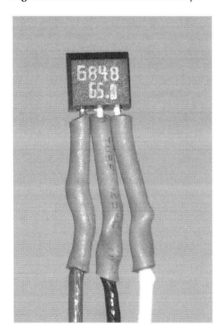

Figure 8-5. Hall Sensor construction step 2

Robot Mouse

Scientific research has proven that mice actually don't like cheese! However, the myth that mice love the smelly stuff will probably never die. This robot mouse has a Hall Effect Sensor for a nose and thinks a magnet is its cheese.

The NXT Quick Start Vehicle is an excellent starting point for the robot mouse. All you need to add is a little boom to hold the Hall Sensor out in front, as shown in Figure 8-6. The height is adjusted so that the sensor just passes over the magnet without touching it. In this case, the magnet is a LEGO train car coupler, but it could be any small permanent magnet.

Figure 8-6. *NXT robot mouse with Hall Effect nose*

The NXT-G mouse program shown in Figure 8-7 has two parallel branches. The top branch simply keeps sweeping the robot back and forth with a slow forward motion. The bottom branch waits for the Hall Sensor to "smell" something; it then brakes the motors and stops the program. You might add some sniffing sounds and maybe a final yummy sound at the end.

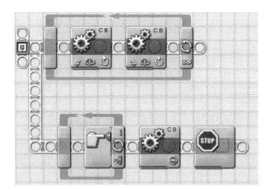

Figure 8-7. *NXT-G robot mouse program*

Transistor Buffer

Not every sensor you want to hook up to the NXT can connect as easily as the DN6849SE. Either the 10kΩ resistor inside the NXT is too much load or the 5V supply causes trouble. A transistor buffer, shown in Figure 8-8, is the perfect solution to the problem. The transistor does the dirty work of driving the NXT input and isolating the 5V supply from the sensor. This design is not foolproof; if you plug it into a motor port it will most likely be damaged. (In the section "Enhancing the Transistor Buffer" we'll suggest an enhancement that fixes that problem.)

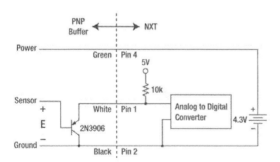

Figure 8-8. *Transistor buffer with NXT sensor input circuitry*

The transistor in the circuit is a PNP type, and the symbol for it is shown in Figure 8-9 along with its pin out. The transistor doesn't need much gain, faces only low voltages, and handles practically no current. Probably the most common small-signal PNP transistor such as this in a leaded package is the 2N3906. Radio Shack sells these transistors in packages of 15.

Figure 8-9. *PNP transistor symbol and 2N3906 pin out*

This one transistor circuit is called a *voltage follower* because the voltage on the transistor emitter just follows the voltage on the base without any gain. In fact, the emitter voltage does follow the base, but with an offset voltage of about 0.6V, as you can see in Figure 8-10.

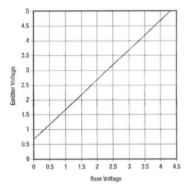

Figure 8-10. *Follower base and emitter voltages*

The emitter voltage is the same as the input to the NXT analog-to-digital converter, so you can easily figure out the Raw value. However, if the NXT thinks it has a LEGO Light Sensor connected, it scales the Raw value into a range from 0–100 (see Figure 8-11), otherwise known as the Percent scale. It isn't really the mathematical percent of anything; it just looks like a percent.

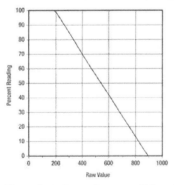

Figure 8-11. *Raw value versus light value*

This equation defines the conversion where P is limited to the range of 0–100:

$$P = 127 - \text{int}\left(\frac{Raw}{7}\right)$$

We can combine all this knowledge to produce a graph of percent reading and the voltage on the transistor base (see Figure 8-12). With a little bit of fringe on the ends, the 0–100 range nicely maps the voltage range you're likely to get from a sensor powered from 4.3V.

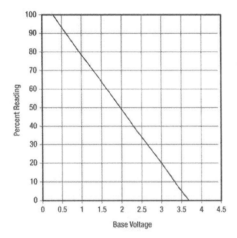

Figure 8-12. *Base voltage versus percent reading*

Construction of the buffer (see Figure 8-13) requires only connecting the transistor to the end of a cut NXT cable, much like the Hall Sensor. Power for the sensor is available on the green wire. The black wire is connected to the collector of the transistor and is the ground for the sensor. The base terminal of the transistor is where the sensor signal is connected, and the white wire is connected only to the emitter of the transistor.

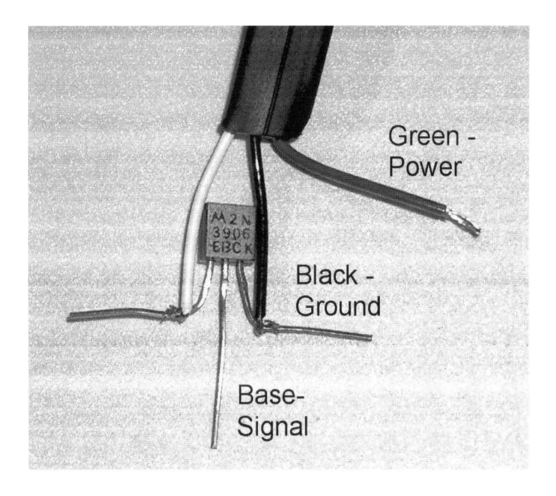

Figure 8-13. *PNP transistor buffer construction*

Infrared Rangefinder

Figure 8-14 is a photograph of the Sharp GP2D12 (Acroname #R48-IR12), which is a self-contained infrared rangefinder. It measures distances from 4 inches (10cm) to 31 inches (80cm). Infrared rangefinders are typically used in equipment such as copy machines to measure the location of paper or other moving parts. One advantage of the GP2D12 over the NXT Ultrasonic Distance Sensor is that it's unaffected by other distance sensors that might be operating nearby.

Figure 8-14. *GP2D12 infrared rangefinder*

It works by sending out a short burst of infrared light from an LED every 32ms. The beam is dark red and barely visible to the naked eye. If you look at it with a digital camera, you can clearly see the beam, as in Figure 8-15. The beam is fairly narrow and is only about 2 inches (6cm) in diameter at a distance of 31 inches (80cm).

Figure 8-15. *Infrared beam as seen with a digital camera*

The block diagram of the sensor is shown in Figure 8-16. A type of one-dimensional camera called a Position Sensing Device (PSD) is then used to receive the reflection of the beam from an object in front of the sensor. The distance to the object is directly related to where the spot lies along the one-dimensional image. The sensor outputs a voltage between 0.4V and 2.4V, and is roughly inversely proportional to the distance. That is, the farther away the object, the lower the output voltage.

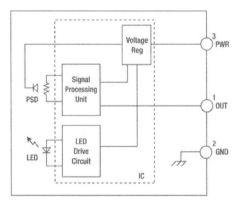

Figure 8-16. *GP2D12 block diagram*

Unfortunately, the GP2D12 cannot be connected directly to the NXT sensor input. The sensor should not have the output pin pulled above the power supply, but the 10kΩ pull up resistor inside the NXT tries to do just that. The GP2D12 also doesn't have enough output power to handle the load of the 10kΩ resistor. Fortunately, the transistor buffer is here to save the day.

Interface Construction

The GP2D12 has a tiny connector known as a JST. Make sure that you order the matching prewired connector when you order the sensor. Although it's possible to solder directly to the connector, we wouldn't recommend it. The three pins in the connector are laid out as shown in Figure 8-17, but you probably need to use this only if the prewired connector you buy is not color-coded. Otherwise, use Table 8-1 and Figure 8-18 to build the interface.

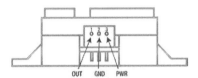

Figure 8-17. *GP2D12 outline and pin out*

Table 8-1. *Connections for the GP2D12*

Pin	Function	GP2D12 Wire Color	NXT Cable Color
1	Output	Yellow	Transistor Base
2	Ground	Black	Black
3	Power	Red	Green

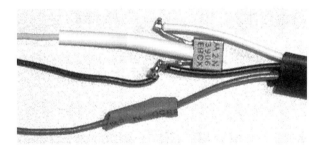

Figure 8-18. *Transistor buffer for the GP2D12 interface*

Operation of the Sensor

When you use the infrared rangefinder, configure the sensor input port to be an NXT Light Sensor. The reading will be in the Percent scale, and the value will range from 30 for a distance of about 4 inches (10cm) to 100 for a distance of 31 inches (80cm). As you can see in the plot in Figure 8-19, the value is not linear with distance. Nobody seems to know exactly why, but at distances shorter than 4 inches (10cm), the relationship actually reverses and the Percent values increase.

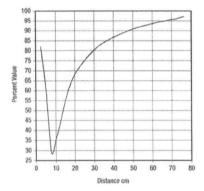

Figure 8-19. *Plot of distance and Percent value*

▓ **Note** The pulsing of the LED creates a lot of electrical noise in the NXT. You can't hear it, but the LEGO Sound Sensor picks it up through its power supply connection. The Sound Sensor picks up so much noise this way, it's essentially useless. There doesn't seem to be any practical way to allow the two sensors to coexist when connected to the same NXT.

Wall Follower

Wall following is a basic function for maze-running robots. The NXT Quick Start robot is the ideal platform, and the infrared rangefinder is the ideal sensor for the task. The mounting holes on the GP2D12 are the wrong size and spacing to mount directly to Technic beams. However, you can arrange four Technic double-axle rubber joiners as in Figure 8-20 to give the right amount of compliance to hold the sensor tightly to the side of a bent lift arm beam. The GP2D12's mounting ears slip perfectly between the beam and the axles. The sensor is tilted back so it looks ahead of the robot.

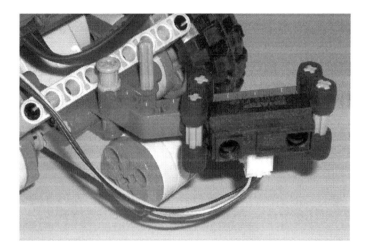

Figure 8-20. *Wall follower*

The NXT-G program is shown in Figure 8-21. A Move block makes programming the wall follower easy because it has a single steering command that simultaneously controls two motors. It turns by an amount proportional to the steering command, with zero going straight. The desired distance to the wall, in this case 90, is subtracted from the distance reading, and it becomes the steering command value. The value of the sensor is also displayed for debugging.

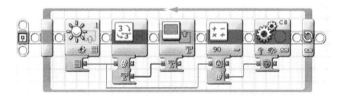

Figure 8-21. *NXT-G wall follower program*

Differential Light Sensor

Occasionally, the measurement you really need is the difference between two levels, not the levels themselves. Measuring the two levels and calculating the difference in software not only uses two input ports but can also limit the accuracy of the result. For example, suppose that you just want to know the difference in the amount of light in two places. The overall range of light levels could be huge, but the range of conversion is limited. The difference between a light reading of 85 and 90 is a big difference in light level, but would be numerically only 5. One way around this problem is to design a sensor that subtracts the difference before the conversion.

Cadmium Sulfide LDRs are resistors that change in value with the light level (refer to Chapter 5). If you put a voltage across two identical LDRs in series (see Figure 8-22), the center connection will be exactly half of the voltage. As long as the amount of light is the same, the voltage will always be half. If one sensor receives less light, its resistance will increase, and the center voltage will move proportionally.

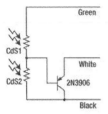

Figure 8-22. *Differential Light Sensor circuit diagram*

It would be nice just to hook this center point up to the sensor input of the NXT, but there would be a problem: the 10kΩ pull-up resistor inside the NXT would throw everything off. In low light conditions, the LDRs would each have a resistance of around 100kΩ. Being 10 times smaller, the 10kΩ would dominate the resistance, and you would mostly measure it, not the LDRs. So, you need to use a transistor buffer again.

Construction

The two CdS sensors are constructed just like those in Chapter 5. You need to connect them in series, tying the center point to the base of the transistor buffer. The CdS sensors in Figure 8-23 are outside the borders of the photo to the left. Tie one of the two ends to the power supply (green) wire and the other to the ground (black) wire. You can use heat shrink to protect and insulate the connections.

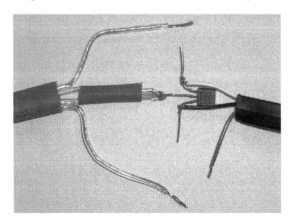

Figure 8-23. *Center point of CdS sensors tied to the transistor base*

Figures 8-24 and 8-25 take you step by step through the rest of the process.

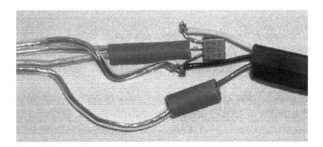

Figure 8-24. *Connect the 4.3V power to a remaining wire and the ground to the other.*

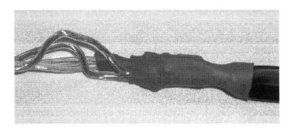

Figure 8-25. *Heat shrink tubing goes over the entire assembly.*

Digital Sundial

A sundial is one of the world's oldest inventions. Most sundials are just objects to block the sun, called the *gnomon*, and dials with time values printed on them. They work by casting a shadow of the gnomon onto the dial. You can use the differential Light Sensor to make a sundial that tries not to cast a shadow by keeping its gnomon pointed directly at the sun.

The gnomon sits between the two Light Sensors, as seen in Figure 8-26. The whole assembly is mounted directly on an NXT motor shaft so it can rotate to track the sun. Over the course of a day, the sun travels across the sky in an arc from east to west. The plane of the arc is at an angle that changes throughout the year. It will be low in the sky in the winter and practically overhead in the summer.

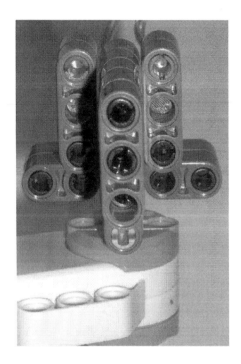

Figure 8-26. *Close-up of differential Light Sensor and gnomon*

The tracking motor is on an adjustable mount, seen in Figure 8-27, that can be tilted to point at the sun. You should point the NXT due south before starting the program.

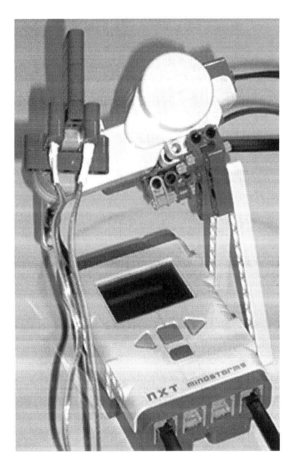

Figure 8-27. *Digital sundial*

The sundial program tries to keep the value of the differential Light Sensor near the balanced light position by turning the motor. You might think that the balanced value would be 50 because that's in the middle of the 0–100 range, but it isn't. If the supply voltage is 4.6V, half the supply voltage would be 2.3V. Looking up 2.3V in Figure 8-11 says the balance point is around 45. Allowing a small amount of imbalance prevents the motor from constantly tracking back and forth around the point. It moves only when the value is less than 40 or greater than 50.

The first thing the program does is swing the gnomon around till a beam contacts a touch switch at the six o'clock position (see Figure 8-28). This establishes the angular zero point.

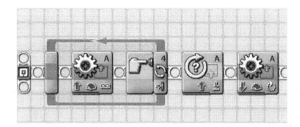

Figure 8-28. *Sundial program initialization*

Then the program goes into an endless loop that orients the gnomon and displays the time (see Figure 8-29). Depending on which side of the gnomon your CdS Light Sensors are mounted, you might need to reverse both of the Motor block directions. If you have them backward, the sundial will actually try to avoid the sun.

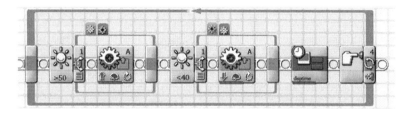

Figure 8-29. *Sundial program main loop*

You compute the time by converting the motor angle into hours and minutes (see Figure 8-30). The My Block conversion isn't fancy. It doesn't do a.m. and p.m. or daylight savings time, and when the minute is less than 10, it doesn't even add the customary leading zero.

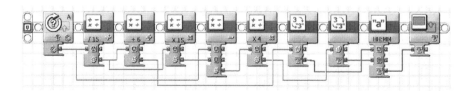

Figure 8-30. *Angle to time display My Block*

The time display does add a colon between the hours and minutes, as shown in Figure 8-31.

Figure 8-31. Sundial time display

Protecting the Transistor Buffer

The NXT has only one type of cable for both motors and sensors. That means you can accidentally plug a sensor into a motor port. As you might expect, LEGO has gone to great lengths to make sure this won't damage its sensors. However, the transistor buffer isn't so forgiving. If you want to make your transistor buffers more foolproof, the addition of a 470Ω resistor in series with the emitter and white wire will protect the transistor if the sensor is plugged into the wrong place. Figure 8-32 is a schematic that shows you where to put the new resistor.

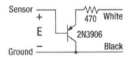

Figure 8-32. Protected PNP buffer

CHAPTER 9

■■■

Two-Wire Powered Sensors

The original LEGO MINDSTORMS brick, the RCX, used a two-wire powered sensor interface. The NXT has a backward compatibility mode with the old RCX sensors, and that mode offers some advantages for homebrew sensors that need higher voltages than the 4.3V supply described in Chapter 8. It's a natural choice for sensors that need to take full advantage of the 5V analog-to-digital conversion. Conveniently, the two wires are the same two wires you already used for passive sensors: the white and black wires in the NXT cable, or pins 1 and 2 on the port connector.

Signals

Power and sensor readings are combined on two wires by splitting the functions in time. First, the sensor signal is read, with exactly the same method as the passive sensors described in Chapters 4 through 7, except the signal is read only during a short 0.1ms window of time. After that, power is applied to the two wires for about 3ms. Figure 9-1 graphically shows the timing, but the passive time interval is much shorter than the power. The NXT keeps cycling between these two intervals as long as the port is configured as a two-wire powered sensor.

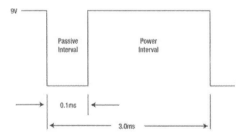

Figure 9-1. *Timing for the two-wire powered sensor (not drawn to scale)*

Figure 9-2 shows a minimal two-wire powered sensor. Diode D1 separates the power part of the cycle from the passive. Diodes act like one-way valves for current, and (oriented in the direction shown) D1 conducts only when the NXT voltage is greater than the voltage on C1. The diode symbol looks like an arrow pointing at a line, and the line end of the part is called the *cathode*. The physical part has a line painted on the cathode end, too. The other end is called the *anode*. With new batteries, the voltage on C1 approaches 9V, but with weak ones it might only be 6V. Either way, it will always be greater than the 5V used by the NXT to read the sensor.

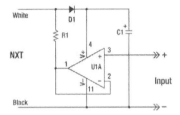

Figure 9-2. *Minimal two-wire powered sensor*

The large triangle symbol in the circuit is an operational amplifier, or *op-amp* for short. There are many kinds of op-amp, but the pin numbers in Figure 9-2 correspond to the LM324. Actually, the LM324 contains 4 op-amps like this in the same 14-pin package. Explaining exactly how an op-amp works is beyond the scope of this book, but basically it's an amplifier whose output is on the corner of the triangle on the left. The NXT reads whatever voltage the op-amp output has through resistor R1.

Remember that the NXT has a 10kΩ resistor pulling the white wire up to 5V. If the op-amp output is 0V, then the voltage the NXT reads will be the result of a voltage divider R1, which is 1kΩ, and the internal 10kΩ resistor to 5V. That results in 0.45V, or a Raw value of 93. If the op-amp output is 5V, the NXT input voltage will also be 5V, which results in a Raw value of 1,023. So, at best, this sensor creates Raw values between 93 and 1,023. Op-amps such as the LM324 can bring their outputs down to only about 0.65V, so the low end of the range is actually limited to something like 214. General instructions for building this type of sensor are given in Appendix A.

Power Supply

The power capability of the two-wire power supply can be seen in Figure 9-3. Getting 9V depends on the condition of the batteries and the amount of load. You can draw up to 14 mA before the voltage rapidly falls off. This is a generous amount of current, considering that the LM324 requires only about 1.5 mA, but you still need to be careful with overall sensor power. You can use up the entire 14 mA with only a 650Ω load to ground.

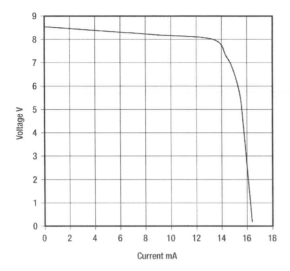

Figure 9-3. *Two-wire power supply*

Programming

NXT-G has a block for the RCX-style Light Sensor called the Legacy Light* block. Instructions for importing blocks like this were given back in Chapter 2. You will use it for all two-wire powered sensors (see Figure 9-4). There's an output from the block with the usual 0–100 light value, but we're more interested in the Raw value output that has a wider operating range.

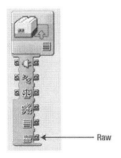
Raw

Figure 9-4. *NXT-G Legacy Light* block*

The little NXT-G program shown in Figure 9-5 just reads the Raw value and puts it on the NXT display. Because the amplifier has a gain of 1, a 5V input will display 1023. However, because of limitations previously mentioned, the Raw value will go down to only about 200 when the input is 0V. There is a plot showing the complete relationship between input voltage and Raw values in Appendix A.

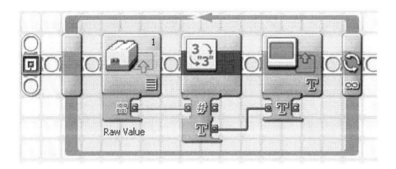

Figure 9-5. NXT-G Read Raw Program

Half-Volt Sensor

Figure 9-6 shows the circuit for a voltage sensor that reads input voltages between –0.5V and +0.5V. Diode D2 has been added to the basic Figure 9-2 design to provide an offset voltage. When diodes conduct, they behave a little like a 0.58V battery.

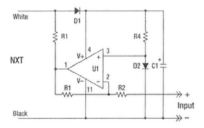

Figure 9-6. Half-Volt Sensor circuit

The positive input on the op-amp in this circuit with the components listed in Table 9-1 will have a gain of 1+R1/R2, 1+330/100, or 4.3. With no voltage on the negative input, the output of the op-amp will be offset by 0.58 × 4.3 or 2.49V. This offset will allow you to measure negative voltages (as well as positive ones).

Table 9-1. Bill of Materials

Component	Part Number	Description	Radio Shack
U1	LM324	Quad op-amp	276-1711
D1, D2	1N4148	Small signal diodes	276-1122
R1	330k	1/4 W 5% Carbon film resistor (orange-orange-yellow-gold)	271-312 For all resistors
R3	1k	1/4 W 5% Carbon film resistor (brown-black-red-gold)	See R1
R2	100k	1/4 W 5% Carbon film resistor (brown-black-yellow-gold)	See R1
R4	10kΩ	1/4 W 5% Carbon film resistor (brown-black-orange-gold)	See R1
C1	22uF	16V or higher electrolytic capacitor	272-1014

The gain of the negative input is R1/R2 or 3.3. The negative input inverts the voltage so a positive input subtracts from the output voltage. For example, with an input of +0.5V, the op-amp output will be the offset 2.49V minus 1.65V, which equals 0.84V. Notice that the more positive the input voltage, the smaller the op-amp output voltage, the smaller the NXT input voltage, and the smaller the Raw value.

The usable range of the voltage sensor is limited by the low-voltage capability of the op-amp and how weak the NXT batteries are. It should give excellent results, between –0.5V and +0.5V, with the relationship of input voltage to Raw value shown in Figure 9-7. After all the circuit gains and offsets, the 0V input is offset by about 560, and the slope is 1.6mV per Raw value over a range of +/– 0.6V.

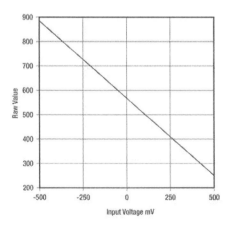

Figure 9-7. Input voltage versus Raw value for Half-Volt Sensor

Construction of the sensor follows the same techniques described in Appendix A. Figure 9-8 shows the circuit built on a solderless breadboard.

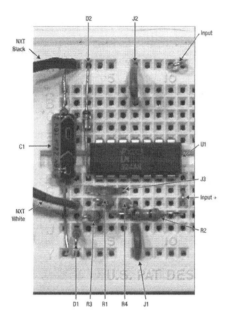

Figure 9-8. *Half-Volt Sensor built on solderless breadboard*

Table 9-2 shows the step-by-step instructions for connecting the parts.

Table 9-2. Component Placement

Component	Start	End
U1 pin 1	F4	
C1 + –	Y1	X1
J1	Y7	J7
J2	X7	B7
D1 anode cathode (the cathode is the end with the line)	J2	Y2
D2 anode cathode	F3	X3
J3	G6	G3
R3 (brown-black-red-gold)	I2	I4
R1 (orange-orange-yellow-gold)	H4	H5
R2 (brown-black-yellow-gold)	I5	I11
R4 (brown-black-orange-gold)	H6	H7
NXT black-white	X2	H2
Input + –	G11	X11

Figure 9-9 shows the sensor moved to a PC board.

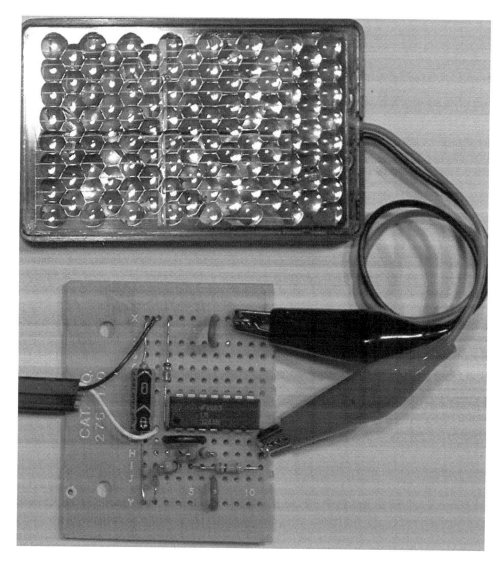

Figure 9-9. *Half-Volt Sensor on PC board measuring a Solar cell output*

The voltmeter program (see Figure 9-10) converts the Raw sensor value into mV and displays the result on the NXT display. Because of variations in electrical components, you might need to adjust the exact offset and scale values for your sensor to get the best zero and voltage calibration. To keep precision with the NXT integer math, the scale value is 10 times larger than it should be to start with, and the result is divided by 10 to make up for it. If you added 5 before you divided, then it would be the same as rounding the number. Of course, second-generation NXT software works with floating-point numbers, and you don't need to be as careful when scaling calculations like this.

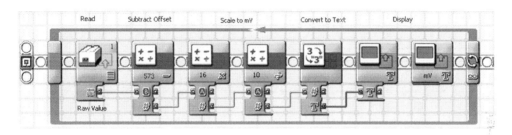

Figure 9-10. *Voltmeter program*

An interesting use for the Half-Volt Sensor is characterizing the output voltage of a solar cell. A single silicon solar cell (Radio Shack 276-124 for example) has an output voltage approaching 600mV in bright sunlight. However, with dimmer light or with any kind of load on its output, the voltage will fall within the range easily measured with the sensor.

Current Sensor

You can use a voltage sensor to measure electrical current by using Ohm's Law. That is $V = I \times R$, where the voltage V equals the current I multiplied by the resistance R. The resistance in this case is of a component known as a *shunt resistor*. Shunt resistors are connected in series with a circuit, as shown in Figure 9-11, and must have a low resistance so they don't significantly affect the current flowing to the load.

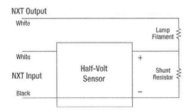

Figure 9-11. *Current sensor circuit*

This shunt resistor is made from four 10Ω resistors in parallel to make a 2.5Ω resistor. You can use a single 2.5Ω resistor, but it's harder to find resistors less than 10Ω. Using Ohm's Law again, you can

153

calculate that 0.2A will be flowing through the 2.5Ω resistor when the voltage is 0.5V. If you want to measure higher currents, you need to use a lower shunt resistor value. For example, you can measure up to 0.5A with a 1Ω resistor.

Electronic Whistler

Back in Chapter 5 you learned that some components, such as thermistors, change resistance value with temperature. An incandescent light bulb filament is another interesting example. When the bulb is cold, the filament resistance is low, but as it heats up to produce light, the resistance increases by more than a factor of 10. It's an interesting example because the heat that's raising the temperature of the filament is coming from the filament itself.

Objects lose heat by convection, conduction, and radiation. *Convection* is cooling by air moving over an object, and the faster the air moves, the more the cooling. *Conduction* is loss by touching other objects, and *radiation* is loss by emitting light or infrared energy. Ordinarily a lamp filament can only radiate energy because it's in a vacuum and barely touching anything. You can add convection cooling by removing the glass bulb.

Figure 9-11 shows the Half-Volt Sensor combined with a shunt resistor to measure the current flowing through a lamp filament. If you use a filament from a light bulb intended for household power, it will barely get hot with the paltry 9V the NXT can output. Because the filament isn't very hot, the radiation part of the heat loss is essentially zero. The current will heat the filament to a point where the convection heat loss equals the electrical energy going into it. Because the filament resistance depends on its temperature, a measurement of the current is about like measuring the speed of the wind cooling it. In the scientific world, this instrument is called a *hot wire anemometer*.

Exposing the Filament

Getting the filament out of a light bulb without destroying it isn't as easy as just breaking the bulb. If you try that, you'll find that the vacuum inside the bulb causes an implosion that sends glass fragments in every direction, tearing the filament to shreds. Instead, you need to let air back into the bulb in a slower, more controlled way.

▓ **Caution** The following operations are dangerous and require the proper safety measures. Be careful: wear safety glasses and gloves. When working with an open flame, make sure there is nothing combustible nearby. Work where it will be easy to clean up any glass fragments that might fly off. Make sure you have adult supervision.

The best way to let air gently back into the bulb is to melt a spot on the glass envelope and let the vacuum do the work of sucking a small hole. Figure 9-12 shows a small torch heating the tip of a 40W 120V chandelier bulb. A similar wattage 240V bulb would probably also work for this. You can use a larger torch intended for soldering plumbing, too, but heat only the very tip of the bulb.

Figure 9-12. Melt the tip of the bulb

You can see where the tip of the bulb has turned into a hole in Figure 9-13. It makes a pop sound when it does this.

Figure 9-13. The hole in the glass bulb

The next step is to break the bulb by pinching it in a vise or C-clamp, as shown in Figure 9-14. The bulb has been wrapped in a paper towel to contain the small pieces of glass.

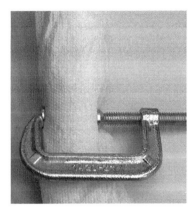

Figure 9-14. *Break the bulb with a C-clamp*

Do not touch the filament or support structure because they're extremely fragile. Remove any remaining pieces of glass (see Figure 9-15) with needle-nose pliers; then carefully screw the bulb into its socket.

Figure 9-15. *Remove the remaining glass with needle-nose pliers*

Whistler Construction

The finished electronic whistler is shown in Figure 9-16. Mounted to the side of the NXT, the filament is exposed so you can blow air on it.

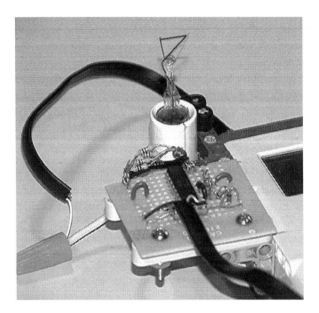

Figure 9-16. Finished electronic whistler

The Whistler program (see Figure 9-17) reads the sensor, displays the value, and produces a whistle tone whose frequency is proportional to the value. As you blow on the filament, the pitch of the tone will increase. Just waving air at the sensor with your hand or moving it around will change the tone.

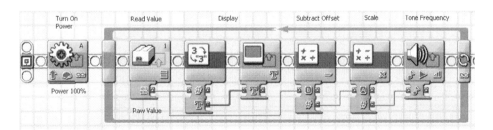

Figure 9-17. Whistler program

Pressure Sensor

Back in Chapter 6 you made an elementary pressure sensor using LEGO pneumatics. Now that you can make op-amp circuits, you can make a more accurate sensor using the bridge pressure transducer shown in Figure 9-18. This is a Model 1230-030D-3L PC board mountable pressure transducer from Measurement Specialties (see Table 9-3 for the full bill of materials). It can measure up to 30psi (2,068hPa or 2 Atmospheres) and it reads the difference in pressure between the two ports.

■ **Caution** You can use this sensor only to measure the pressure of a gas. Do not try to measure the pressure of liquids or let any moisture get into it—it will ruin the sensor element.

Figure 9-18. *Bridge pressure transducer*

Table 9-3. *Bill of Materials*

Component	Part Number	Description	Radio Shack
U1	LM324	Quad OpAmp	276-1711
D1	1N4148	Small Signal Diode	276-1122
D2	1N4733A	5.1V 1W Zener Diode	276-565
R1	100k	1/4 W 5% Carbon Film Resistor (brown-black-yellow-gold)	271-312 For All Resistors
R2, R4	10k	1/4 W 5% Carbon Film Resistor (brown-black-orange-gold)	See R1
R3	1k	1/4 W 5% Carbon Film Resistor (brown-black-red-gold)	See R1
R5	1meg	1/4 W 5% Carbon Film Resistor (brown-black-green-gold)	See R1
R6	470	1/4 W 5% Carbon Film Resistor (yellow-violet-brown-gold)	See R1
P1	1230-030D-3L	Measurement Specialties	Digi-Key MSP6822-ND
C1	22uF	16V or Higher Electrolytic Capacitor	272-1014

The pressure transducer is component P1 in the circuit shown in Figure 9-19. Internally, it is four resistive elements in an arrangement known as a Wheatstone bridge. With 5V applied to the top of the bridge, the measurement of interest is the difference of the two voltage dividers, and this difference is only 100mV full-scale. Op-amp followers U1B and U1D condition the two voltage-divider values so the differential amplifier made with U1A can subtract and then amplify the difference by 10.

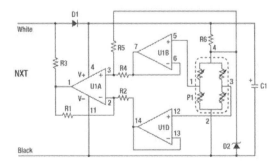

Figure 9-19. *Pressure sensor circuit*

159

Diode D2 is a Zener-type diode that creates a constant 5V for the pressure transducer. Resistor R5 offsets the output of U1A so that the sensor can measure negative pressures. Figure 9-20 shows the pressure sensor built on a solderless breadboard.

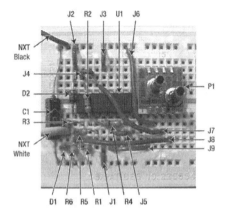

Figure 9-20. *Pressure sensor on solderless breadboard*

Table 9-4 shows the step-by-step construction of the whole sensor.

Table 9-4. *Component Placement*

Component	Start	End
U1 pin 1	F4	
C1 + −	Y1	X1
J1	Y7	J7
J2	X7	B7
D1 anode cathode	J2	Y2
J3	X3	B3
J4	C4	C5
D2 anode cathode	C3	F3
R2	D4	G5

Table 9-4. *Component Placement (continued)*

Component	Start	End
R3	G2	G4
R4	F10	F6
R1	J5	J4
R6	Y3	J3
R5	H3	H6
J5	H9	H10
P1 pin 1	F13	
J6	X10	G14
J7	D6	H15
J8	I3	I16
J9	J8	J13
NXT white black	H2	X2

After you build the pressure sensor, it needs to be calibrated. With nothing connected to the transducer ports, the pressure reading should be zero because the pressure difference is zero. However, the sensor reading is deliberately offset by a Raw value of approximately 580 so it can measure negative pressures. You can use Boyle's Law to calculate the slope of the relationship between Raw value and pressure. Boyle's Law says that the product of the pressure and volume of a gas is a constant. In other words, if you halve the volume of a gas, you double its pressure.

You can get disposable 10ml oral syringes such as the one shown in Figure 9-21 from pharmacies. Set the syringe for exactly 10ml and connect it to the lower pressure port with a very short piece of LEGO pneumatic or other tubing. There's about 0.5ml of air in the tubing and sensor that is not measured by the syringe, so you need to compress the syringe to 3ml to cut the volume to exactly one-third.

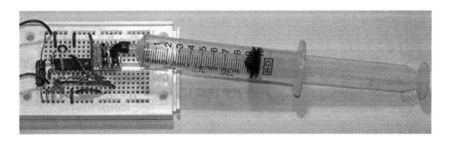

Figure 9-21. *Calibrating the pressure sensor with Boyle's Law*

Boyle's Law says the pressure is now three times as high as it was initially. The initial pressure was atmospheric, which is about 14.7psi (1,014hPa or 1atm), so now it is 44.1psi (3,041hPa or 3atm). The pressure transducer reads the difference between the two ports, and the other port is still seeing atmospheric pressure. So, the pressure sensor should be reading 29.4psi (2,027hPa or 2atm). This should lead to a slope of approximately 6.2 Raw values to 1psi.

When you're done calibrating the sensor, you should be able to generate a plot like the one shown in Figure 9-22.

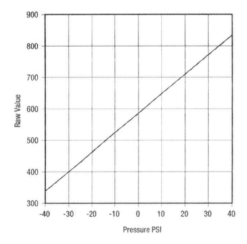

Figure 9-22. *Plot of pressure versus Raw value*

Figure 9-23 is a NXT-G program that automatically converts the Raw values to psi and displays the value on the NXT. It will work with any generation NXT software because it scales the value before the divide.

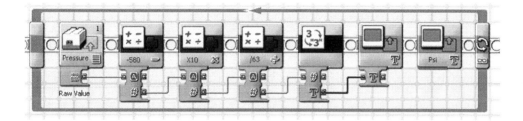

Figure 9-23. Pressure display program

■■■

CHAPTER 10

Light Sensor with LED Control

Back in Chapter 5 we showed you how to build your own light sensors with CdS Light Dependent Resistors (LDRs). However, they lacked the capability to generate light like the LEGO sensor does. This capability is particularly useful for sensing objects by reflecting light off of them instead of just measuring the ambient light level. In this chapter we will show you how to add the same LED illumination control as the LEGO Light sensor.

LED Control Circuit

Pin 5 of the NXT sensor input port, or the yellow wire in cable, controls the state of the LED in the Light Sensor. Unfortunately, the strength of the signal from the NXT is just not strong enough to directly power an LED. We need to add a simple transistor amplifier for that (Figure 10-1 shows the circuit for a CdS LDR Light Sensor that has LED control).

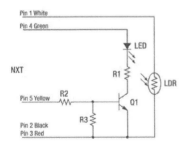

Figure 10-1. *LED control circuit*

The black triangle with little arrows in the circuit is the electronic symbol for an LED. You will really get to know LEDs when we show you how to connect them to outputs in Chapter 12. Figure 10-2 shows the typical package of a light emitting diode and the corresponding symbol. The symbol is the same as the diode discussed in Chapter 9, except for the added arrows that represent the light being emitted. Instead of a painted line on the body of a convention diode that signifies the cathode end, the LED has a flat space in the flange directly next to that lead. The cathode lead is also a little shorter than the anode lead.

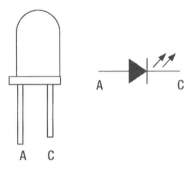

Figure 10-2. *LED outline and circuit symbol*

You already learned about PNP transistors in Chapter 8, where they were used as a buffer to isolate sensors from the NXT measurement circuitry. In this circuit, Q1 is a 2N3904 NPN type transistor. The NPN symbol (see Figure 10-3) is identical to the PNP, except that the little arrow on the emitter leg points away from the base. The physical pin outs are exactly the same, but the parts are *not* interchangeable.

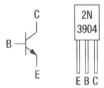

Figure 10-3. *NPN transistor symbol and 2N3904 pin out*

The transistor circuit is generically known as a *grounded emitter amplifier. Ground* is just an old electronics term for the part of the circuit that is at zero volts. If the voltage on the base of Q1 becomes positive enough, the collector will become effectively connected to the emitter. It is much like closing a switch. LED and R1 are connected in series to the 4.3V power supply and the collector of Q1. When Q1 switches on, it completes the circuit to ground and the LED lights up. Q1 needs only a small amount of current from the NXT into its base to turn on, and R2 and R3 are there to limit that current.

Table 10-1 has the complete bill of materials for the CdS sensor with LED control.

Table 10-1. *Bill of Materials*

Component	Part Number	Description	Radio Shack
Q1	2N3904	NPN transistor	276-2016 or -1617
LED	LED	any color T1-3/4 LED	
R2 and R3	10kOhm	1/4 W Resistor	271-312
R1	150 Ohm	1/4 W Resistor	see R1
LDR		Light Dependent Resistor	276-1657

Table 10-2 is the step-by-step placement guide for building the sensor on the prototype board, as shown in Figure 10-4. The most likely mistake in building the circuit is connecting the LED backward. The leg next to the flat is the one connected to R1. The blue wire in the NXT cable isn't connected to anything in the circuit and should be cut short.

Table 10-2. *Component Placement*

Component	Start	End
Q1 Emitter Base Collector	G1	G3
LDR	E1	F1
LED Anode Cathode	X3	A3
R1 (brown green brown gold)	E3	F3
R3 (brown black orange gold)	E2	F2
R2 (brown black orange gold)	H1	H2
NXT Green Yellow	X1	A2
NXT White Red	C1	I1
NXT Black	J1	

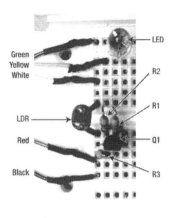

Figure 10-4. *Light control circuit on prototype board*

Testing the circuit doesn't even require a program because the NXT-G environment communicates with the NXT and its sensors while you are configuring them. Plug your prototype to sensor input port 3, connect the NXT to your computer with the USB cable, turn it on, and bring up the NXT-G environment. Start a new program and place a Light Sensor block on the program beam. With the Light Sensor block selected, the configuration window will look something like Figure 10-5. The light value should be displayed like the 84, and selecting and deselecting the Generate light field should turn the LED on and off.

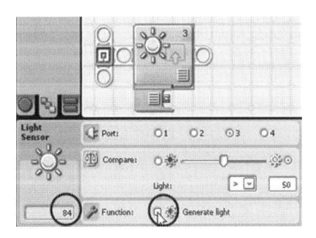

Figure 10-5. *Testing the prototype*

After testing the circuit, move the components to the PCB, as shown in Figure 10-6. It is a good idea to connect the CdS LDR through a short length of speaker wire. That way it can be separated further away from the LED. It is also a good idea to feed the wire through a beam before soldering it, just as we did in when building Light Sensors in Chapter 5. The diameter of the T1-3/4 package LED makes it easy to press-fit it into a hole of a second beam.

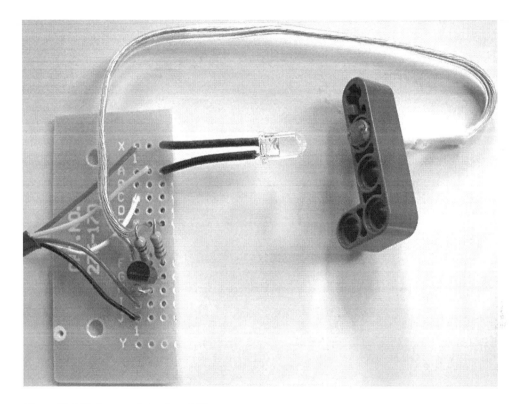

Figure 10-6. *Light control circuit on PCB*

Reflected Light Sensor

The Light Sensor can now be configured to detect objects by having the light either reflect off or be obstructed by the object. The LEGO Light Sensor's LED is permanently arranged so you can only reflect light directly back from an object. This version can reflect the light at an angle (as shown in Figure 10-7) if you want.

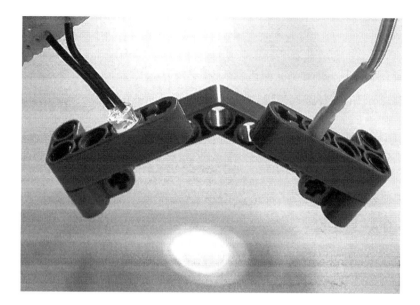

Figure 10-7. *Reflected light application*

When an object moves in front of the sensor, the light from the LED is reflected back at the LDR, and the measured light level increases. The problem with depending only on light level is that the ambient light can also increase, creating a false detection. The way around this problem is to take a light reading without the LED turned on to establish the ambient level and then a second reading with the LED on.

The two readings will be equally affected by the ambient light, but only the one with the LED turned on will be affected by light reflected off the object. It is a simple matter of subtracting the two readings to get a number that is sensitive only to the presence of an object. The NXT-G program in Figure 10-8 continuously displays the value of the difference of the two readings. The Display Value My Block was developed back in Chapter 2 and simply puts the current value on the NXT display.

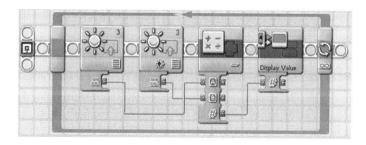

Figure 10-8. *Object detection program*

When the program is running, the LED will be flashing many times a second as it is rapidly turned off and then back on to make the two measurements. Move an object closer and farther away from the sensor. The closer the object gets, the brighter the reflected light from the LED will become, and the higher the difference will become. However, with no object present, the value will be close to zero no matter what the ambient light level is.

Transmissive Light Sensor

Another way to detect an object is for it to block the light. This is called a Transmissive Light Sensor. Figure 10-9 shows a gate where an object can roll between the LED and the LDR. Without an object in the gate, the light level will be 100, but it will drop to about 40 when the light is obstructed.

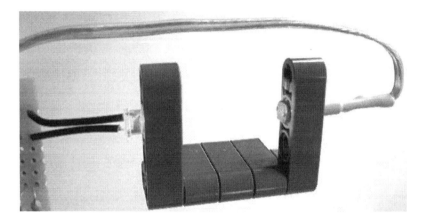

Figure 10-9. Transmissive light application

The program in Figure 10-10 will count how many times something has obstructed the light. First it waits for the light to become dark and then it waits for the light to become bright again. The Display Value My Block is used to put the Count value from the While Loop on the display.

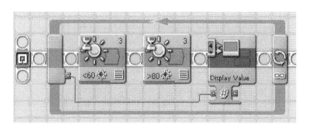

Figure 10-10. Counting program

There is an important concept illustrated by the program called *hysteresis*. The plot on the left in Figure 10-11 shows the light level as an object passes through the gate. If we greatly magnify the signal where it crosses the threshold, we would see a plot that looked something like the one on the right. The light level actually wiggles back and forth rapidly across the threshold because of the roughness on the object surface. If you set only a single threshold for light and dark, the program would count up several times while the object was only starting to obscure the light.

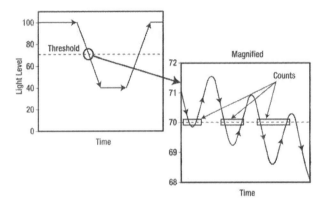

Figure 10-11. *Single threshold*

To prevent this, the dark threshold is set much lower than the light threshold. This dual threshold scheme is called hysteresis, and Figure 10-12 shows the two thresholds. Now, when the dark threshold is crossed, the light level would never wiggle back up to the light threshold. The program counts only when the object has completely passed through the gate.

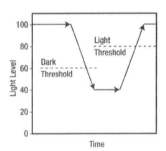

Figure 10-12. *Two thresholds*

■ ■ ■

CHAPTER 11

LEGO Motor Interfaces

The easiest way to extend the reach of your NXT inventions is to use the motors that came with it to operate the electronic controls of appliances and other equipment. The motor simply needs to be mechanically arranged to push the buttons, turn the knobs, or flip the switches on the external device to control it. The NXT motor makes it easy because it has a lot of torque and has built-in position feedback.

Another easy way to{ " LEGO motors:extending NXT with " } extend the NXT is to use other LEGO motors. LEGO makes several other motors that are designed for use with less sophisticated sets. The shape and size of these motors may allow you to build creations that would be impossible with the NXT motors. Adapter cables are available that enable you to connect them directly to the NXT, but we'll show you how to make your own.

The Clapper

Buttons are common controls, and you can arrange the NXT motor to push them instead of you doing it. The exact mechanical design will vary from device to device, but you can operate anything from expensive laboratory equipment to disposable cameras this way. When you push buttons on a remote control, the NXT can practically control the world—at least anything plugged into the wall.

For example, Radio Shack sells a little handheld remote control that transmits to a base station with an electrical outlet in it. All kinds of lights and appliances can be plugged into it. In fact, this is the safest way to control this kind of power, and we highly recommend it. Figure 11-1 shows the handheld remote control and the mechanism used to push the on and off ends of the channel one button. The gears are being used only for their peg holes, not their teeth. The top gear acts as a driver, and the lower one acts as a guide. When the motor turns forward, the linkage pushes the on-end of the button; when the motor reverses, it pushes the off-end.

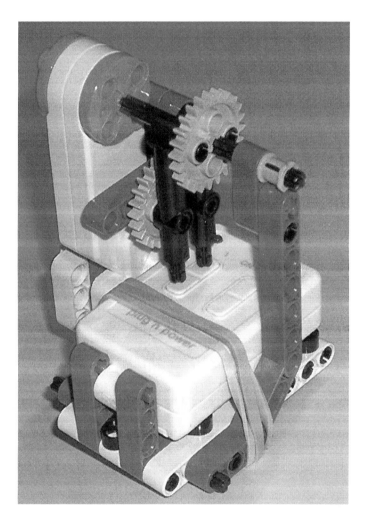

Figure 11-1. Remote control button pusher

Figure 11-2 is an NXT-G program to reproduce a simple remote-control product called *the Clapper*. The Clapper turns something on or off when it hears a loud sound. The program waits till the Sound Sensor picks up a noise louder than 25; then it pulses the motor forward with the Motor block. This pushes the on-end of the remote control button. It then waits for a second loud sound. This time it pulses the motor in reverse, which pushes the off-end of the button. The program loops back and waits for another sound.

Figure 11-2. *The Clapper program*

The buttons don't require a lot of force, so the NXT-G Motor block shown in Figure 11-3 uses only 50% power. A 0.3-second pulse is all that's needed to rotate the mechanism far enough to push the button. Because the Next Action in the Motor block is coast, the motor naturally springs back to a neutral position.

Figure 11-3. *Motor block from button pusher*

The Etch-A-NXT

Volume, tuning, position, brightness, and many other analog controls are rotary types. Designed for human fingertips, they can also be turned with an NXT motor. The built-in position feedback in the NXT motor really comes in handy for this type of control. All you need is a coupler to attach the LEGO axle to the knob of the control you want to turn. The coupler might need to be custom made, but gears, pulleys, wheels, or tires can usually be used to attach the control knob to an axle.

Etch-A-Sketch is a drawing toy from Ohio Art that uses two knobs to control a cursor that draws a line on a screen. The right knob controls the vertical movement of the cursor, and the left knob controls the horizontal movement of the cursor. Drawing with it is particularly challenging because the cursor always draws a line. You can't just move to a new location and start drawing again. You also need to coordinate the movement of both knobs when you want to draw anything but a straight horizontal or vertical line. You can eliminate this difficulty by driving the knobs with the NXT creating the Etch-A-NXT.

Figure 11-4 shows the little assembly that holds the two motors in position. The particular Etch-A-Sketch in the picture is the pocket version, which is smaller than the original.

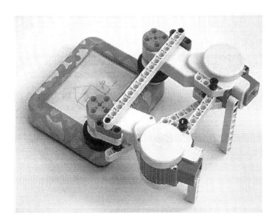

Figure 11-4. Etch-A-NXT

Couplers for the knobs are made using the #2994 30.4x14 VR wheels and the #6578 very small balloon tires. They were parts in the original MINDSTORMS Invention Kits, and are found in a variety of LEGO model car kits. One tire rim is on the wheel and the other is on the knob, as shown in Figure 11-5. It grips both well enough to drive the knobs without any slippage. The larger balloon tires that come with the NXT version of the MINDSTORMS kit fit nicely on the knobs on the bigger original Etch-A-Sketch.

Figure 11-5. Etch-A-NXT knob coupler

The NXT-G program shown in Figure 11-6 uses a My Block to take care of reading values from a text file and turning the knobs accordingly. The movements are stored in the text file as relative horizontal and vertical distances. The short wait allows the motors to come to a full stop before continuing on to the next point.

Figure 11-6. *Etch-A-NXT main program loop*

The My Block file_move3 is shown in Figure 11-7. Inside the two File blocks is the name of the text (.txt) file where the distances are stored. You must keep this file name the same in both blocks if you change it. When the last distance has been read, the STOP block is executed, and that ends the program.

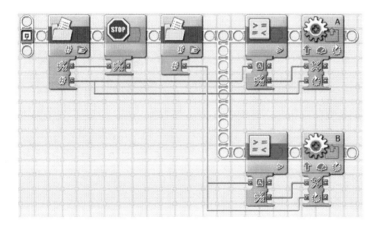

Figure 11-7. *My Block file_move3*

The distances are stored as text, one value per line, with the horizontal distance first, followed by the vertical, as seen in Listing 11-1. You need to use a simple text editor program such as Notepad to generate these files because other word-processing programs add unwanted formatting information. Pairs of distances are read and fed in parallel to the Motor blocks. A Motor block ignores the sign or direction of the distance value. The direction of the command is determined by comparing the value to 0 and feeding that logical result to the direction input of the Motor block.

Listing 11-1. *Drawing File Format*

```
Horizontal_1
Vertical_1
Horizontal_2
Vertical_2
Horizontal_3
Vertical_3
...
```

The example drawing file box.txt contains the distance commands to create a simple box that's 200 units on a side (see Listing 11-2).

Listing 11-2. *Listing for Drawing File box.txt*

```
200
0
0
200
-200
0
0
-200
```

MyFile.txt, available from the book web site (go to the Source Code/Download area at http://www.apress.com), is considerably more ambitious. It draws the picture of a house and a waving stickperson next to it (shown in Figure 11-8). The text files must be downloaded to the NXT before running the Etch-A-NXT program.

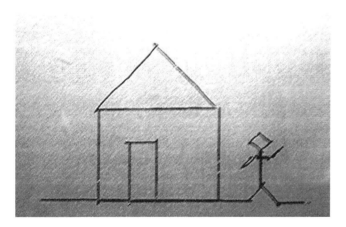

Figure 11-8. *Drawing created from MyFile.txt*

The first step of downloading a drawing text file is to open the NXT window in the NXT-G programming environment. Click the upper-left button in the control cluster shown in Figure 11-9.

Figure 11-9. *Button to bring up the NXT window*

The window shown in Figure 11-10 displays. It has two tabs: Communications and Memory.

Figure 11-10. *NXT Communications and Memory window*

Select the Memory tab, and you'll see the window shown in Figure 11-11, in which you need to pick the Other file type under NXT Memory Usage. However, the first time you do this you won't see the Other category. Either way, press the Download button. In the window that opens, you need to change the "Files of type" to include All Files (*.*), or you won't see files with the .txt extension. When you've found the file you want to download to the NXT, just double-click its name.

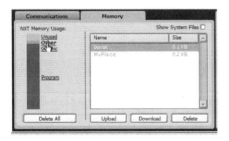

Figure 11-11. *Select the Other file type and download the file to the NXT*

Pneumatic Gripper

Toggle switches are common control devices you'll want to operate. LEGO pneumatic cylinders are controlled by toggle-switch–type valves that select one of two tubes that will receive air pressure. Because they're already LEGO components, connecting them to the NXT motor is easy. The switch operator is the same size as a Technic axle, and you can connect a linkage to it, as shown in Figure 11-12, to move it between the two operating points. In the mechanical engineering world, this is called a *four bar linkage.*

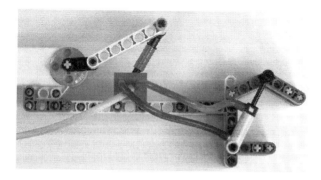

Figure 11-12. *Open pneumatic gripper*

Robotic grippers are a good application for pneumatic control. The force provided by a pneumatic cylinder is gentle, and it's a compact way to deliver the force directly to the jaws. The simple one-sided gripper, shown open in Figure 11-12 and closed in Figure 11-13, is operated by rotating the NXT motor between two positions 180 degrees apart.

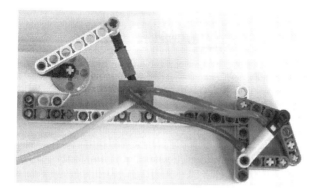

Figure 11-13. *Closed pneumatic gripper*

A NXT-G program to control the gripper is shown in Figure 11-14. Every time you push the left button on the NXT, the motor rotates 180 degrees, and that toggles the gripper open and closed.

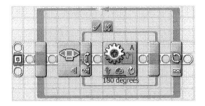

Figure 11-14. *Program to toggle gripper*

The details of the Motor block are shown in Figure 11-15, in which you can see the 180-degree Duration value. Before running the program, you need to rotate the motor by hand so the valve starts out in one of the two positions.

Figure 11-15. *Motor block showing 180-degree movement*

RCX 9V Motor

The RCX motor (see Figure 11-16) is internally geared down, but not as much as the NXT motor. Available from LEGO Education as part number W775225, it might be appropriate when you need high speed but low torque because the motor isn't as powerful as the NXT motor.

Figure 11-16. *RCX 9V motor*

181

The DC motor brushes are visible on the back of the motor in the breakout photograph in Figure 11-17. It requires the conversion cable (LEGO #8528) to connect it to the NXT. A unique feature of the old RCX-style connector is that depending on the orientation of the mating connectors, you can reverse the motor direction without changing the software.

Figure 11-17. *Motor breakdown*

The RCX motor is particularly handy because of its smaller size. Figure 11-18 is an example of just how compact the motor is. It is used here with a pulley to power a wheel that can be steered by a second NXT motor. Making anything similar to this with only the NXT motors would result in a construction that was considerably taller. The electrical connections would also be less convenient.

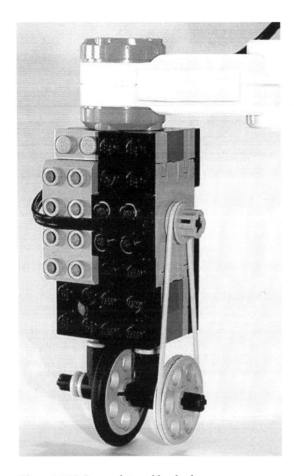

Figure 11-18. Powered steerable wheel

NXT Conversion Cable

LEGO sells an RCX-compatible cable for the NXT (see Figure 11-19). The large rectangular block in the middle of the cable protects the electrical connections. It allows the NXT to use both RCX motors and the Legacy Sensors.

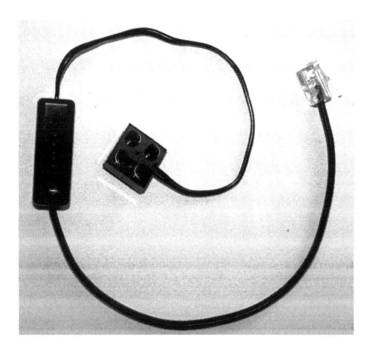

Figure 11-19. *NXT conversion Cable*

You can make your own with an NXT cable and an RCX cable. The adapter connects a 9V RCX cable to wires 1 and 2 (white and black) of an NXT cable. You should refer to Chapter 3 for instructions on cutting and preparing NXT cables.

First, we'll describe how to make one with a screw terminal (you can see the different elements needed for a homebrew compatibility cable in Figure 11-20):

Figure 11-20. *Elements needed to build a compatibility cable*

1. Split the two wires of the RCX cable and strip them.

2. Fold the ends of the cables before screwing them in the terminal.

3. Strip the black sheath of the NXT cable with a cutter and cut all color cables except the black and white ones.

4. Strip the black and white wires of the NXT cable and fold them. The prepared cable should look like the ones in Figure 11-21.

Figure 11-21. Prepared cables

5. Screw all the wires under the screw terminals (see Figure 11-22). Folding the ends and tightening the insulating material under the screw provides some strain relief.

Figure 11-22. Attaching wires to the screw terminal

185

6.   The final cable is illustrated in Figure 11-23: it connects an RCX motor to the NXT.

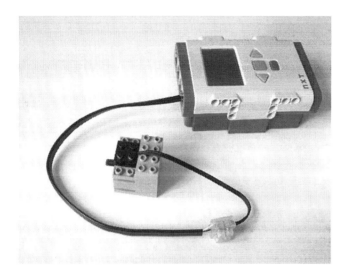

Figure 11-23. *NXT driving a 9V RCX motor*

Of course, it's also possible to make a soldered version of this cable using some heat shrink tubing to insulate and join the two sections of the cable, as shown in Figure 11-24.

Figure 11-24. *Solder RCX and NXT wires together. Don't forget to insert heat shrink tubing!*

Figure 11-25 shows such a cable connecting an RCX Light Sensor to the NXT.

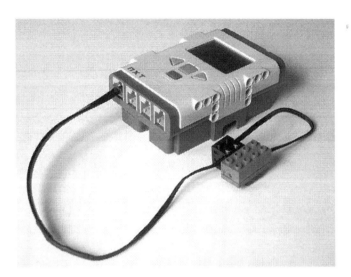

Figure 11-25. Using an RCX Light Sensor with the NXT

Power Functions Motors

LEGO Power Functions is a family of products designed to motorize the Creator and Technic line of construction kits. It consists of large and medium-sized motors, a battery box, and an infrared remote control. The motors can be used with the NXT, but require two adapter cables. The first is the NXT conversion cable previously described and a second cable that converts the Power Functions connector to the RCX 9V style connector. Of course, we'll show you how to make the conversion yourself.

The medium-sized, or M-Motor (LEGO Shop PN#8883), is shown in Figure 11-26. It has the classic stud-style mounting system on the bottom as well as the studless style used with the NXT on its face. The motor speed is faster than, but not as powerful as, the NXT motor. However, it is both faster and more powerful than the RCX motor.

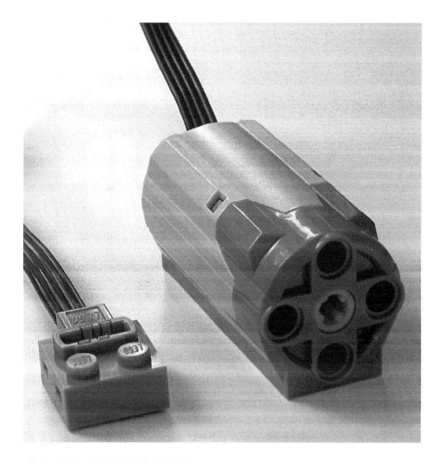

Figure 11-26. *Power Functions M-Motor*

One excellent use for the M-Motor is vehicle propulsion. Figure 11-27 shows how efficiently the motor can be connected directly to a wheel through the beam that makes up the side of the chassis. This method also works well for tracked vehicle designs. A symmetrically arranged motor on the opposite side of the vehicle allows for steering as well as propulsion. The disadvantage of using Power Functions motors is that you lose the position feedback built in to the NXT motors.

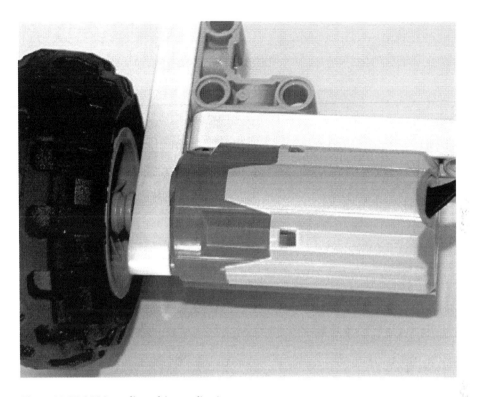

Figure 11-27. M-Motor direct drive application

The larger Power Functions XL-Motor (LEGO Shop PN#8882) is shown in Figure 11-28. It has only the studless NXT construction and for good reason. This motor produces so much torque it can easily disassemble weakly designed drive trains. An excellent choice for direct drive propulsion, it is highly geared down internally, making it the slowest LEGO motor.

Figure 11-28. Power Functions XL-Motor

Power Functions Cabling

A closer look at the Power Functions connector reveals that it has four electrical connections in the small rectangular section. Figure 11-29 shows both the top and bottom view of the connector. The battery power is always available as the 0V and 9V connections. Switching elements, like the infrared remote control, selectively connect the battery power to C1 and C2. Motors are connected only to C1 and C2.

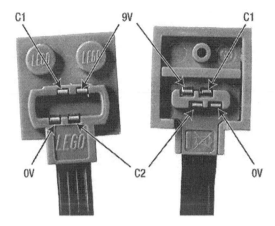

Figure 11-29. Top and bottom of the Power Functions connector

The Power Functions extension wire (LEGO Shop PN#8886) is an extension cord 8 inches (20cm) long, but more importantly it is an adapter to the RCX 9V–style connector system. Figure 11-30 shows the bottom of the adapter end and the bottom of the Power Functions end. The top side of the ends looks like the regular Power Functions connector top. C1 and C2 are connected to the two connections of the RCX 9V connector.

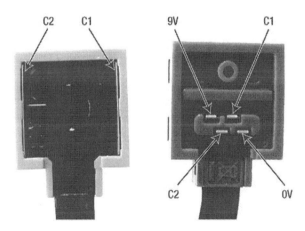

Figure 11-30. Power Functions extension wire connector bottoms

Having made our own NXT conversion cable, we already know the RCX 9V connector is connected to pins 1 and 2 (white and black) of the NXT cable (Figure 11-31).

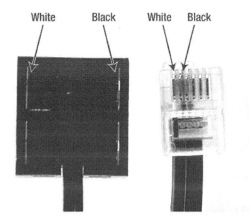

Figure 11-31. *NXT conversion cable ends*

If you want to connect directly from the NXT to a Power Functions motor, you only need to connect the black and white wire from the NXT cable to the C1 and C2 wires in the motor cable:

1. You might want to refer to Chapter 3 for instructions on cutting and preparing NXT cables. Cut the Power Functions (see Figure 11-32) connector off the motor, but make sure you leave about one inch (2.5cm) of cable on the connector so it can be used for something else later.

Figure 11-32. *Cut Power Functions connector off the motor*

2. The inner two wires of the cable are C1 and C2. You can cut the outer two wires back because you will not be using them. Prepare an NXT cable with only the black and white wires, leaving enough room for short pieces of heat shrink to be slid on them (see Figure 11-33). An additional larger piece of heat shrink should be slid on the Power Functions cable that will serve to cover the entire splice.

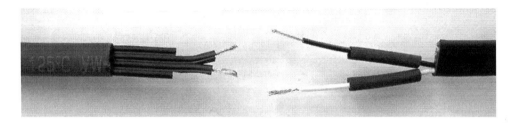

Figure 11-33. Slip heat shrink tubing on wires before soldering

3. Solder the black wire to C1 and the white to C2, as shown in Figure 11-34. It is all right if you get these mixed up because it only eventually affects which direction the motor rotates when given a forward command.

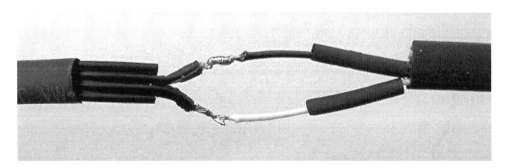

Figure 11-34. Solder black and white wires to Power Functions middle wires

4. Slide the small heat shrink tubes over the solder joints and apply enough heat to shrink them. Then slide the larger heat shrink over the whole splice and shrink that. When you are done, you will hardly be able to detect the connection (see Figure 11-35). If you need a longer cable to reach between the motor and the NXT, splice in a length of 18 gauge (0.8mm2) speaker wire to extend the cable.

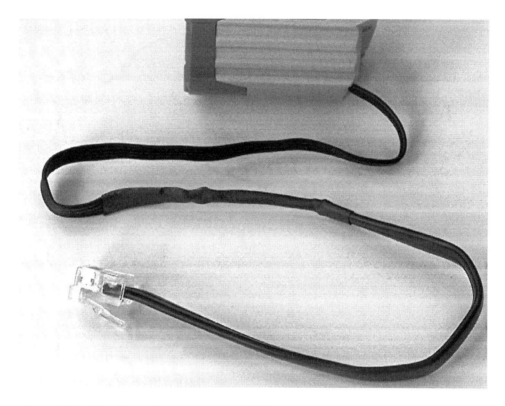

Figure 11-35. Finished Power Functions motor with NXT connector

CHAPTER 12

Beyond LEGO Motors

The NXT has three output ports with variable power and polarity control that you can use to activate a variety of devices above and beyond LEGO motors. (The sophisticated pulse width modulation circuitry behind these ports was already described in Chapter 3.) The NXT output power is on the same two wires that we used for passive sensors: the black and the white wires in the NXT cable, or pin 1 and pin 2 on the output port connector. The white wire will be positive, and the black will be negative, when the motor output is set to forward. For most of the projects that follow, we'll show only 18 gauge ($0.8mm^2$) speaker wires, and you can presume that they are attached to these two NXT connections.

The Motor Block

Three NXT-G blocks control the output ports. The Move block is specifically designed for simultaneous control of two outputs for steering vehicles and is not generally useful for controlling single outputs. The Motor block makes full use of the built-in NXT feedback, while the Motor* block is designed for older, less-sophisticated LEGO 9V motors. Figure 12-1 shows the Motor block in its expanded form. In this form, a variety of data inputs and outputs are available, but most of them are concerned with the built-in angle feedback. For now, we're interested in only the Power and Direction inputs because they directly control the voltage on the output port.

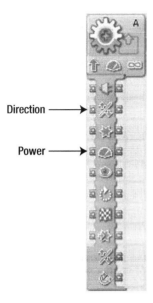

Direction

Power

Figure 12-1. Expanded Motor block

Output Control Program

It would be nice if the NXT came with a control panel that allowed you to adjust the output power directly with a "Try Me" type of menu, but it doesn't. The NXT-G program laid out in Figures 12-2, 12-3, and 12-4 is handy for debugging the projects that follow. Pushing the right NXT button increases the motor power up to 100, and pushing the left button decreases the power to –100. A –100 power is actually a power of 100 in reverse.

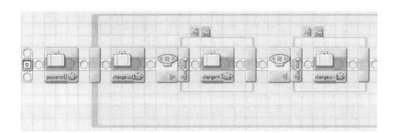

Figure 12-2. Output control program—initalization and button detection

The power level is stored in the variable *power*, and the increment amount—+1, 0, or –1—is stored in the variable *change*. When the value of *power* reaches +101 or –101, you need to set it back to the limit. The sign of the value of *power* is determined by comparing it to zero. The result of this comparison becomes the direction input for the Motor block.

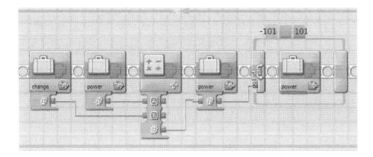

Figure 12-3. *Output control program—change and limit*

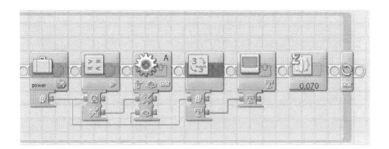

Figure 12-4. *Output control program—output and display*

Lamps

By far, the simplest non-LEGO device you can connect to an NXT output port is an incandescent lamp. Lamps don't care about polarity, which means you can hook the black and white wires either way, as shown in the circuit diagram in Figure 12-5. About the only problem is that the 9V output of the NXT is an uncommon voltage for lamps. Higher-voltage lamps aren't very bright, while you can burn out lower voltage lamps by accidentally putting full power to the output.

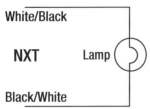

Figure 12-5. *Lamp circuit*

Figure 12-6 shows a small lightbulb and plastic socket available at Radio Shack. The lamp is designed to operate from 7.5V, so you shouldn't set Motor block power to more than about 90 to keep from burning it out. Simply screw wires to the two terminals of the socket, and you're ready to create light on command.

Figure 12-6. *7.5V lamp in socket*

Muscle Wires

Muscle Wires are a type of shape memory alloy (SMA) made from an alloy of nickel and titanium called Flexinol. Due to their crystal structure, SMAs change shape at different temperatures. Below a critical transition temperature, Muscle Wires can stretch by as much as eight percent, but they recover their original length when heated. You can use this contraction to create motion without the usual need for motors. You can supply the heat externally or you can generate it internally by passing electrical current through the wire. The time it takes to heat or cool the wire is measured in seconds, and that greatly limits the places where it can be used.

The easiest way to start experimenting with Muscle Wires is to buy the "Muscle Wires Project Book and Sample Kit" from the Robot Shop (RB-Dyn-31). Figure 12-7 shows a basic lever demonstration built with one of the Flexinol 150LT wires that comes in the kit. The Muscle Wire runs from the base of the tower to the short side of the lever, and a bag of coins on the long side of the lever provides the force to stretch it. When the NXT output passes current through the Muscle Wire it will be heated, causing it to contract and lift the bag.

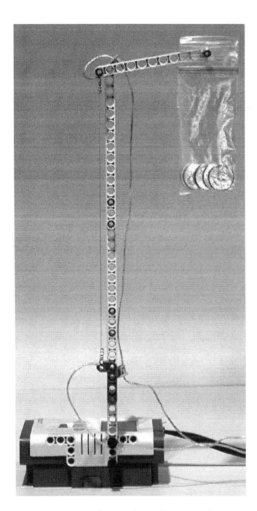

Figure 12-7. *Muscle Wire lever demonstration*

Making good connections to a Muscle Wire is challenging because it's brittle and cannot be soldered. The kit comes with little crimp connectors that are used to fasten the Muscle Wire to an anchor and an electrical wire. Crimp the Muscle Wire to one end of the connector and then crimp a loop of solid hook-up wire the same size as a Technic peg and a length of speaker wire on the other end. While holding the Muscle Wire end of the connector with needle-nose pliers to keep it cool, solder the other end with the loop and speaker wire together. When you're done, the connector should look like Figure 12-8. Repeat this process for the other end.

Figure 12-8. *Crimp assembly*

You attach the Muscle Wire to the base of the tower and lever using black Technic pegs, as shown in Figure 12-9.

Figure 12-9. *Anchor at base of tower*

The NXT-G program in Figure 12-10 applies power to the output for five seconds. The power level needs to be only about 25 to get full contraction. The voltage on the wire should be less than 0.3V/cm to prevent it from overheating. Then the program waits five seconds to let the wire cool down and stretch. Audible "Start" and "Stop" sounds are generated with Sound blocks, so you can tell when the NXT is switching the power on and off.

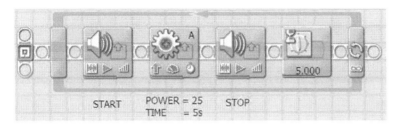

Figure 12-10. Muscle Wire program

Electromagnets and Solenoids

A motor is just a fancy kind of electromagnet, and it probably isn't too surprising that you can hook up an electromagnet to an output instead of the NXT motor. A *solenoid* is also an electromagnet that includes a metal rod that moves in and out of the winding, called the *armature*. It's like a motor that goes back and forth rather than around.

Kinetic Sculpture

Normally, a swinging pendulum eventually stops due to friction. If a small amount of energy is pumped into the pendulum at the right time, like pushing a child in a swing, it will keep on going. That's the secret behind the kinetic sculpture shown in Figure 12-11. An electromagnet in the base is pulsed on to attract a small metal globe as it swings by. You control the timing by using an NXT Light Sensor to detect when the globe is in the correct position.

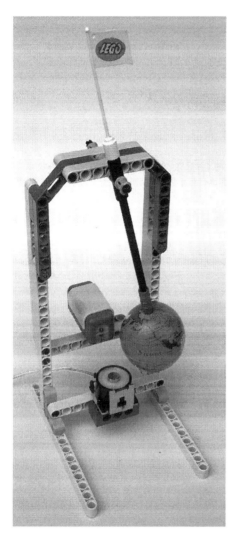

Figure 12-11. *Kinetic sculpture*

The metal globe is from the small toy pencil sharpener shown in Figure 12-12. You can probably find these in the stationery department of a variety store. The mounting hole in the North Pole of the globe is enlarged, and a blue Technic axle peg is pressed into it to allow it to be connected to Technic axle components.

Figure 12-12. *Globe pencil sharpener*

The electromagnet (see Figure 12-13) is a coil removed from a device known as a *relay*. The relay is a Potter and Brumfield KRPA-11DG-6, which has a 6VDC coil (the correct use of relays is discussed in the following section). It's all right to use a lower-voltage coil because the 9V of the NXT is only briefly applied to the coil, and the voltage is much less than 6V on average. You can attach the coil to the structure with a rubber band or double-face tape.

Figure 12-13. *Electromagnet coil from 6V relay*

The NXT-G program shown in Figure 12-14 loops till the globe casts a shadow on the Light Sensor, making its value less than 50. The program then gives the electromagnet a short pulse on with the Motor block and makes a little click with the Sound block. After that, it waits till the sensor is exposed to the light again as the globe swings past. It keeps looping until the globe swings back from the other direction, which starts the whole process over again.

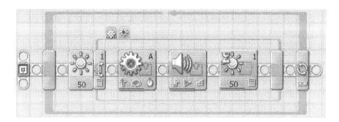

Figure 12-14. *Kinetic sculpture program*

There has to be enough light in front of the sculpture so that the globe casts a shadow on the Light Sensor. Then you need to start the pendulum swinging by hand. After that, it keeps swinging and making a sound like a metronome. You can use it to provide animation for small objects such as flags or Minifigs.

Relays

Relays are controlled switches that use an electromagnet to move electrical contacts on and off. Usually relays have both normally open (NO) and normally closed (NC) contacts with a shared common connection. The common connection is also known as the *pole*. When the electromagnet is energized, the pole is pulled toward the NO contact to close it and away from the NC contact to open it. Figure 12-15 shows the basic relay circuit. The load can be a device operating at a different voltage than the NXT, and also something that requires substantially more power than the NXT can deliver.

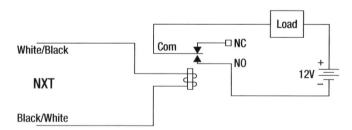

Figure 12-15. *Basic relay circuit*

■ **Caution** Although you could use a relay to control household electricity, we strongly advise you to stay away from it. Even the slightest mistake can be lethal. Stay safe by sticking with devices that operate from low voltages, and preferably from batteries.

One of the most important characteristics of a relay is its coil voltage. Just like with lightbulbs, 9V is a fairly uncommon voltage for relay coils. Even if you could find a 9V relay, the output voltage of an NXT with weak batteries would be too low to operate it. Your best bet is to buy a 6V relay and operate the NXT output with less than full power. Limit the power value in the Motor block to 80 to keep the voltage on the relay coil around 6V.

The Potter and Brumfield KRPA-11DG-6 is an excellent choice for a relay, but it's expensive and requires an additional octal socket that will add a lot of cost to your project. A good alternative is the Potter and Brumfield PE014006, which is substantially smaller and cheaper. It's designed for mounting on a printed circuit board, but you can solder wires directly to the pins, as shown in Figure 12-16.

NXT   Normally
                                                        Open
                                                        Contact

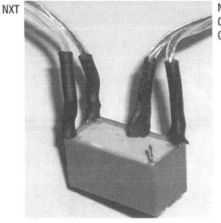

Figure 12-16. Relay

Relays are good for operating devices that were originally designed for automotive or marine applications. The NXT is a real weakling compared with equipment that operates at up to 13.8VDC with several amps of current. An automobile vacuum cleaner could be the basis of your own robotic vacuum cleaner. Portable air compressors can supply a constant source of pressure for pneumatics. Boat bilge pumps, as shown in Figure 12-17, can move liquids in hydroponic gardens or water fountains. It's more economical to run these devices with power supplies that deliver 12V from household electricity, but it's much safer to use batteries.

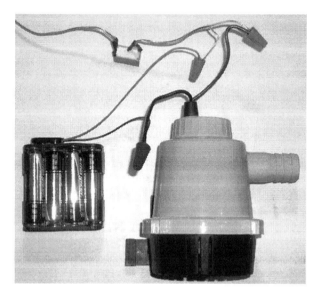

Figure 12-17. *Relay control of a 12V bilge pump*

Doubling Outputs

Diodes are the one-way valves of the electrical world. The physical package and circuit symbol are shown in Figure 12-18. They have two leads like a resistor, but unlike the resistor the leads are not interchangeable. A diode has an anode and a cathode lead, and a line is painted on the cathode end of the part. Electrical current can flow only from the anode to the cathode. In that direction, the diode looks about like a solid piece of wire. However, in the reverse direction, the diode looks like an open circuit.

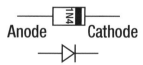

Figure 12-18. *Diode and circuit symbol*

If you connect a diode in series with a lightbulb, as shown in Figure 12-19, it will light only when the current flow is in one direction and not the other. Because you can control the polarity of the NXT output using the direction input on the Motor block, the bulb will light only in forward or reverse, but not both.

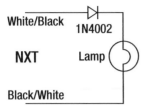

Figure 12-19. *Diode and lamp circuit diagram*

An inexpensive way to get small lights is to cut apart long strings of tiny Christmas tree lights. Up to 50 of these lights are connected in series, which means each light only operates on a few volts. You should only set the power in the Motor block to a low value such as 20, or you'll burn out the light.

Figure 12-20 shows how to connect the diode in series with the light. It's a good idea to solder the connections to make them more permanent.

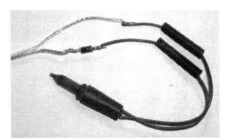

Figure 12-20. *Christmas tree light with diode*

Figure 12-21 shows how you can cover the entire diode and the connections with heat shrink tubing to insulate and protect them.

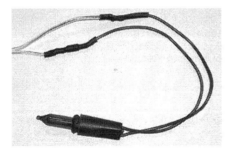

Figure 12-21. *Heat shrink tubing covers the diode and connections*

207

The whole idea of connecting a diode in series might sound pretty useless, but there is a method to the madness. If you connect two lights to the same output with diodes facing in opposite directions, like the schematic in Figure 12-22, one lamp will light in forward and the other in reverse. In a way, you've doubled the number of NXT outputs because you can control six different lights. The only drawback is that you can light one light per output at a time.

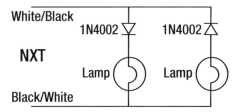

Figure 12-22. *Two lights connected to one output*

Many different types of diodes are available. The best ones to use for NXT outputs are the 1N400X rectifier diodes. The X in the model number has to do with the voltage capability of the part, and the higher the number, the higher the voltage. All of them can handle the current and voltages present on an NXT output. This book shows the 1N4002, which is good to 100V.

When controlling anything but a resistive load such as a lamp or Muscle Wire, the circuit gets a little more complicated. Figure 12-23 shows how you should add an additional diode to the circuit when operating motors or relays. It's beyond the scope of this book to explain exactly why this diode is necessary, but it has to do with diverting energy that's stored in motors and electromagnets when they get turned off. Not using it will probably damage the other diode. Just like with the lights earlier, now you can control six different motors or relays.

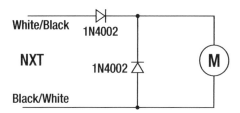

Figure 12-23. *Motor or relay circuit diagram*

You can combine the contacts from two relays controlled by the same output to get voltage polarity control on an output. Figure 12-24 has two of the circuits in Figure 12-23 and an arrangement of relay contacts that switch 12V on the motor to make it go forward with Relay 1 energized or reverse with Relay 2.

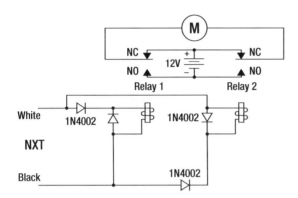

Figure 12-24. *Directional voltage control using two relays*

Although you could use the point-to-point wiring schemes shown so far, it's better to build the circuit shown in Figure 12-24 on a printed circuit board (PCB). Figure 12-25 shows how you can connect the relays and diodes in a sturdy and compact way on a prototype PCB. Speaker wires are used to input the 12V and NXT signals and output the load voltage.

Figure 12-25. *Directional voltage control assembly*

Light Emitting Diodes

Figure 12-26 shows the typical package of a light emitting diode (LED) and its electrical circuit symbol. The symbol is the same as the diode we've already discussed, except for two little arrows that symbolize the light being emitted. Instead of a painted line to signify the cathode end of the LED, like a conventional diode, the LED has a flat space in the flange directly next to that lead. The anode lead is also a little longer than the cathode lead.

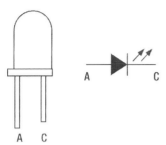

Figure 12-26. *LED outline and circuit symbol*

An LED needs a resistor connected in series with it to limit the amount of current flowing through it. Unlike an incandescent lamp, the voltage across the LED is fixed and only about two volts. If you connect an LED to a voltage greater than that, it won't just shine brightly it will also be permanently damaged.

The calculation of the resistor value is a little mathematical. The first thing you need to know is the power supply voltage from which you intend to run the LED. In the case of the NXT, the output voltage is 9V. The second thing you need to know is the LED voltage drop, and that depends on the particular LED you have. Table 12-1 shows typical values, but it's better to check the datasheet for your particular device. Finally, you need the amount of current that should flow through the LED. That should also come from the datasheet, but Table 12-1 also has typical values.

Table 12-1. *Typical LED Data*

Color	V Drop	Current	R
Red	1.7 V	20mA	330Ω
High-efficiency red	1.9	20	330
Orange and yellow	2	20	330
Green	2.1	20	330
White, blue, and pure green	3.4	25	220

Subtract the LED voltage from the power supply voltage and then divide the result by the LED current. For example, suppose that you have a 9V power supply, a 2V LED voltage drop, and you want 20mA (0.020A) of current. The calculated resistor value is 350Ω, but you would need to use a 330Ω resistor because that's the closest standard resistor value.

$$R = \frac{V - VDrop}{I} \; [\Omega]$$

$$R = \frac{9-2}{0.02} = 350 \; [\Omega]$$

LEDs produce light only when they are *forward biased*. That means the current needs to flow in the same direction as the arrow of the diode in the LED symbol. This also means the anode voltage must be positive with respect to the cathode. LEDs don't produce light when they are connected backward, or *reverse biased*. In fact, they can be damaged if the reverse voltage is greater than about 5V. Because the NXT output voltage polarity can be positive or negative, you must protect the LED with another diode to prevent it from being damaged this way.

Figure 12-27 shows the circuit diagram of an LED output, and Figure 12-28 shows the assembly. The value of resistor R is computed using the equation, and the 1N4148 is a small diode used to protect the LED from reverse voltage. You could use a 1N4002, but the 1N4148 is smaller and more appropriate for the current in the LED. Hooking the white NXT cable wire to the resistor and the black to the LED cathode will make an LED that lights when the Motor block output is set to forward. Reversing the white and black connections will make an LED that lights when the Motor block is in reverse.

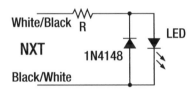

Figure 12-27. Basic LED circuit

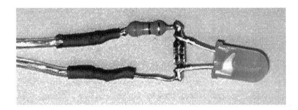

Figure 12-28. LED assembly

You can also use another LED in place of the 1N4148, as shown in the circuit in Figure 12-29. They can share the same series resistor if the LEDs are similar enough. Only one LED will light at a time: LED1 when the Motor block output is in forward and LED2 when it is in reverse.

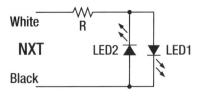

Figure 12-29. *Two-LED circuit*

Use LEDs in the T13/4 package, which is about 5mm in diameter because they can be pushed partway into Technic holes for mounting, as in Figure 12-30.

Figure 12-30. *T13/4 LEDs in Technic beam*

It's easier to create the parallel connection between the LEDs by bending one lead of each LED over to the other LED. Make sure that the LEDs are mounted with the cathode flat spot on opposite sides. This gives you two leads to connect to that are separated by enough distance that they won't easily touch and short. Figure 12-31 shows the parallel connection.

Figure 12-31. *LEDs connected in parallel*

Figure 12-32 shows the addition of the series resistor.

Figure 12-32. Add common series resistor

Finally, Figure 12-33 shows heat shrink covering the connections.

Figure 12-33. Heat shrink to insulate connections

Assuming that executives make important decisions that are about as good as flipping a coin, you can make a contraption that makes yes/no decisions at the push of a button (see Figure 12-34). You make the yes/no indicator using the circuit shown in Figure 12-28, with one red and one green LED.

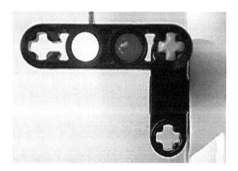

Figure 12-34. *Green light on the left is a favorable decision*

The NXT-G program is shown in Figure 12-35. Pushing the center button on the NXT turns the output off, clearing the previous decision. When the button is released, the Random block picks a number 0 or 1, with equal probability. Depending on the number, the output is either turned on in forward or reverse, making the green/yes or the red/no light up. If you reduce the power level in the Motor block, you could also use two Christmas tree lights connected as shown in Figure 12-22.

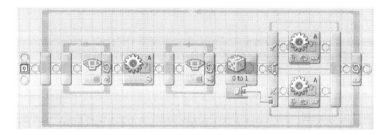

Figure 12-35. *Decision maker program*

More Power

Relays are great for turning on and off equipment that requires power beyond the capability of the NXT. The NXT creates variable power by turning on and off the output thousands of times a second, but relays are way too slow to be operated this way. You can use a solid-state device known as a metal oxide semiconductor field effect transistor (MOSFET) like a relay, but it can switch as fast as the NXT. Unlike relay contacts, the MOSFET conducts in only one direction, so it's useful only for DC applications.

One MOSFET Amplifier

Figure 12-36 shows the basic N-channel MOSFET amplifier using the IRF510. The MOSFET is the complicated symbol in the center of the drawing. It has three leads: the gate, source, and drain. The diode in the symbol is usually not drawn for simplicity, but it's always a part of the device. When the voltage between the gate and source is greater than about 4V, the MOSFET will switch the connection between the drain and the source on. The 10k resistor prevents the gate voltage from floating around when it isn't connected to anything, and the 1N4002 is there to divert the power stored in the motor when it is turned off.

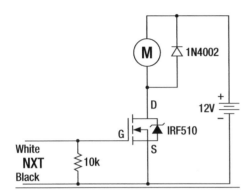

Figure 12-36. *MOSFET unipolar amplifier circuit*

The IRF510 comes in the TO-220AB package shown in Figure 12-37. The drain is connected to both the center lead and the large flange. You can use a small screw and nut to turn the flange into a handy terminal for connecting the load. However, if you need for the IRF510 to carry more than about 2A, you'll need to attach a heat sink to the flange.

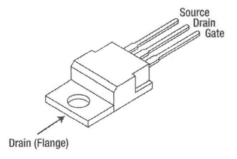

Figure 12-37. *MOSFET package*

A terminal strip version of the MOSFET amplifier is shown in Figure 12-38. The drain lead is bent up and out of the way because the flange is used to make the connection. The wires to the load are soldered to the leads of the 1N4002 to make connecting easier. Make sure you have the cathode (end with the band) of the diode toward the positive power terminal.

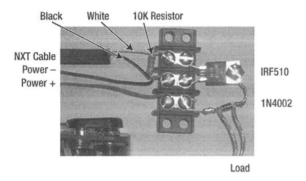

Figure 12-38. MOSFET amplifier assembly built on a terminal strip

Because you often need variable speed, motors are the natural application for the MOSFET amplifier. Figure 12-39 shows an automobile electric window motor connected to the amplifier. A variety of motors such as this are used in automobiles for power equipment and windshield wipers. They are geared down much like the NXT motor, but they often use a worm gear that locks the shaft when the motor isn't turning.

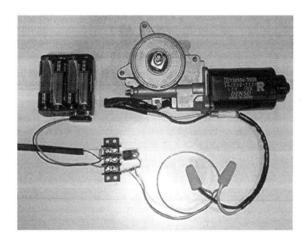

Figure 12-39. MOSFET amplifier controlling an automotive electric window motor

Bipolar MOSFET Amplifier

You can vary motor speed with the one MOSFET amplifier, but not the direction. This can be a serious shortcoming for vehicle designs for which you need to go both forward and reverse. Extending the design to control both speed and direction requires the more complicated bipolar amplifier shown in Figure 12-40.

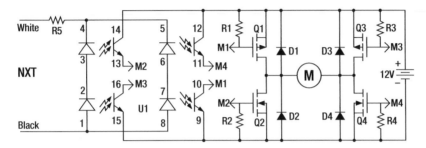

Figure 12-40. *Bipolar amplifier*

Table 12-2 shows the bill of materials.

Table 12-2. *Bill of Materials*

Component	Part Number	Description	Digi-Key
Q1, Q3	IRF9530PBF	P Chan MOSFET	IRF9530PBF-ND
Q2, Q4	IRF520NPBF	N Chan MOSFET	IRF520NPBF-ND
R1–R4	330 Ohm	1/2 W Resistor	PPC330BCT-ND
R5	100 Ohm	1/4 W Resistor	P100CACT-ND
U1	PS2501-4	NEC Quad Opto-isolator	PS2501-4A-ND
D1–D4	STTH2R06RL	Fast Recovery Rectifier Diode	497-4409-1-ND

The heart of the design is the H-bridge made from four MOSFETs. You can see the H pattern where the motor symbol M is in the middle of the horizontal line of the letter H. The upper MOSFETs—Q1 and Q3—are P-channel; the lowers—Q2 and Q4—are N-channel like the IRF510. P-channel MOSFETs work like their N-channel brothers, but have a negative gate voltage. The arrow in the gate part of the symbol is reversed to differentiate it from the N-channel.

You use the MOSFETs in pairs to connect either the positive voltage or ground to either end of the motor. The forward pair is Q1 and Q4, and the reverse is Q3 and Q2. U1 is an opto-isolator that contains four LEDs and four phototransistors. When the light from an LED shines on a corresponding phototransistor, it turns on. The LEDs are cleverly arranged to turn on the right pairs of MOSFETS to preserve the polarity of the NXT output voltage.

You should first build the bipolar amplifier on a solderless prototype board, and then transfer the working design over to a matching prototype PCB. Figure 12-41 shows the first step in populating the prototype board.

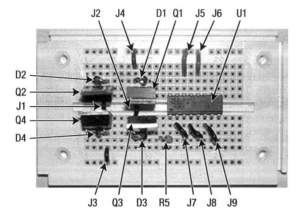

Figure 12-41. *Step one*

Follow Table 12-3 for step-by-step construction, making sure that every part is in the correct hole. The MOSFET legs fit tightly in the prototype board and require gentle rocking to minimize the insertion force. Pay special attention to the direction of the diodes—it's easy to accidentally connect them backward.

Table 12-3. *Component Placement Step One*

Component	Start	End
Q2 Gate Drain Source	D2	D4
J1	E4	F4
Q4 Gate Drain Source	G2	G4
D2 Anode Cathode	C4	C3
D4 Anode Cathode	H4	H3
Q1 Gate Drain Source	D10	D8
J2	E8	F8
Q3 Gate Drain Source	G10	G8

Table 12-3. *Component Placement Step One (continued)*

Component	Start	End
D1 Anode Cathode	C9	C8
D3 Anode Cathode	H9	H8
J3	X8	A8
U1 Pin 1	F13	
J4	J4	Y4
R5	I12	I13
J5	X15	B15
J6	X17	B17
J7	G14	H15
J8	G16	H17
J9	G18	H19

Figure 12-42 shows additional parts, with Table 12-4 giving the step-by-step construction that goes with it. Notice that resistors R1–R4 need to be the larger 1/2 W type because of the power they dissipate.

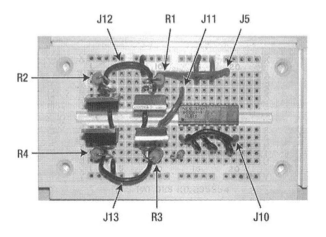

Figure 12-42. *Step two*

Table 12-4. *Component Placement Step Two*

Component	Start	End
R2	B2	B4
J12	B3	B9
R1	B8	B10
R4	I2	I4
J13	I3	I9
R3	I8	I10
J11	A10	A19
J10	G13	G20
J14	C13	F10

Figure 12-43 shows the complete circuit with connections to 12V, the NXT, and the load. Again, step-by-step instructions are in Table 12-5.

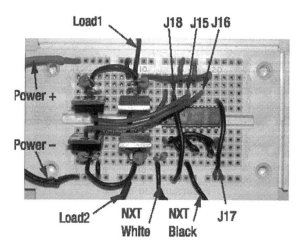

Figure 12-43. *Step three*

Table 12-5. *Component Placement Step Three*

Component	Start	End
Power +12V GND	X1	Y1
Load 1 Load 2	A9	J9
J18	C14	Y14
J17	D20	Y20
J15	C16	E2
J16	C18	F2
NXT White Black	J12	J16

Double-check your connections before connecting the 12V to the circuit. If you accidentally connect the 12V power backward to the amplifier, it will probably be destroyed. Connect the motor and then the 12V, but not the NXT. The motor should not run, and the circuitry should remain cool. When the circuit passes that test, connect the NXT and run the power control program discussed earlier. With a power level of about 10, you should hear the high-pitched noise of the PWM coming from the motor. By the time you advance the power to 50, the motor should be turning. The circuit should operate the same way for negative power, except that the motor will turn in the opposite direction.

You could use the amplifier built on the prototype board, but moving it to a PCB will make it much more reliable. Figure 12-44 shows the final assembly, in which components were moved one at a time from the prototype board. The amplifier is capable of controlling up to 15V at 2A without additional heat sinks.

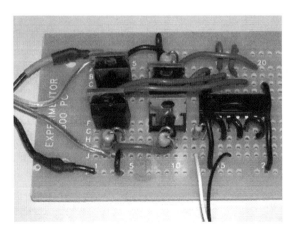

Figure 12-44. *Step four*

The bipolar amplifier is well suited for controlling motors for vehicle propulsion. Figure 12-45 shows a good-sized 24VDC motor that runs nicely on 13.8V from a lead acid battery–based power supply. You usually don't need the high speed of a DC motor, so it's better to buy motors with built-in gear reduction, called *gear head motors*, because they already have lower speed and higher torque. However, you can lower the ratio externally with drive belts where the smaller pulley, such as the one in Figure 12-45, is on the motor, and the larger one is on the axle connected to the wheel.

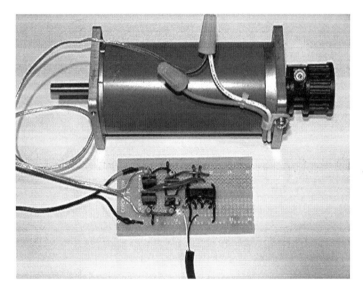

Figure 12-45. *Bipolar amplifier connected to a large DC motor*

RC Servo Interface

RC Servos were originally intended for operating the flight surfaces of radio-controlled model airplanes, but have found a new home in robotics. They contain a highly-geared-down DC motor and a shaft feedback circuit that allows accurate position control over a 180-degree range of motion. Control comes in the form of a series of pulses (illustrated in Figure 12-46). The control pulse width varies from 1ms for 0 degrees to 2ms for 180 degrees. Some Servos can rotate beyond this range, but one standard among the many available Servos is that a 1.5ms pulse will place the shaft at its midpoint.

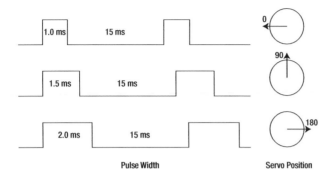

Figure 12-46. *Pulse width and shaft angle*

Unfortunately, the output of the NXT can't be used to directly create the control pulses for a couple of reasons: the voltage is too high, and you can't generate pulses as short as a few ms. However, you can make a little interface circuit that will generate the proper size pulses and use the NXT output to control the width of those pulses. The heart of the interface circuit is the LTC555 CMOS timer (see Figure 12-47).

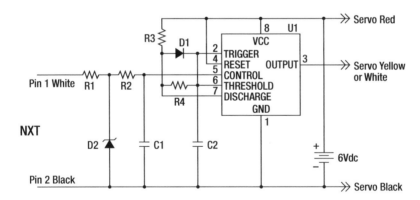

Figure 12-47. *RC Servo interface circuit*

Resistors R3 and R4, along with capacitor C2 and diode D1, determine the pulse width and the time between pulses. Resistor R1 and Zener diode D2 guarantee that the PWM output level of the NXT is limited to 5V, while resistor R2 and capacitor C1 smooth out the NXT PWM to a DC level. The plot in Figure 12-48 shows how the power level is related to the DC level. This DC level is fed into the control input of the TLC555 to vary the Servo pulse width. The Servo also needs its own 6V power supply, which can be easily provided by batteries.

223

▓ **Tip** It is a good idea to include an on/off switch to turn off power to the Servo when it is not in use.

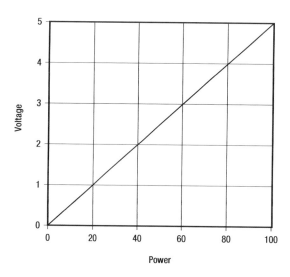

Figure 12-48. *Plot of output power vs control voltage*

Figure 12-49 shows the RC Servo interface built on a solderless breadboard. The complete bill of materials for the circuit is in Table 12-6, along with the step-by-step instructions in Table 12-7. With the component values listed, the interface will produce pulses shorter than 1ms for an output power level of 0 and longer than 2ms for a level of 100. An output power level of about 50 will be close to the 1.5ms (90-degree) center point. Connectors for Servos are available from the same suppliers as the Servos themselves.

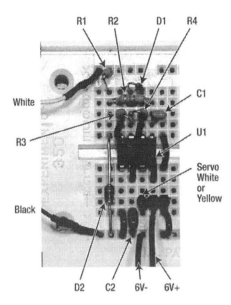

Figure 12-49. *RC Servo interface on solderless breadboard*

Table 12-6. *Bill of Materials*

Component	Part Number	Description	Radio Shack
R1	1K Ohm	1/4 W Resistor	271-312
R2	47K Ohm	1/4 W Resistor	See R1
R3	10K Ohm	1/4 W Resistor	See R1
R4	100K Ohm	1/4 W Resistor	See R1
C1	0.1uF	Metal Film or Ceramic	272-135
C2	0.22uF	Metal Film or Ceramic	272-1070
U1	TLC555	CMOS Timer	276-1718
D1	1N4148	Small Signal Diode	276-1122
D2	1N4733	5.1V Zener Diode	276-563

Table 12-7. *Component Placement*

Component	Start	End
U1 pin 1	F3	
D2 anode cathode	Y2	E2
J1	Y3	J3
C2	Y4	J4
J2	Y7	J7
J3	F7	E7
J4	D3	G6
J5	G4	D5
R1	X2	A2
R2	B2	B6
R3	C3	D4
R4	C4	C5
C1	C6	C7
D1 anode cathode	A4	A5
Servo White or Yellow	I5	
Servo Red Black	I6	I7
6V Red Black	J6	Y5
NXT White Black	X1	Y1

The completed RC Servo and interface can be seen in Figure 12-50. The little 6V battery box conveniently included an on/off switch. The NXT-G output control program from earlier in this chapter is perfect for exploring the operation of the RC Servo. At first, with the output power at 0, the Servo should rotate fully counterclockwise. As you increase the power level, the Servo will start to move clockwise. Eventually the Servo will stop moving when the power level approaches 100.

■ **Caution** It is generally not a good idea to drive the Servo beyond its normal range of motion (for my Servos, it relates to power levels from 20 to 80).

Figure 12-50. Completed RC Servo interface

■ ■ ■

CHAPTER 13

I²C Bus Communication

The I²C communication bus capability of the NXT is a powerful feature that allows practically unlimited expansion of inputs and outputs. Originally developed by Philips Inc., I²C stands for Inter-Integrated Circuit. Although physically located on the NXT sensor input ports, it's actually used for expanding both inputs and outputs.

Only three wires are necessary for I²C because the data is transmitted serially, or one bit at a time. One wire is used for sending and receiving data (SDA), while the other provides a synchronizing clock signal (SCL). On the input port connector, SDA is pin 6, and SCL is pin 5, or blue and yellow in the NXT cable. You need a third wire for ground, which is either pin 2 or 3, black or red in the NXT cable.

■ **Note** The original NXT firmware had some problems with I²C communications, so make sure that you're running at least version 1.04 firmware before trying any of these projects.

■ **Note** If your I²C programs appear to hang or crash, cycle the power to the I²C hardware by unplugging and then plugging the sensor connector back in the NXT port.

I²C Communications

Fortunately, the NXT takes care of the low-level details of communication with I²C, but you should understand a few basic things that are going on. An I²C bus has one master—the NXT—and up to 127 slave devices. However, there is a hardware limit of only about eight slaves for each NXT port. Each slave has a unique 7-bit address. When the NXT wants to communicate with a device, it sends the 7-bit address of the device plus a single bit to tell whether it intends to read or write. Then the device replies with a single-bit acknowledgment of the transmission. If the master is writing the device, the data follows right after the acknowledgment. If the NXT is reading the device, it expects the slave to start sending its data immediately after the acknowledgment. You often combine the functions to have a write followed immediately by a read. Figure 13-1 shows the transfers graphically.

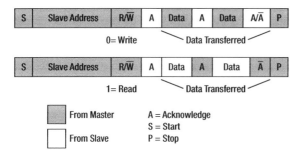

Figure 13-1. *I²C protocol*

PCF8574

One of the most useful I²C devices is the PCF8574 remote I/O expander. It's a single integrated circuit that includes eight pins that can be either inputs or outputs. Figure 13-2 shows the basic block diagram of the part, in which the 8 I/O pins are labeled P0 to P7. The figure doesn't show the part's interrupt pin because you won't be using it for any of the projects in this book.

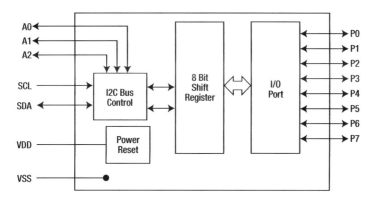

Figure 13-2. *PCF8574*

You use address pins A0, A1, and A2 to generate one of eight possible addresses for the expander. That means you can have eight PCF8574s on the same I²C bus by connecting the address pins either high to VDD or low to VSS. A PCF8574 with all address lines tied to VSS will have the address 40 hexadecimal (0x40) or 64 decimal. There's an alternate version of the part with an *A* suffix that has a base address of 70 hexadecimal (0x70) or 112 decimal. Figure 13-3 illustrates how to compute the address for the two devices.

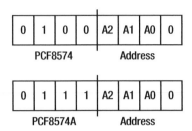

Figure 13-3. *PCF8574 and PCF8574A address*

When used as outputs, the pins can only sink current (that means they can only be expected to pull a load to ground). This can be confusing because turning a load on means you must write a zero to the pin, not a 1. For example, writing a zero will light an LED whose anode is tied to the positive power supply through a resistor. Each output can sink up to 25 mA, and is latched. That means if your program crashes, they'll remain in whatever state they were in last. Fortunately, when first powered up, the default condition of the pins is high, and the loads will be off.

Eight Outs

Figure 13-4 shows a PCF8574 driving eight LEDs. The LEGO hardware documentation specifies that resistors R1 and R2 must be 82kΩ to terminate the I²C bus properly. Instead of using eight discrete LEDs, you can also use a single bar graph display that has multiple LEDs in the same package. This particular display has the anodes of ten LEDs along the side with the little notch cut in the corner.

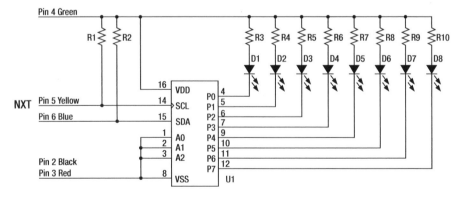

Figure 13-4. *Eight Outs circuit*

Table 13-1 has the complete list of parts you'll need, and Table 13-2 takes you through the placement on the solderless breadboard step by step. Figure 13-5 shows the completed construction. To

231

simplify the wiring, resistors R3 to R10 have insulation stripped from hook-up wire slid over their leads to prevent them from shorting to each other. The solderless breadboard lacks a hole at column 18, where one of the display pins needs to go. Bend the appropriate pin of the display over to an adjacent pin and wrap it around to make its connection.

Table 13-1. *Eight Outs Bill of Materials*

Component	Part Number	Description	Digi-Key
U1	PCF8574 or PCF8574A	I²C Digital Port	296-13109-5-ND
D1–8	LED	LED Bar Graph Display	160-1068-ND
R1 and R2	82k	1/4 W 1% Film Resistor	P82.0KCACT-ND
R3–R10	150Ω for Eight Outs Ror 100Ω for Wand	1/4 W 1% Film Resistor	P150CACT-ND or P100CACT-ND

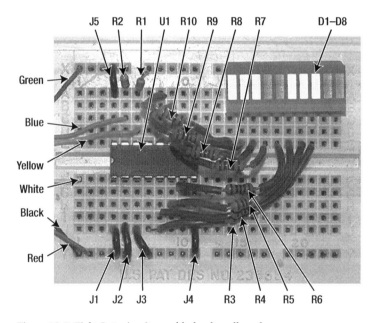

Figure 13-5. *Eight Outs circuit on solderless breadboard*

Table 13-2. *Eight Outs Component Placement*

Component	Start	End
U1 pin 1	F4	
R1	A6	X7
R2	A5	X5
J1	Y4	J4
J2	Y5	J5
J3	Y7	J6
J4	Y11	J11
J5	X4	A4
NXT Green White	X1	H1
NXT Red Black	Y2	Y1
NXT Blue Yellow	C5	C6
R3	J7	E21
R4	I8	E20
R5	H9	E19
R6	G10	E18
R7	D11	E17
R8	C10	E16
R9	B9	E15
R10	A8	E14
D1–D8 Anodes on X	X23	

You need to import two blocks into the NXT-G environment to control I²C devices such as the PCF8574. Instructions for importing new NXT-G blocks can be found back in Chapter 2. I²CbusW is for writing, and I²CbusR is for reading, and because the Eight Outs project has only outputs, we will look at I²CbusW first.

The Blink program shown in Figure 13-6 uses the eight LEDs to display the binary value of the loop counter. I²CbusW needs to know the Port on the NXT and the decimal value of the I²C address of the device. In this case, we are using Port 1 and an A series part that has an Address of 112, but you would use 64 for the base PCF8574 part.

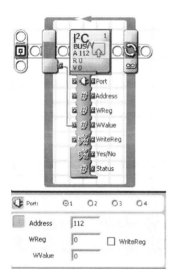

Figure 13-6. *I²CbusW in Blink NXT-G program*

Sophisticated I²C devices are typically configured through registers. First, you send the device the register number you want; then you read or write that register's value. However, the uncomplicated PCF8574 doesn't have registers, so you don't enter a register number and you uncheck the WriteReg box in the block's configuration window. WValue is just the value that will be sent directly to the output port pins. The error output Yes/No is True if there has been some sort of communications error, and Status is a code for the error. For now, if there is an error, we'll just ignore it and keep going.

While the program is running, all eight of the LEDs will be blinking on and off. The least-significant bit LED will blink so fast it will just look dim, but the most significant bit will take several seconds to blink on and off. The direction of the count might seem backward because an LED is lit when the output value is actually zero.

Most likely, if you're using I²C communications, you're also ready to try some NXC programming. Listing 13-1 is for an NXC program that does exactly the same thing as the Blink NXT-G program. The two #define lines take care of specifying the Port and I²C address for the whole program. We declare and initialize a 2-byte array called WriteBuf to be used for I²C communications. WriteBuf[0] is the device address, and WriteBuf[1] is the data.

Listing 13-1. *Blinkall.nxc Program*

```
#define I2Cport S1        // Port number
#define I2CAddr8574 0x70 // I2C address x040 8574 or 0x70 for 8574A
byte WriteBuf[]={I2CAddr8574,0x00}; // write buffer is addr and data

task main() {
  int nbytes;
  SetSensorLowspeed (I2Cport);        // Configure I2C port
  while (true) {
    WriteBuf[1]++;                     // update data byte
    I2CWrite(I2Cport, 0, WriteBuf);  // send buffer
    while(I2CStatus(I2Cport, nbytes)==STAT_COMM_PENDING); // wait
  }
}
```

The program configures the sensor port as an I²C type device with the SetSensorLowSpeed function. Then it enters a while loop in which the data value is repeatedly incremented and sent to the device. The actual transmission of WriteBuf takes some time, and I²C Write only initiates the transmission; it doesn't wait around for it to be finished. Before you can call it again, you must make sure the transmission has completed by checking the I²C status with the I²CStatus function. That is what the second while loop is doing.

Magic Wand

If you waved the bar graph display back and forth fast enough while changing the LED pattern, it would give the appearance of a multicolumn display. That's the magic behind the next project. You've probably seen digital clocks and message displays that work on this principle.

All you need is the Eight Outs circuit with the display mounted on a separate little integrated-circuit breadboard such as the Radio Shack #27-159 shown in Figure 13-7. We've broken with tradition a little here and mounted the PCF8574 on one of the little boards as well. Allow enough connection wire between the boards so the display can move freely. The 100Ω LED resistors are soldered in series with the connection wire and covered with heat shrink tubing. The lower resistance value makes the display a little brighter and easier to see. However, there's a 180 mA limit to the current you can draw from the 4.3V power supply.

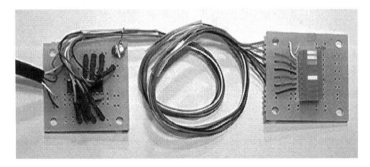

Figure 13-7. *Magic wand on printed circuit*

The spacing of the mounting holes in the PCB allows you to connect it directly to a LEGO beam with small screws and nuts. The simple contraption shown in Figure 13-8 just waves the beam back and forth as fast as it can. You use the touch switch to tell the program when the beam has advanced to the far left end of its travel and is ready to start spelling out the message.

Figure 13-8. *The magic wand*

If you want a larger display, use discrete LEDs and mount them to a beam, as shown in Figure 13-9. The display can be much brighter because more efficient LEDs are available in discrete packages than the bar graph displays.

Figure 13-9. *Close-up of wand construction*

Figure 13-10 shows the longer wand in action, but the program is exactly the same.

Figure 13-10. *Longer magic wand with discrete LEDs*

An NXT-G program would be too slow to produce the patterns fast enough for the magic wand. (The complete NXC program listing for the magic wand can be found in Appendix C.) Listing 13-2 shows just the part of the program that has to do with generating the data patterns for the letters. Only L, E, G, O, N, X, and T are already defined in the program, but you can generate any pattern you want that's 8 segments high and up to 15 columns wide. It's easy to lay out the pattern on graph paper and then convert the pattern to hexadecimal numbers in which 1s are the lit LEDs. For example, 0x80 would only be the lowest segment lit, and 0xFF would be all segments.

Listing 13-2. *Magic Wand Pattern Declarations*

```
// Display patterns
// Each byte represents a column of dots
// Bit set to 1 means lit LED.
// Least significant bit is at top of column.
// Last byte must be all 0
// Maximum number of bytes par pattern: 15

byte L_[] = {0xff, 0x80, 0x80, 0x80, 0x80, 0x80, 0x80, 0x80, 0};
byte E_[] = {0xff, 0x89, 0x89, 0x89, 0x89, 0x81, 0x81, 0};
byte G_[] = {0x7e, 0x00, 0x81, 0x81, 0x81, 0x81, 0x91, 0x90, 0x72, 0};
byte O_[] = {0x7e, 0x00, 0x81, 0x81, 0x81, 0x81, 0x81, 0x00, 0x7e, 0};
```

Four Ins and Outs

It might be exaggerating a little, but the circuit in Figure 13-11 more than doubles the number of inputs and outputs on the NXT—that is, if you only wanted to have only switch-type inputs and LED-type outputs—but it is the basic circuit you can use to expand the NXT for bigger things.

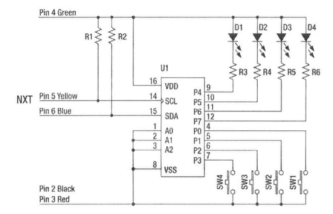

Figure 13-11. *Four Ins and Outs schematic*

The most important thing to learn from Figure 13-11 is how the PCF8574 inputs work. Although the port pins can't source current, they do have weak pull-up resistors to VDD built in. If you want to use a pin as an input, you must write a 1 to it first. Then, when an input switch is closed, it pulls the pin down to VSS. It might seem confusing at first, but when an input switch is pressed, it is actually read as a bit with the value zero.

Table 13-3 is the complete bill of materials, and the step-by-step construction instructions are in Table 13-4.

Table 13-3. *Four Ins and Outs Bill of Materials*

Component	Part Number	Description	Digi-Key
U1	PCF8574	I²C Digital Port	296-13109-5-ND
D1–D4	LED	4 Different Color LEDs	
R1 and R2	82kΩ	1/4 W 1% Film Resistor	P82.0KCACT-ND
R3–R6	150Ω	1/4 W 1% Film Resistor	P150CACT-ND
SW1–SW4	Tact Switches	PCB NO Switches	EG2495-ND

Table 13-4. Four Ins and Outs Component Placement

Component	Start	End
U1 pin 1	F4	
R1	A6	X7
R2	A5	X5
R6	D11	D22
R5	C10	C19
R4	B9	B16
R3	D8	E13
J1	Y4	J4
J2	Y5	J5
J3	Y7	J6
J4	Y11	J11
J5	X4	A4
J6	Y14	J14
J7	Y17	J17
J8	Y20	J20
J9	Y23	J23
D1 Anode Cathode	X13	A13
D2 Anode Cathode	X16	A16
D3 Anode Cathode	X19	A19
D4 Anode Cathode	X22	A22
J10	J7	J21
J11	J8	J18
J12	J9	J15

Table 13-4. *Four Ins and Outs Component Placement (continued)*

Component	Start	End
J13	J10	J12
SW1	I21	I23
SW2	I18	I20
SW3	I15	I17
SW4	I12	I14
NXT Green White	X1	H1
NXT Red Black	Y2	Y1
NXT Blue Yellow	C5	C6

The circuit built on a solderless breadboard is shown in Figure 13-12. The little circuit-board mount buttons are called "tact" switches and are really handy for building projects like this.

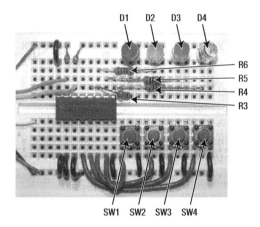

Figure 13-12. *Four Ins and Outs on solderless breadboard*

I²C busR block can be seen in the little program shown in Figure 13-13. The block has the same inputs and outputs as the I²C busW block, except that it has a Raw Value output instead of the WValue input. This Raw Value output is just the 1 byte value it reads from the device. The program maps the four input switches to the four output LEDs. Because the inputs are on the low 4 bits of the port and the outputs are on the high 4 bits, we cleverly call the program Low²High.

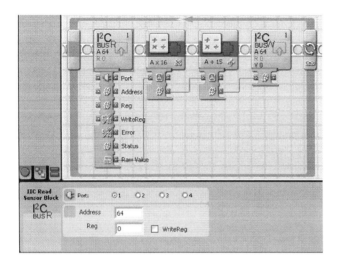

Figure 13-13. *Low²High NXT-G Program*

The program reads the PCF8574 and moves the value of the 4 low bits up by multiplying by 16. This is the same thing as shifting the value up by 4 bits. If we wrote this shifted value to the PCF8574, the correct LEDs would light to correspond to whatever buttons were being pressed. However, we must also rewrite ones to the input pins so when we loop back around to the I²CbusR again, the pins can be read as inputs. That is why we add 15 to make the each of the low 4 bits one.

The Low²High NXC program shown in Listing 13-3 does the same thing as the NXT-G program. However, it takes care of both the read and write with a single function called I²CBytes. This high-level function writes a 1 byte data (WriteBuf[1]), waits for the transmission to finish, and then reads 1 byte of data back from the device (ReadBuf[0]).

Listing 13-3. *low2high.nxc Program*

```
#define I2Cport S1 // NXT sensor port 1
#define I2CAddr8574 0x40 // 0x40 8574 or 0x70 for 8574A
byte WriteBuf[] = {I2CAddr8574, 0xFF}; // Sent to 8574
byte ReadBuf[];    // Receive from PCF8574
int RdCnt=1;       // Number of bytes to read

task main (){
  SetSensorLowspeed (I2Cport); // Configure NXT port
  while (true){
    // write output data and read back port value
    I2CBytes(I2Cport, WriteBuf, RdCnt, ReadBuf);
    // shift left 4 bits and make lowest 4 bits 1
    WriteBuf[1] = (ReadBuf[0] << 4) + 0x0f;
  }
}
```

Simon Game

Simon, a take-off of the electronic toy with the same name, is a deceptively simple game in which the NXT generates a random ever-lengthening sequence that you must reproduce purely from memory. Moving the Four Ins and Outs project to a circuit board makes the game look more professional, and Figure 13-14 shows how the circuit was built on the PCB. We used the opposite end of the PCB because the other end was already used for a different project.

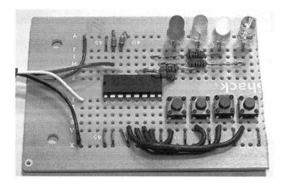

Figure 13-14. *Simon game*

The complete listing of the Simon NXC program is located in Appendix C, but let's take a quick look at how the program reads the buttons in Listing 13-4. I²CBytes sends WriteBuf[1] which equals all ones (hexadecimal FF). That turns off the LEDs with the high 4 bits, and establishes inputs for the low 4 bits. Then I²CBytes reads the port value into ReadBuf. Remember, 1 means the button is not pressed, so the do-loop repeats while the reply is all 1s or no buttons are pressed. When a button has been pressed, the for-loop checks each bit to figure out which button it was.

Listing 13-4. *GetButtons from Simon.NXC Program*

```
int GetButtons()
{
  WriteBuf[1] = 0xff;
  do
  {
    I2CBytes(I2Cport, WriteBuf, RdCnt, ReadBuf);
  }
  while (ReadBuf[0] == 0xff)
  for(int i=0; i<4; i++)
  {
    if((ReadBuf[0] & 1) == 0) return i;
    ReadBuf[0]>>=1;
  }
}
```

Keypad Input

You might want to change some threshold, set point, limit, or other constant number's value in your NXT program. Because the NXT has only three input buttons, entering numeric values means that you have to use the computer to edit the value in the program and then download it all over again. However, with the Keypad Input shown in Figure 13-15, you can enter numbers directly into the NXT without the computer.

Figure 13-15. Keypad Input built with the Mindsensors Prototype Board

You could build the Keypad Input using the construction methods we have already discussed, but Mindsensors sells a PCF8574 prototype board that is perfect for the job. (More information about this board can be found in Appendix A.) All you need is to combine it with a 16-button matrix keypad such as the Grayhill 96BB2-056-R (Digi-Key #GH5011-ND). That is a 4-by-4 style keypad in which the buttons are connected in a row-and-column format (see Figure 13-16). The columns are connected to the top 4 bits, while the rows are connected to the bottom 4 bits of the PCF8574.

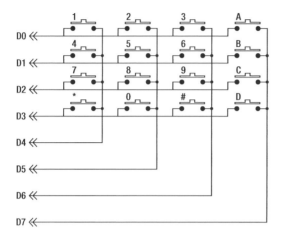

Figure 13-16. *Keypad schematic*

The eight connections to the keypad matrix are arranged as pins in a row that can be soldered directly into the holes of the Mindsensors prototype board I/O connector. The connector is labeled D0 to D7, but they are really just pins P0 to P7 of the PCF8574. Make sure that you use the middle eight holes in lower row, as shown in Figure 13-17. You don't need the outer holes that are for VCC and ground. It is a good idea to physically space the keypad as high above the top of the circuit board as possible and still have the pins reach all the way through to the bottom of the board.

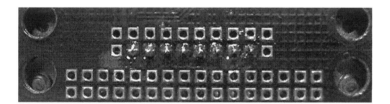

Figure 13-17. *Soldered connections on bottom of circuit board*

A complete listing of an NXC keypad data entry program can be found in Appendix C. The program builds up a number one digit at a time; when you are done, it saves the number in a file with the name A, B, C, or D.txt, depending on which letter key you press. Pressing the asterisk (*) button clears the number, and pressing the pound sign (#) button changes the sign of the number. A program that actually uses the number simply opens the appropriate file and reads the value out of it. The keypad can be temporarily connected or more permanently attached to the side with beams, as shown in Figure 13-18.

Figure 13-18. *NXT data entry terminal*

The trick to reading a 16-matrix keypad is to "look" only at one column at a time. Listing 13-5 shows the code used to read just the leftmost column with buttons 1, 4, 7, and the asterisk. First, we select the column by writing a zero to its bit and 1s to all the rest (hexadecimal EF). Then if you press any of the buttons in that column, you will see zero in the appropriate input bit. If you press buttons in the other columns, they won't register anything because their column line is 1. The button value decoding is done with four if statements that check each of the input bits and assign the correct numeric value for the button. The asterisk is given the special value of 14.

Listing 13-5. *Read and decode left column*

```
WriteBuf[1]=0xEF; // Col 1
I2CBytes(I2Cport, WriteBuf, RdCnt, ReadBuf);
if(ReadBuf[0]==0xEE) return(1); // Row 1
if(ReadBuf[0]==0xED) return(4); // Row 2
if(ReadBuf[0]==0xEB) return(7); // Row 3
if(ReadBuf[0]==0xE7) return(14);// Row 4
```

Relay Outputs

You probably don't want to only blink LEDs and play games with your I²C bus. Making the outputs useful requires adding circuitry that allows higher voltages and currents than the PCF8574 can handle. One of the easiest ways is to use a relay, and you can buy reed relays—for example, Radio Shack #275-232 or Digi-Key #306-1019-ND—that operate directly off the feeble 25mA available from the output pin.

Figure 13-19 is a schematic for an I²C interface with two relay outputs. Obviously, you could control all eight outputs in the same way. As you learned in Chapter 12, diodes D1 and D2 (1N4148) are necessary to protect the PCF8574 when the relays RL1 and RL2 are turned off.

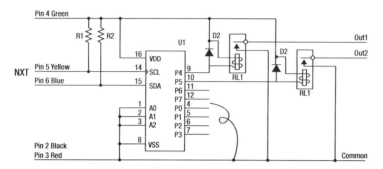

Figure 13-19. *Relay output*

The circuit is essentially the same as the previous designs, and it should be easy to figure out how to build it onto a solderless breadboard, as shown in Figure 13-20. The short wire lead is used to make contact temporally with pins 4 or 5 on the PCF8574 while running the Low²High program to test the relay operation.

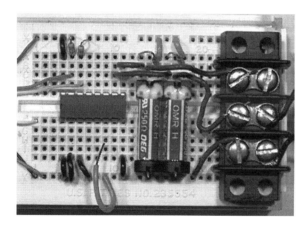

Figure 13-20. *Relay output on solderless breadboard*

Finally, Figure 13-21 shows how to use one of the relays in the project to control an old RCX-style motor. The LEGO battery box has a built-in switch that can be used to turn the power off when the PCF8574 is not under program control.

Figure 13-21. *Relay output controlling an RCX-style stepper motor*

Stepper motors turn in small controlled steps in which a typical step is fewer than 10 degrees of rotation. Accurate motion is achieved by making only a precise number of steps. Stepper motors are available with a shaft like most motors for rotary output or a threaded *lead* screw that creates linear motion. There are *bipolar* and *unipolar* coil configurations, but we will pursue only unipolar types here because they are the easiest to drive.

The PCF8574 can drive LEDs or small low-voltage relays directly, but stepper motors need something a little more substantial. The ULN2003A (see Figure 13-22) is an array of seven inverting amplifiers that can switch up to 50V. Inverting means that when the input to the amplifier is 1, its output will be zero. One nice thing about the ULN2003A is that the diode needed with inductive loads like motors or relays is built right in.

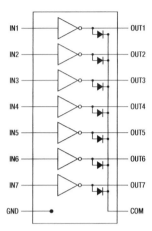

Figure 13-22. *ULN2003A*

Like the PCF8574, the ULN2003A only sinks current. Because the reset condition of a PCF8574 output is 1, the reset condition of any loads connected through a ULN2003A will be on. The output current capability of each amplifier actually depends on how many of the amplifiers are on at any given time. You can usually count on at least 200 mA per amplifier, and with 12V that works out to a minimum coil resistance of about 60Ω. Going much below this runs the risk of overheating the part.

A stepper motor circuit combining the ULN2003A and the PCF8574 is shown in Figure 13-23. Pull-up resistors R3–R6 are 3.3kΩ are necessary because the ones inside the PCF8574 don't quite provide enough current for the inputs of the ULN2003A. Connecting the correct color wire from the stepper to the ULN2003A is critical. The colors shown are only for the 35DBM10B2U-L (Digi Key #403-1034-ND) and will vary with model and style of stepper motor. It is a good idea to include a power switch so you can turn off the 12V when the motor is not in use.

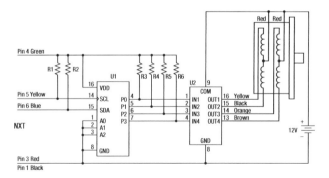

Figure 13-23. *Stepper motor circuit*

Figure 13-24 shows just the carriage assembly for a little scanner built using the 35DBM10B2U-L linear stepper motor. The lead screw of the stepper is prevented from turning because it has been screwed into the beam end of the two triangle plates that serve as the slider. As the lead screw is pulled (or pushed) through the stepper, these plates slide back and forth and are held straight by two long axles. The movement of the slider is very precise because the total travel is about 2 inches (5cm) and takes more than 1,600 steps to traverse.

Figure 13-24. *35DBM10B2U-L with linear carriage*

Figure 13-25 graphically shows the voltage pattern needed to produce continuous motion. The coils are in pairs: yellow/black and orange/brown. The members of a pair are never turned on at the same time because this is a unipolar device. It takes four steps before the pattern repeats, and the four values that need to be sent to the PCF8574 are shown at the bottom of the figure.

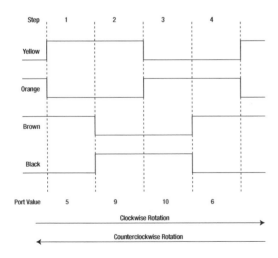

Figure 13-25. *Stepper motor voltage pattern*

There are really two programs shown in Figure 13-26. Running the first will sequence the values 5, 9, 10, and 6 repeatedly 400 times for a total of 1,600 steps. The slider will move almost the entire length of the carriage to the right. The second program produces the sequence in reverse order and will cause the slider to return exactly back to the starting position.

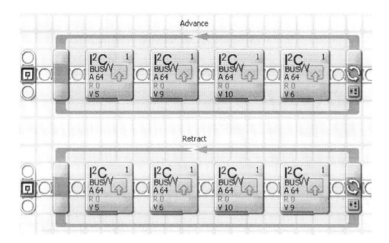

Figure 13-26. *Advance and Retract stepper motor programs*

PCF8591

Another useful I²C integrated circuit is the PCF8591 8-bit analog-to-digital (A/D) converter. It has four channels of analog input and a single channel of analog output. You can see the basic functionality of the part in Figure 13-27. The 8-bit A/D is made by comparing the output of the digital-to-analog (D/A) converter to the selected analog input. A process called *successive approximation* determines the correct value in just eight clock cycles. The digital results range from 0 to 255, and if you multiply the result by 4, it will look like the Raw values from the NXT A/D.

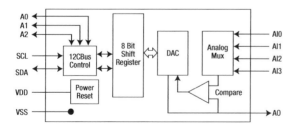

Figure 13-27. *PCF8591 8-bit A/D and D/A*

Each PCF8591 has three address pins that allow you to connect up to eight PCF8591s on a single I²C bus. With all address lines tied to VSS, the base address is 144 decimal (hexadecimal 90), and you can use Figure 13-28 to derive the other address values. Unlike the PCF8574, there is no A series version with an alternate base address.

Figure 13-28. PCF8591 addressing

The PCF8591 has several options that are configured by writing a control byte, and Figure 13-29 is a diagram of the control byte. The input Mode bits can be thought of as a single 2-bit number with values from 0 to 3.

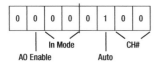

Figure 13-29. Control byte

Figure 13-30 illustrates the four input Modes. When the Auto increment bit at 1, the conversions will start with channel 0 and automatically increment to the next channel for every byte that is read from the part.

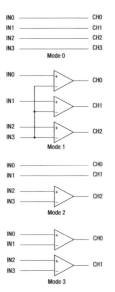

Figure 13-30. 8591 Input Modes

251

Basic programming for the part requires first writing the control byte with the Auto increment bit set and then reading 5 bytes back. The first byte read is actually an old conversion value and should be ignored. The last 4 bytes are the new values for channels 0 through 3. You could select and read one channel at a time, but reading all of them this way is easier and just as fast.

Four Analog Ins

Figure 13-31 shows a PCF8591 circuit that can read four analog inputs. Channels 0 and 1 have 10kΩ pull-up resistors, and you could use any of the sensors from Chapters 4, 5, 6, and 8 with them. These sensors would connect between either CH0 or CH1 and GND. Channels 2 and 3 have potentiometers connected, but unlike the pots in Chapter 6 they read a voltage linearly related to the shaft angle. That's because they're voltage dividers for the full power supply voltage, not just a divider with the 10kΩ pull-up inside the NXT.

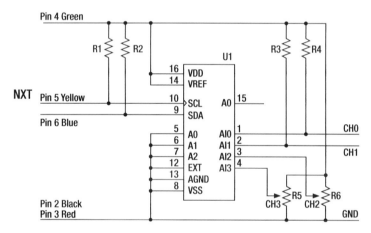

Figure 13-31. Four Analog Ins circuit

The bill of materials is in Table 13-5 and the step-by-step instructions are in Table 13-6.

Table 13-5. Four Analog Ins Bill of Materials

Component	Part Number	Description	Digi-Key
U1	PCF8591	I²C Quad Analog Input	568-1087-5-ND
R1 and R2	82kΩ	1/4 W 1% Film Resistors	P82.0KCACT-ND
R3 and R4	10kΩ	1/4 W 1% Film Resistors	P10.0KCACT-ND
R5 and R6	10kΩ	Potentiometers	3310C-001-103-ND

Table 13-6. Four Analog Ins Component Placement

Component	Start	End
U1 pin 1	F3	
R1	X9	A9
R2	X10	A10
R3	D5	G4
R4	D3	G3
R5 left center right	J12	J14
R6 left center right	A14	A12
J1	X3	A3
J2	X5	A5
J3	D6	G7
J4	D7	G8
J5	J7	Y7
J6	J8	Y8
J7	J9	Y9
J8	J10	Y10
J9	I10	I12
J10	F12	E12
J11	F14	E14
J12	C14	X16
J13	C13	G6
J14	H5	H13

Table 13-6. *Four Analog Ins Component Placement (continued)*

Component	Start	End
NXT Green White	X1	H1
NXT Red Black	Y2	Y1
NXT Blue Yellow	C10	B9

Figure 13-32 shows the complete construction of the Four Analog Ins on a solderless breadboard. Although the potentiometers are shown attached directly to the breadboard, most likely they would be connected on long wires to measure the angle of a joint some distance from the circuit.

Figure 13-32. *Four Analog Ins on solderless breadboard*

Using the PCF8591 in a NXT-G program requires importing the custom 8591 block. We prefer this PCF8591 block because it is simpler to use and seems more reliable than the one from Mindsensors. As you can see in Figure 13-33, the 8591 block has inputs for port number, I²C address, and analog output value. The values for the four channels of A/D values are displayed using the Display Value MyBlock developed in Chapter 2.

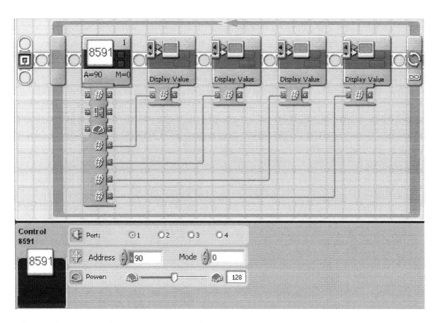

Figure 13-33. *Read4 NXT-G program with 8591 block*

Without anything connected, channels 0 and 1 will read 255, as shown in Figure 13-34. You need to customize this design for your particular needs. You might want all potentiometer inputs, or you might want to connect four passive-style sensors. In Chapter 14, we'll show you how to combine the Four Analog Ins project with a graphics program to make a Pong video game.

```
Chan 0 = 255
Chan 1 = 255
Chan 2 = 4
Chan 3 = 213
```

Figure 13-34. *Read4 NXT-G program with 8591 block*

The Read4 NXC program shown in Listing 13-6 reads all four channels and just displays their values on the NXT display. This is a handy program for debugging PCF8591 sensors. Only the Auto increment bit is set in the control byte (hexadecimal 04) so it is in input Mode 0. ReadBuf[0] contains an old conversion value and is not displayed.

Listing 13-6. *Read4 program*

```
#define port S1                      // sensor port 1
#define I2CAddr8591 0x90             // PCF8591 address
byte WriteBuf[] = {I2CAddr8591, 0x04}; // write buffer
byte ReadBuf[];                      // read buffer
int RdCnt=5;                         // read 5 bytes

task main(){
  SetSensorLowspeed(port);           // make port I2C
  while(true){
    // Write config byte and read back 5 bytes
    I2CBytes(port, WriteBuf, RdCnt, ReadBuf);
    NumOut(0,24,ReadBuf[1],true);    // Chan 0
    NumOut(0,16,ReadBuf[2]);         // Chan 1
    NumOut(0,8,ReadBuf[3]);          // Chan 2
    NumOut(0,0,ReadBuf[4]);          // Chan 3
  }
}
```

2-D Light Sensor

Way back in Chapter 5 you learned how to build a light-seeking robot called the Braitenberg Vehicle that required two separate Light Sensors and two NXT sensor ports. Then in Chapter 8 we combined two Light Sensors into a single Differential Light Sensor that only needed a one NXT port. Now let's see how to use the four analog inputs of the PCF8591 to build a light-seeking vehicle that will move toward bright light regardless of its direction.

Figure 13-35 shows just the part of the circuit with four Light Dependent Resistors (LDRs) and their pull-up resistors. The rest of the circuit is built like Figure 13-31 with R3-R6 removed. The four LDRs share a common connection to the AGND input of the PCF8591 and, through 10kΩ pull-ups, to VREF.

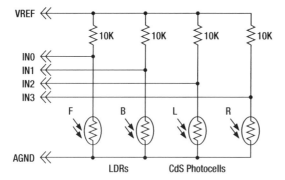

Figure 13-35. *2-D Light Sensor Circuit for PCF8591*

For simplicity, we built our 2-D Light Sensor using the Mindsensors PCF8591 prototype board. You can find out more about this board in Appendix A. Long pieces of wire insulation have been slipped over the leads of the LDRs in Figure 13-36 to keep them from accidentally connecting to each other. Part of the prototyping area of the board was used to attach the four pull-up resistors. It is critical that you get the input channel and physical direction of the LDRs correct for the light seeker to work.

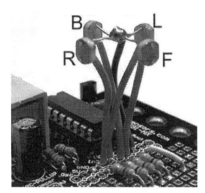

Figure 13-36. *LDRs on Mindsensors PCF8591 prototype board*

Figure 13-37 shows the 2-D sensor attached on top of the Quick Start Vehicle to make a light-seeking robot.

Figure 13-37. *Light-seeking robot*

Because the input to the PCF8591 is in Mode 3, the Light Seeker program shown in Figure 13-38 can be made remarkably simple. Mode 3 causes the value of channel 0 to be the difference of input 0 and 1, which is the difference of the light from front to back. The bigger the light difference is, the more power will be sent to the motors. If the difference is negative, the direction will be reversed. The difference between the light from left to right is read by channel 1, which is fed to the Steering input of the Move block. No matter where the brightest light is coming from, the robot will always move toward it.

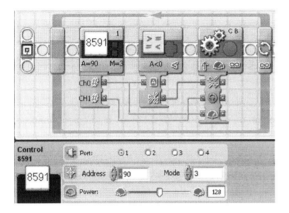

Figure 13-38. *2-D Light Seeker NXT-G program*

RC Servo Controller

In Chapter 12, we showed you how to build a RC Servo motor controller that used the power to a NXT motor output to create the control voltage for a TLC555. That voltage determined the pulse width that was used by a RC Servo to establish its shaft angle. The analog output of the PCF8591 can also be used to provide this control voltage.

Figure 13-39 is the schematic diagram for the PCF8591 RC Servo controller. The PCF8591 has a slightly lower output voltage range than the NXT motor output. To compensate, we reduced the 47kΩ coupling resistor to 33kΩ. Otherwise, the TLC555 circuit is the same, and the Bill of Materials for it is in Table 13-7.

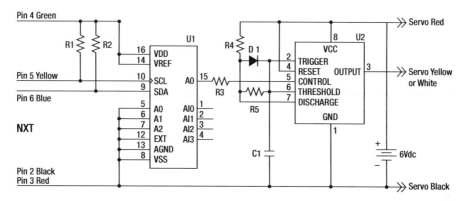

Figure 13-39. *RC Servo control with PCF8591 circuit*

Table 13-7. *Bill of Materials*

Component	Part Number	Description	Radio Shack
R3	33K Ohm	1/4 W Resistor	See R1
R4	10K Ohm	1/4 W Resistor	See R1
R5	100K Ohm	1/4 W Resistor	See R1
C1	0.22uF	Metal Film or Ceramic	272-1070
U2	TLC555	CMOS Timer	276-1718
D1	1N4148	Small Signal Diode	276-1122

The circuit was built on a solderless breadboard first and then transferred to a printed circuit, as shown in Figure 13-40.

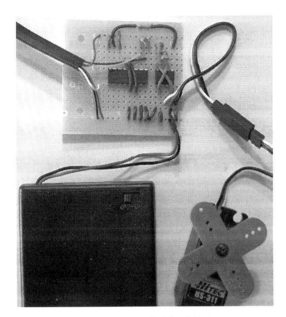

Figure 13-40. RC Servo control with PCF8591

The 8591 block has an input to set the value of the PCF8591's analog output. The range is from 0 to 255, and the inner loop of the program in Figure 13-41 just counts over this range. Zero will position the shaft fully counterclockwise; 255 positions it fully clockwise. The design provides a slightly wider range of pulses than the Servo can travel, so there might not be motion at the extremes.

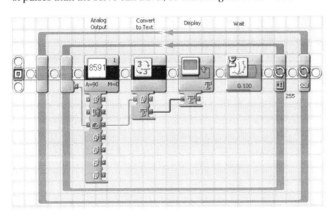

Figure 13-41. PCF8591 Servo test program

Color Sensor

You can use an NXT sensor port as both an I²C interface and as a passive sensor input at the same time. You'll put that feature to good use by building a reflective light Color Sensor. LEDs are used to flood an object with light at each of three colors: red, green, and blue. This is just like the LEGO Color Sensor, except the LEDs are discrete devices. The amount of reflected light from each color is measured with our old friend, the CdS LDR. It's an excellent sensor for this job because it can be easily read by the NXT input and has a spectral sensitivity close to human vision. Figure 13-42 shows the cluster of three LEDs surrounding the LDR and how heat shrink tubing has been fitted around them to keep their light from directly hitting the LDR.

Figure 13-42. *LEDs and LDR for Color Sensor*

The Color Sensor schematic is shown in Figure 13-43. Values for R3, R4, and R5 are carefully selected to make the LEDs produce a balanced amount of light, and you might need to adjust their values for your particular LEDs. Use the brightest LEDs you can get and a "pure green" green LED if possible. The resistors are adjusted by calibrating the sensor to a white object and making all three colors read the same value.

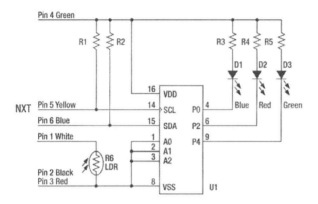

Figure 13-43. *Color Sensor schematic*

Table 13-8 has the complete bill of materials.

Table 13-8. *Color Sensor Bill of Materials*

Component	Part Number	Description	Digi-Key
U1	PCF8574	I²C Digital Port	296-13109-5-ND
R1 and R2	82k	1/4 W 1% Film Resistors	P82.0KCACT-ND
R3	390	1/4 W 1% Film Resistor	P390CACT-ND
R4	100	1/4 W 1% Film Resistor	P100CACT-ND
R5	820	1/4 W 1% Film Resistor	P820CACT-ND
R6	CdS LDR	CdS Photoresistor	PDV-P8001-ND
D1	Blue LED		160-1610-ND
D2	Red LED		160-1499-ND
D3	Green LED		160-1615-ND

Listing 13-7 is just the Red part of the ReadRawColor subroutine from the Readhue program. (You can find the full program listing in Appendix C.) LEDs are turned on one at a time by sending the appropriate bit pattern and then the light level is measured with the LDR. The sensor type is switched between I²C (Lowspeed) and Touch so that the same port can be used for two different functions. Waits are introduced because it takes the LDR time to settle after the color has changed.

Listing 13-7. *NXC Code to Read the Red Value*

```
SetSensorLowspeed (port);
WriteBuf[1] = RED ^ 0xff;
I2CWrite(port, 0,  WriteBuf);
Wait(20);
SetSensorTouch (port);
Wait(80);
RawRGB.Red = 1024 - SensorRaw (port);
```

Construction on the solderless breadboard is straightforward, as shown in Figure 13-44. Start with step-by-step assembly instructions from the Eight Outs project in Table 13-2 until you get to R3; then start following the instructions in Table 13-9.

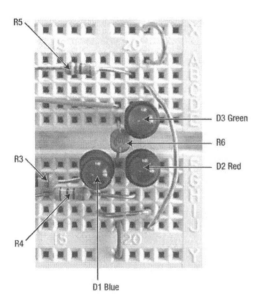

Figure 13-44. *Color Sensor on solderless breadboard*

Table 13-9. Color Sensor Component Placement

Component	Start	End
R3	G7	G17
R4	H9	H20
R5	B20	B11
R6	E19	F19
D1 anode cathode	F18	F17
D2 anode cathode	F21	F20
D3 anode cathode	E21	E20
J6	D19	G1
J7	Y19	J19
J8	I18	I21
J9	J21	C21
J10	X21	A21

The sensor can be left on the solderless breadboard and mounted, as shown in Figure 13-45, to make the finished Color Sensor. You might notice that this breadboard layout is different from the one you just developed, but it works exactly the same way.

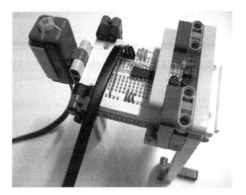

Figure 13-45. Finished Color Sensor

You can program the Color Sensor and a robot arm to sort blocks into separate bins. The blocks in Figure 13-46 are actually made from four 2-by-8 stud bricks. The arm first moves the block over to the Color Sensor and then drops it into the correct bin after the color has been determined.

Figure 13-46. T-56 robot sorting colored bricks

Going Further

We have just scratched the surface of I²C expansion. Integrated circuits are available that have real-time clocks, memory, and other interesting functions. You can even use the bus to interconnect with other computers. For example, the LEGO Ultrasonic Sensor has its own processor and communicates through the I²C bus to the NXT. Third-party suppliers provide compasses, accelerometers, and other sophisticated sensors that would be impossible without the functionality available from the I²C bus.

CHAPTER 14

■ ■ ■

Cool Combinations

In this chapter, we'll investigate some examples of the cool things you can do when you combine your NXT with other software, hardware, and the coolest thing of all: yourself.

Data Logging

Some experiments take a long time to perform, and waiting around for hours to write down the data every few minutes can be mind-numbing. Also, some experiments happen so fast you couldn't write down the data fast enough. Fortunately, the NXT can automatically log data from any of its sensors into a file. Light level, color, temperature, sound level, and distance can all be logged. You store the numbers in the file with a text format that spreadsheet programs can easily import. Once the data is in a spreadsheet, you can process and plot it to produce graphs for a lab report.

Figure 14-1 is a basic data-logging program written in NXT-G. It should be easy to modify it for your particular application. Notice that you must include the Keep Alive block or the NXT will fall asleep during your experiment and ruin everything.

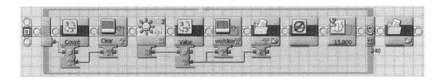

Figure 14-1. *Light level data-logging program*

You put data into a file whose name is set in the File Access block menu shown in Figure 14-2. It's also important to close the data file when the program is done, which is what the final File Access block is doing.

Figure 14-2. *File Access menu*

The Wait block at the end of the loop sets the time between samples—in this case, 15 seconds. The number of samples is set by Until: in the loop count menu shown in Figure 14-3. If the loop count is set to 240 and the time between samples is 15s, the total data logging time is 3,600 seconds, or one hour. When you first try to do data logging, you might want to set Wait to a few seconds and take only a few samples to make sure that everything is working correctly. The sensor used in this example is the LEGO Light Sensor. You could also use the Color Sensor with the Action set for light or even one of the Light Sensors you built from Chapter 5. Remember to turn off any light generation the sensor might have or else it will spoil the reading. The first data point is taken immediately when you start the program, so you need to have everything ready at the start.

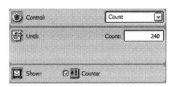

Figure 14-3. *Loop menu*

Every time you run the program, you need to go into the NXT-G environment to retrieve the data file. First, click the NXT window button (see Figure 14-4).

Figure 14-4. *NXT window button*

Then select the Memory tab (see Figure 14-5).

Figure 14-5. *Select the Memory tab*

On the Memory page, click the Other file type (see Figure 14-6). Select the appropriate data file name and click the Upload button. Save the file somewhere on your computer where you can feed it to your spreadsheet program. Make sure that you delete the file from the NXT, or else the next time you run the program it will just add the new data to the end of the old file.

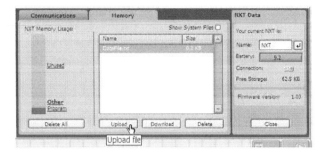

Figure 14-6. Memory tab

You're probably familiar with the handheld light sticks used as emergency flashlights. They also make a tiny version that is used for fishing lures, and you can purchase these light sticks at sporting goods stores. The smaller light stick is easier to enclose in a box made out of LEGO bricks, as shown in Figure 14-7. Seal around the Light or Color Sensor with black electrical tape to make sure that no stray light bothers the experiment.

Figure 14-7. Black box to hold the light stick

269

When you're ready, break the little vial inside the glow stick to energize it, quickly put it in the box, put the lid on, start the program, and come back in an hour. Retrieve the data file and open it with a text-based editor such as Notepad. You can see the first few lines of the data file in Figure 14-8. In the Edit pull-down menu, pick Select All and then Copy.

Figure 14-8. *DataFile opened with Notepad*

Open your spreadsheet program and select cell A1. Then in the Edit pull-down menu, choose Paste. All the data numbers should fill the A column, as shown in Figure 14-9.

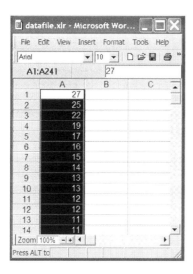

Figure 14-9. *Data pasted into the spreadsheet*

270

Next, in the Tools pull-down menu, select Chart, or follow whatever procedure generates plots for your particular program. A wizard (see Figure 14-10) allows customization of the chart for your experimental data.

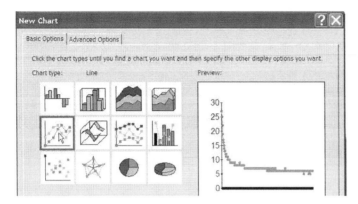

Figure 14-10. *Data plotted in the spreadsheet*

As you can see in the finished plot shown in Figure 14-11, the brightness of the light quickly drops and then stabilizes. You could make this into more of a scientific project by making multiple runs with sticks that are at different temperatures.

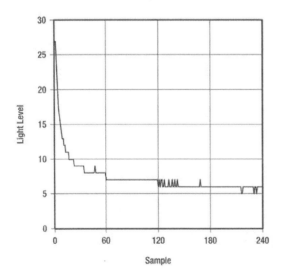

Figure 14-11. *Light level over time*

271

Another interesting long-term experiment is to observe the temperature of a disposable hand warmer over time (see Figure 14-12) using the Temperature Sensor from Chapter 5. Hand warmer devices work by an exothermic chemical reaction that creates rust inside a porous bag. There's some iron dust in the bag, along with some other ingredients that cause the iron to rust quickly and heat up when it's exposed to moisture in the air. It can take ten hours to fully use up the supply of chemicals in the bag.

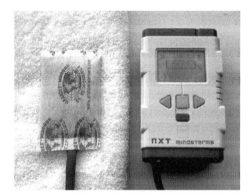

Figure 14-12. Data logging the temperature of a hand warmer

NXT-to-NXT Bluetooth Remote Control

For this project, you'll combine two NXTs. An NXT can communicate with another NXT using a wireless technology called Bluetooth. One NXT has the back-mounted joystick from Chapter 6 and is running a program called bluesend. The other is the NXT Quick Start Vehicle running a program called bluereceive. Figure 14-13 shows the pair ready for action.

Figure 14-13. Joystick remote control and Quick Start Vehicle

When the bluesend program starts, the joystick should be in the centered position. The Raw values for the two pots are recorded as Pzero for the power and Szero for the steering, as shown in Figure 14-14. Whenever the joystick is returned to the starting position, the vehicle will be going straight but at zero speed.

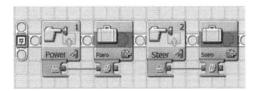

Figure 14-14. Remote-control bluesend program initialization

Figure 14-15 shows the main loop of the bluesend program, which reads each of the joystick pots and subtracts the initial positions. The values tend to be too large for the Motor block in the vehicle, so they're divided by 5. These two values are sent to Bluetooth connection 1 and to mailboxes 1 and 2. It's up to the remote-control vehicle to receive these values and convert them into speed and steering commands.

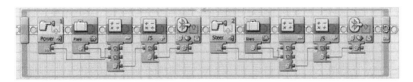

Figure 14-15. Remote–control bluesend program main loop

The NXT Quick Start Vehicle is a convenient starting point for a remote-control vehicle. All you need to do is load the bluereceive program shown in Figure 14-16. The receiver program just gets the steering and power values for a Move block from the two Bluetooth mailboxes. You determine the direction of the power command by comparing it with zero.

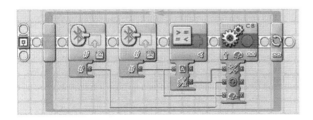

Figure 14-16. Remote–control bluereceive program

You need to use the Bluetooth menu on the remote-control NXT to establish the connection with the vehicle NXT as connection 1 and then run the programs. Refer to the *LEGO MINDSTORMS User*

Guide chapter on Bluetooth for detailed instructions on establishing links between NXTs. It can be tricky and might require several tries to establish a connection.

LEGO Train Station

The NXT is a natural for automating LEGO train control. The variable output power from the NXT is sufficient to operate a train motor, and you can use the Light Sensor or Color Sensor to detect the presence of the train. The power to the tracks uses the same connector as the old RCX (see Figure 14-17). That means you can connect the NXT with the same conversion cable (LEGO #8528) used for the RCX sensors or motor. The prolonged power consumption of operating trains will probably make you wish you had the NXT rechargeable battery pack (LEGO #9798).

Figure 14-17. *Track electrical connections*

The LEGO train track ties have two rows of regular LEGO studs that you can use to mount the sensor using plates, as can be seen in Figure 14-18. You must set the sensor back far enough to avoid being hit by the train as it goes by, but close enough for the reflected light from the train car to be registered by the NXT.

Figure 14-18. *Light Sensor as a train detector*

An NXT-G program to control a train station is shown in Figure 14-19. The train automatically stops at the station long enough to pick up passengers and then pulls away. Power is supplied to the train motor till the Light Sensor or Color Sensor detects the reflection from the locomotive. It then cuts the power to make the engine stop. It waits one second at the station and then pulls away. The on time in the last Motor block guarantees that the train will be clear of the station before the program loops back to the beginning. If the train were on a circular track, it would stop every time it came around to the station.

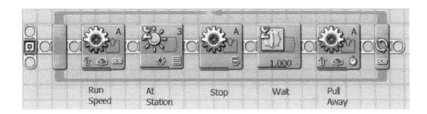

Figure 14-19. *Train station control program*

Panoramic Camera

Panoramic photographs are made by merging many photographs together that have been taken while rotating a camera in one place. The camera used in this example is a Jazz Photo JDC-11, but many similar inexpensive digital cameras are available. You'll need to modify the holder and trigger design from the one shown in Figure 14-20 to suit the particular camera you have. The width of the camera field of view is about 50 degrees. It's important to allow plenty of overlap between images to make merging the photographs easier by only turning 35 degrees between photos. You also want to make sure that the pan is more than 360 degrees to allow some cropping on the ends.

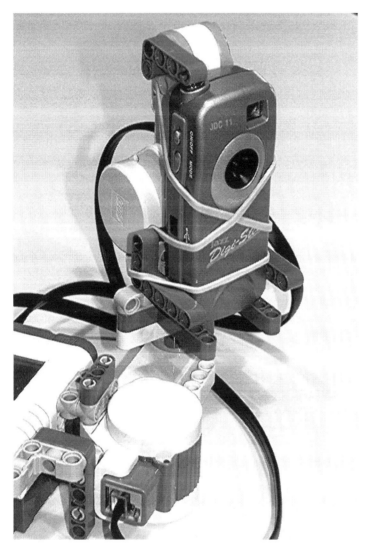

Figure 14-20. *Panoramic camera mount*

The base of the RoboArm T-56 project from the original NXT kit has a turntable (see Figure 14-21) that makes a great platform for rotating a camera to take panoramic photographs, too. The turntable is geared down so much that it takes 168 full turns of the NXT motor for only one rotation of the turntable.

The worm gear advances the 24-tooth gear by only 1 tooth per motor revolution. The turntable has 56 teeth, so the 8-tooth gear makes 7 revolutions for 1 turntable rotation, and 7 times 24 equals 168. That works out to only 2.2 degrees per turn. If you turn the motor 16 times, the camera will move 35 degrees, allowing plenty of overlap between shots. Repeating this 11 times will create a pan of more than 380 degrees.

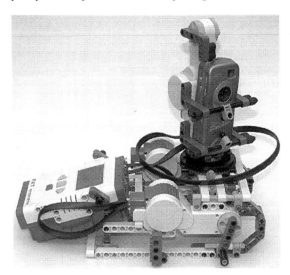

Figure 14-21. *Panoramic camera using T-56 base*

Pushing the camera shutter button requires running the motor forward only long enough to guarantee that the arm has made good contact with it. A short reversal is necessary to make sure the button is fully released. Then rotate the camera 35 degrees and wait a little while to make sure it isn't shaking to take the next photo. The NXT-G program is shown in Figure 14-22. If you are using the T-56 base, you'll need to rotate 16 full revolutions to get 35 degrees.

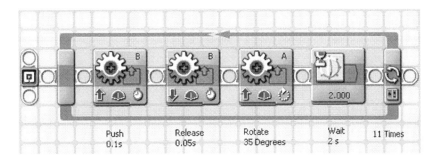

Figure 14-22. *NXT-G panoramic camera control*

You can use just about any photo-editing software to merge the 11 photos into one long panorama. For example, Figures 14-23 and 14-24 show how Microsoft Photo Editor was used. The first photo in the sequence is expanded to have ten times the left margin so that the other photos can be simply cut and pasted into place.

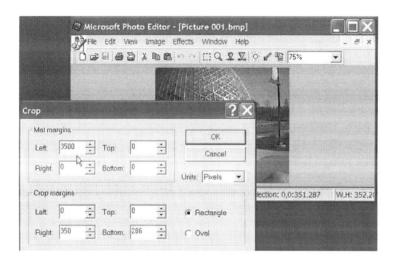

Figure 14-23. Expanding the first photo's width

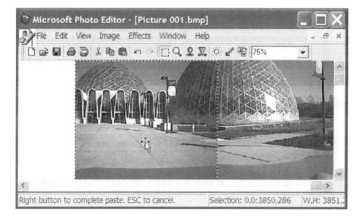

Figure 14-24. The other photos are pasted and adjusted one at a time.

An example of a full 360-degree panorama is shown in Figure 14-25.

Figure 14-25. *Finished 360–degree panoramic photo*

Graphics

A nice freeware program called nxtRICedit by Andreas Dreier lets you create and modify the graphics files used for the NXT display (see Figure 14-26). These files carry the RIC extension, and can be found in a subdirectory of the LEGO software. In fact, all RIC files in that directory will show up in the image selection list for the NXT-G Display block. Conveniently, the default directory for nxtRICedit is also that folder.

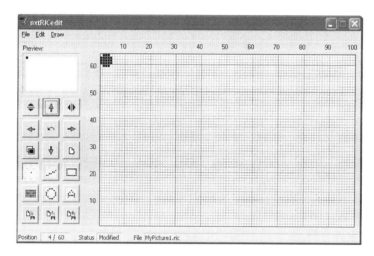

Figure 14-26. *NxtRICedit by Andreas Dreier*

In addition to creating images, the program can convert photographic images to the RIC format. The NXT display is pure black and white with no grayscale, so contrast is a critical adjustment. Figure 14-27 shows part of the Import window where the contrast can be adjusted.

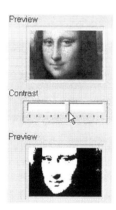

Figure 14-27. *Contrast adjustment in the Import window*

The RIC file is loaded into the NXT automatically when you load an NXT-G program that contains a Display block that uses the file. BricxCC users must manually download the files using the NXT Explorer tool. Figure 14-28 shows the selection of the file created in the preceding example. For full-screen images, you'll want to set the X and Y to 0.

Figure 14-28. *NXT-G Display Options box*

If you're animating small images on the NXT display, you'll need to erase the old image before redrawing it in its new location. You can erase the entire screen and redraw everything, but that can be a problem if you have a lot of other graphics. The best thing to do is draw an all-white image of the same size over the original object to erase it.

For example, if you're moving the little ball image shown being created in Figure 14-26, you'd draw a 5-by-5–pixel white block to erase it and then redraw the ball at its new location. You create this white block image, oddly enough, by adding borders to a blank file. This works because the program normally saves only the minimal area containing black pixels. In nxtRICedit, select File New and then Save As. In the Add Borders part of the Save window, enter a 5-by-5 border, as shown in Figure 14-29. The program then saves a small white box.

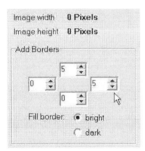

Figure 14-29. *Making a 5-by-5 white box RIC file*

NXT Pong Video Game

You can make a Pong–like video game by combining the nxtRICedit tool to create the graphic elements and the Four Analog Ins project from Chapter 13 for paddle control. Figure 14-30 shows a screen shot of the game, and you can find the complete NXC program listing in Appendix C.

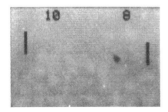

Figure 14-30. *NXT Pong screen shot*

Listing 14-1 is just the four lines of code that update the ball symbol on the screen. W.ric is the all-white image that erases the ball at location bx and by. The values for bx and by are then updated by adding the velocity values bxv and bxy. Finally, the ball is redrawn with B.ric at its new location.

Listing 14-1. *NXC code for updating the ball image*

```
GraphicOut(bx, by, "W.ric");
bx=bx+bxv;
by=by+byv;
GraphicOut(bx, by, "B.ric");
```

Similar code is used to draw the two paddles. The position of the paddles is determined by the values from channels 2 and 3 on the analog-to-digital (A/D) converter. Because the vertical screen resolution is only 60 pixels, the converter value, which can be as large as 255, must be divided by 4 to scale it down. The ball's velocity is changed by the following situations: if it has hit a paddle, bounced off the top or bottom of the screen, or gone off the ends of the field.

Figure 14-31 shows the finished Pong game. The Four Analog Ins project has been moved to a PCB, and 40-tooth gears serve as the player control knobs. The board is attached to a beam with two small screws. The paddles are 2-pixel-wide and 16-pixel-tall black rectangles (P.ric), and their counterpart 2-by-16 white rectangles (N.ric) are needed to erase them. You must use the NXT Explorer in BricXCC to download the image files B, W, N, and P.ric to the NXT before running the program.

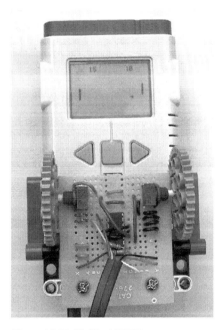

Figure 14-31. *Finished NXT Pong game*

Remotely Guided Vehicle

Inexpensive digital cameras or web cams make great attachments for making remotely guided vehicles. It's as if you're riding along as you pilot your vehicle while watching the live video on the computer screen. The cameras are easily mounted to the Quick Start Vehicle with a just few beams, as shown in Figure 14-32. You'll probably want to buy some USB extension cords to expand the area you can explore, but USB can't be extended much beyond 16 feet (5m) total. If you used Bluetooth for control and a wireless camera, your vehicle would be completely untethered.

Figure 14-32. *Inexpensive digital camera fitted to the vehicle*

Both the second–generation NXT-G environment and BricxCC have built-in remote control windows that give you joystick-like control of the vehicle. Dashboard Designer from RoboDNA and NXT-Remote from Anders Søborg are also suitable programs for remote control. Arrange the live video and the remote control windows to be side by side, as in Figure 14-33, and then try driving while only looking at the video screen as a true remotely guided vehicle. When you see something interesting, you can take a picture of it by pressing the Capture button.

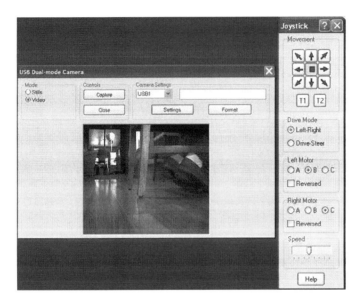

Figure 14-33. *Live Video and BricxCC Joystick Tool*

Usually both the NXT-G environment and BricxCC do a good job of automatically finding the NXT and making a Bluetooth connection for wireless control. The process is called *pairing*, but unfortunately it doesn't always seem to work. Sometimes it helps to establish the Bluetooth connection another way, and we'll go through that process step by step. Start by opening the Windows Control Panel and double-clicking the Bluetooth Devices icon, as shown in Figure 14-34.

Figure 14-34. *Windows Control Panel*

A window with your known Bluetooth Devices shows up, as shown in Figure 14-35. If there's already an NXT device in the window, select it and click the Remove button. Don't worry; you'll reconnect to it in just a moment. When the NXT device icon is gone, click the Add button.

Figure 14-35. *Devices tab of the Bluetooth Devices window*

An Add Bluetooth Device Wizard opens, as in Figure 14-36. Make sure that your NXT is turned on and then select the check mark in the wizard that says "My device is set up and ready to be found." Then click the Next> button.

Figure 14-36. *Add Bluetooth Device Wizard welcome window*

After searching, the NXT Bluetooth icon should show up, as in Figure 14-37. Double-click the icon, and the passkey window opens.

Figure 14-37. *Double-clicking the NXT Bluetooth icon*

In the passkey window (see Figure 14-38), select "Let me choose my own passkey" and enter **1234**. Then select the Next> button. The NXT should make a little chirping noise, and you'll need to confirm the passkey by pressing the orange button.

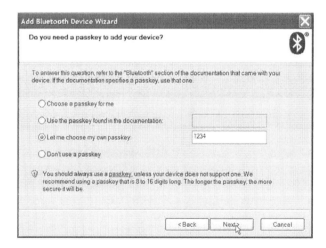

Figure 14-38. *Passkey window*

The Completing the Add Bluetooth Device Wizard window looks like Figure 14-39; it shows the COM ports that the NXT will be using. The lower number of them, COM9 in this case, is the one you need to enter in some of the alternative remote-control programs.

Figure 14-39. *COM port information*

You can check the port numbers at any time by selecting the COM Ports tab on the Bluetooth Devices window, as in Figure 14-40. You should need to go through this whole process only once because your computer and the NXT will remember their paired relationship.

Figure 14-40. *COM Ports tab of the Bluetooth Devices window*

Galvanic Skin Response Meter

Combining you and your NXT is one of the coolest combinations of them all. Galvanic Skin Response (GSR) is the most familiar term for the body's reaction to increased stress by increased sweating. The effect is commonly used for lie detectors and biofeedback monitors. The phenomenon has been observed for more than 100 years, and the modern medical term for it is Electrodermal Response, or EDR.

When subjects become stressed, their sweat glands involuntarily become more active, and this lowers their skin's electrical resistance. The resistance measurement is basically the same as the salinity measurement discussed in Chapter 5. In this case, however, we make two electrodes to attach to the subject's skin. Because the hand has a large number of sweat glands that react with GSR, good locations for the electrodes are adjacent fingers on the same hand, as shown in Figure 14-41.

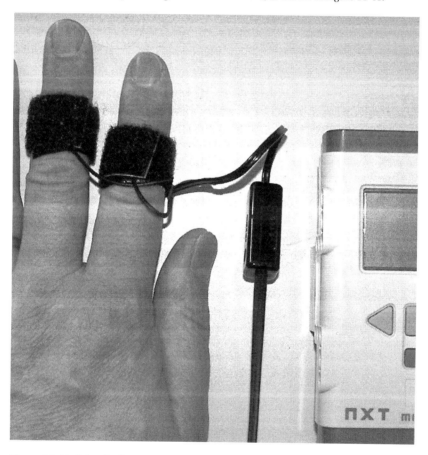

Figure 14-41. *Galvanic Skin Response meter*

Finger electrodes are made by adding some aluminum foil to self-adhesive Velcro. (This type of Velcro comes in long strips and can be purchased from sewing supply stores.) Figure 14-42 shows all the parts of the assembly. You connect the electrode wires to the NXT Sensor Input Pin 1 and 2 (white and black wires) using any of the methods discussed in the previous chapters. Another easy method is to simply cut the LEGO 9V connector from a NXT adapter cable, split the pair of wires, and strip their ends.

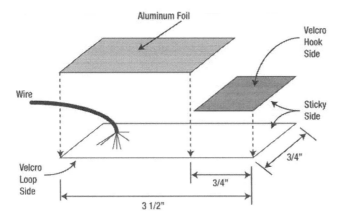

Figure 14-42. *Finger electrode construction*

Figure 14-43 shows the two completed electrodes.

Figure 14-43. *Completed finger electrodes*

The program in Figure 14-44 is about the simplest GSR program you can write. The program makes a continuous tone whose frequency is roughly proportional to the skin's resistance. The first Math block makes the frequency higher for lower skin resistance. That way, increased stress relates to increased frequency. The second block magnifies the range of frequency by a factor of 6. Finally, the Sound block is configured with the window shown in Figure 14-44. Notice that the block is set for Tone, low volume, and not to Wait for Completion. Because the Sound block ignores negative frequency inputs, when the electrodes aren't connected to anyone, there isn't any audible tone.

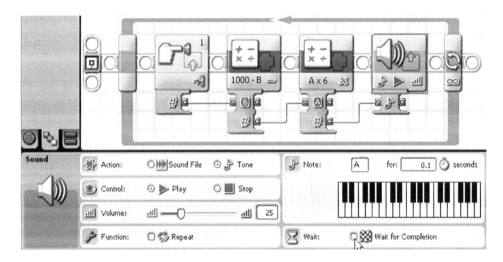

Figure 14-44. *Simple GSR program*

The program can be used for a variety of experiments. For example, in biofeedback conditioning, the objective is to learn to relax your body. This would be the same as lowering the body's stress level, and that can be measured as a rising skin resistance. After connecting the electrodes and starting the program, the goal is to make the tone frequency go lower over time. Most people achieve this by relaxing their muscles, taking slow deep breaths, and clearing the mind of anxiety-producing thoughts. When used as a lie detector, the connected subject is asked a series of questions. If subjects answer untruthfully, their body stress level rises, which can be detected as a rising frequency tone.

APPENDIX A

■■■

Construction Techniques

Building the more advanced projects in this book might require you to learn some new skills. Most electronic products today use construction techniques that involve parts so small you need a microscope to handle them. Fortunately, larger electrical components that you can reasonably work with are still available. Methods to build with these parts have been around for decades, and everything you need is available at Radio Shack or other electronic distributors. For the I2C bus projects in Chapter 13, Mindsensors sells prototype boards for the PCF8574 and PCF8591 integrated circuits. They save you from making many of the connections and include the unique NXT socket that saves you from having to cut cables.

Solderless Breadboard

The first tool to become familiar with is the solderless breadboard. The term *breadboard* dates back to when electronic hobbyists literally built projects on a plank of wood intended for cutting bread. Many styles of breadboards are available, but they all consist of columns of interconnected holes used for connecting components and a few long rows of holes at the top and bottom used for connecting power.

Radio Shack sells a small breadboard (Catalog Number: 276-175) that is big enough to build all the projects in this book (see Figure A-1). A nice feature of this particular breadboard is that it has row- and column-identification marks that make construction easier. Throughout this book, we indicate the exact row and column where you should insert the lead of a device. By following these instructions precisely, your chance of making a mistake will be greatly reduced.

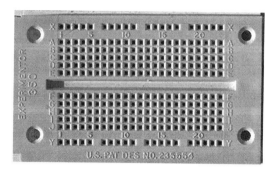

Figure A-1. *Solderless prototype breadboard*

Building on the Breadboard

We demonstrate the construction process through a simple example. Figure A-2 shows a minimal 9V powered sensor design. The design just takes care of separating the power and sensor read parts of the 9V powered interface described in Chapter 9. Nevertheless, the circuit is useful for voltage input where measured voltage is something that can't be loaded by the NXT internal 10kΩ resistor. It has only four parts, listed in the bill of materials in Table A-1.

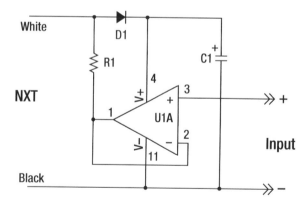

Figure A-2. *Voltage input*

Table A-1. *Bill of Materials*

Component	Part Number	Description	Radio Shack
U1	LM324	Quad OpAmp	276-1711
D1	1N4148	Small Signal Diode	276-1122
R1	1kΩ	1/4 W 5% Carbon Film Resistor	271-1321
C1	22uF	16V or higher Electrolytic Capacitor	272-1014

All the parts have been placed on the breadboard in Figure A-3. Most of the parts have long leads to start with, and you could insert them into the same holes without cutting them shorter, but you run the risk of accidentally touching the leads together, creating short circuits.

Figure A-3. *Components on the solderless breadboard*

Construction consists of going down row by row in Table A-2 and connecting one component at a time. The "start" column corresponds to the first listed end of the part and the "end" corresponds to the last. For example, C1's start is the positive (+) lead, and the end is the negative (–) lead. J1, J2, and J3 are just wire jumpers.

Table A-2. *Component Placement*

Component	Start	End
U1 pin 1	F4	
C1 + −	Y1	X1
J1	Y7	J7
J2	X7	A7
J3	G4	G5
D1 anode cathode	J2	Y2
R1	I2	I4
NXT white black	X2	H2
Input +	H6	I6
Input −	X10	X11

After building the circuit, you'll need to make sure that it works. While running a program that configures the port as an old RCX–type Light Sensor, check that the voltage across C1 is between 9V and 6V. You can add a potentiometer, as in Figure A-4, to input a known voltage.

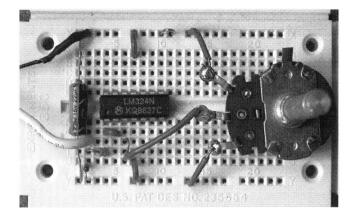

Figure A-4. *Checking the circuit*

Using a voltmeter and a program that reads the Raw sensor value, you can create a plot like Figure A-5. The lower end of the voltage range has a flat region because the LM324 cannot output a value less than about 0.6V.

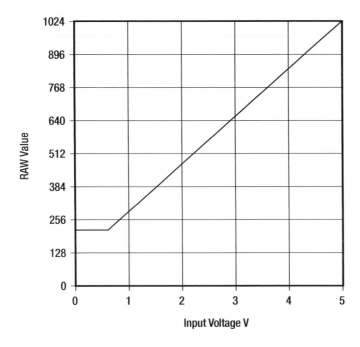

Figure A-5. *Voltage input versus Raw value plot*

You could just leave the circuit on the breadboard for as long as you needed it, but it's better to commit it permanently to a PCB. It will be more compact and much more reliable because it keeps parts from accidentally being pulled out of the breadboard.

Printed Circuit Board

The Global Specialties Experimenter PCB or the Radio Shack 276-170 (see Figure A-6) match the layout of the electronic breadboard exactly, as can be seen in the bottom view in Figure A-7. It has the same row and column markings as the breadboard, so it should be easy to transfer the parts from the breadboard to the PCB. The only problem with the PCB is that it's way too long. That means that one Experimenter PCB could be the source for several sensors.

Figure A-6. *Printed circuit board that matches the solderless breadboard*

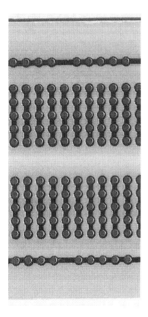

Figure A-7. *Bottom view of the PCB*

Cutting the PCB is a lot easier than you might think: you need only a straight-edge ruler and a sharp knife, as shown in Figure A-8. You score the board by creating a shallow groove in the top and bottom of the board along a column of holes where you want to cut the board. Once the board has been scored, it will snap by bending it at the groove.

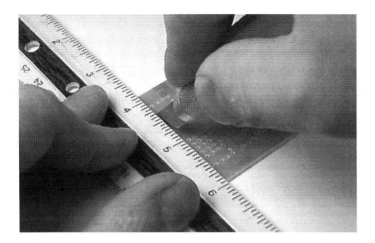

Figure A-8. *Scoring the PC board*

Start by laying the straight-edge ruler along the column of holes where you want to cut the PCB. Take a sharp knife and run it along the straight edge of the entire width of the board. The knife will bump along from hole to hole. At first, don't use very much pressure. Keep running the knife along exactly the same path over and over until a groove develops. It usually takes about ten passes. Repeat the process on the bottom side of the board.

Bracing your thumbs at the groove, as shown in Figure A-9, gently bend the board down on both sides with your fingers. It should snap with only a reasonable amount of force. If it doesn't snap, continue to cut at the grooves to make them a little deeper and try again. You'll be left with a small PCB that's just the right size for your project.

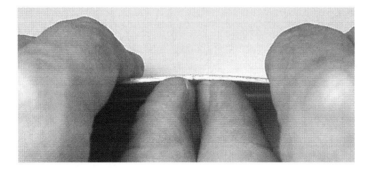

Figure A-9. *Snapping the PC board*

As you cut away other small PCBs, you'll notice that the printed column numbers no longer match the solderless breadboard. The original painted numbers are easily scratched off, and you can re-mark them with permanent marker.

Soldering

Soldering the parts to the PCB is probably the scariest part. It requires a certain amount of skill, but after a few connections you'll find that it really isn't that difficult. Making good solder connections requires following a few basic rules:

- The soldering iron should be a 25-to-40-watt pencil type with a 1/8"-to-3/16" chisel- or cone-shaped tip.
- Always wait at least five minutes for the soldering iron to come up to temperature.
- The solder should be rosin core 60/40 tin/lead content with .062" diameter. Never use acid core or the type used for plumbing.

▨ **Caution** Lead is a poison and has been proven to cause health problems, especially for young children. Never leave solder around where people might handle or eat it.

- Lead-free solder is available and works just as well, but it requires a little higher melting temperature.
- When using a new tip, coat the tip with a good layer of solder and wipe off the excess with a damp sponge.
- The soldering iron must be kept clean by always quickly wiping it on a damp sponge just before making a connection.

▨ **Note** Remember to unplug the soldering iron when you're done using it.

The first step of soldering a component to the PCB is making absolutely sure that you have the component leads in the right holes and that the part is oriented properly. If you have built the circuit on the breadboard first, it's a simple matter of pulling parts off the breadboard and placing them one by one. Push the leads of a component through the holes and spread the leads apart, as shown in Figure A-10, to keep the component from falling out when you turn the PCB over to solder. You can work on one part at a time, but the job will go faster if you place several parts that are close together at the same time and then solder.

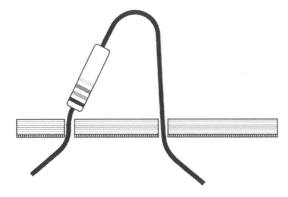

Figure A-10. *Placement of the component on a PC board*

To make a solder joint, touch the soldering iron tip to both the PCB copper pad and the component wire at the same time and allow the connection to heat for a second. Figure A-11 shows the proper placement of the soldering iron tip and the lead.

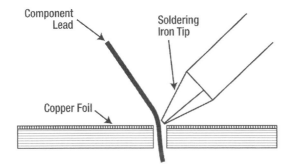

Figure A-11. *Heating the connection*

Now bring the solder to the hot connection (see Figure A-12), not the iron tip.

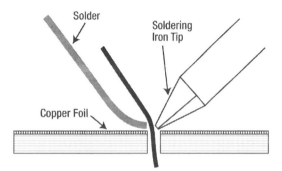

Figure A-12. *Adding solder to the connection*

Allow enough solder to flow around the connection, as shown in Figure A-13. You might think that the components would be instantly damaged by the high temperature of soldering. However, they're designed to tolerate it for fairly long periods, and you shouldn't be afraid to take the time to make a good joint. Remove the solder and iron and then allow the connection to cool for a few seconds before moving anything. The solder should be shiny and look almost wet when it first cools.

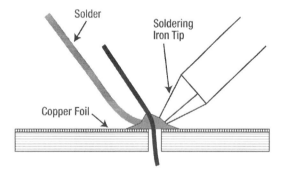

Figure A-13. *Let solder flow around the connection*

Bad solder joints, like those shown in Figure A-14, are usually the result of not heating the joint sufficiently. The joint might have voids as in the top example, or have a blob-like appearance as in the lower example. Bad joints might also look dull. Just reheat the joint and add solder if necessary.

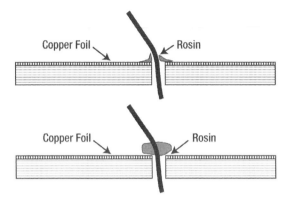

Figure A-14. *Examples of bad solder joints*

Cut off the excess component lead close to the connection with diagonal cutters. The finished joint should look like Figure A-15 in cross-section.

▓ **Tip** Clip leads so the ends won't fly toward your eyes.

Figure A-15. *Cut excess component lead flush with the joint*

Solder bridges are a common problem when soldering this type of PCB. A little too much solder gets into the joint and flows over onto the next trace. Don't panic! Hold the PCB vertically in one hand and bring the soldering iron tip up to the bridge from below, as shown in Figure A-16. The excess solder should flow back onto the tip, where you can wipe it off on the damp sponge. Unsoldering tools are available that you can use to vacuum practically all the solder from a joint.

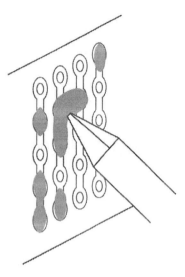

Figure A-16. *Removing a solder bridge*

Another problem is solder covering a hole where you need to insert a part. Usually a technique similar to the bridge removal will work to clear the hole. Just coax the solder down the copper track away from the blocked hole with the soldering iron. You can also melt the solder while pushing the component lead into the hole. Because all the holes in a column are connected anyway, you can substitute placing a part into a nearby hole that isn't blocked. There's also a product called *unsoldering braid* that will wick up extra solder when heated along with the solder.

Building a Printed Circuit Board

Figure A-17 is what the voltage input should look like after it has been moved to a PCB.

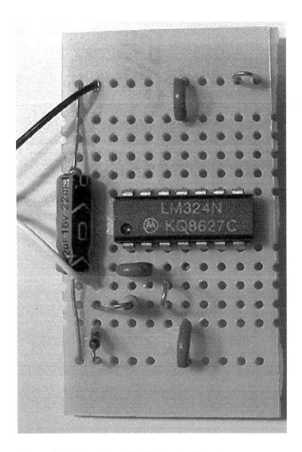

Figure A-17. *Top side of the finished voltage input*

The bottom view is in Figure A-18, and you might notice that the unused pins of the LM324 haven't been soldered at all. You can solder these pins if you want, but the step is unnecessary and you are more likely to create solder bridges.

Figure A-18. Bottom side of the finished voltage input

Prototype Board Kits

Figure A-19 shows all the parts that come with the PCF8574 prototype kit from Mindsensors.

Figure A-19. *PCF8574 kit parts*

One very important part in the kit is the NXT-compatible socket shown in Figure A-20. You can buy extra sockets like these for your other sensor projects, which can save you from cutting cables to connect your project to the NXT. The board also has a location for a second NXT socket, so you can easily daisy chain multiple PCF8574s using the same sensor port. However, each board must have its own I2C address, and you populate the 82kΩ resistors on only one of the boards.

Figure A-20. *NXT compatible socket*

Soldering the components onto the PCB follows the same procedure we have already discussed. There is an area on the board in which you can add your custom circuitry, too. The kit also comes with a connector that can be used to interface the board to other circuitry. Unlike the breadboard PCB, the prototype area holes are not connected together in strips. You have to add short pieces of bare copper wire or create solder bridges to tie holes together. Figure A-21 shows the connector area in which the eight digital I/O pins are connected along with power and ground. Although it is labeled 5V, this is really the 4.3V supply.

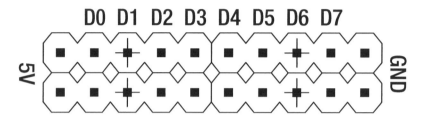

Figure A-21. *PCF8574 connector area*

Figure A-22 shows the completed board. In Chapter 13, we used this prototype board with a 16-button matrix to make a small keypad input for the NXT.

Figure A-22. *Finished PCF8574 PCB*

The PCF8591 prototype board kit is shown in Figure A-23. It has many of the same convenient features of the PCF8574 kit. It includes a 2.5V reference for the analog signals, which means that the range of the analog inputs is 0 for 0V and 255 for 2.5V. The analog output is limited to the 2.5V range.

Figure A-23. *PCF8591 prototype kit*

The connector area for the PCF8591 PCB is shown in Figure A-24. All four analog inputs are available, along with the 2.5V reference and the analog output. In Chapter 13, we use this prototype board to build the Light Compass project. In that project, the four CdS LDRs were pulled up to this 2.5V reference with 10KΩ resistors. Just like the PCF8574 PCB, there is also a connector labeled 5V, but it is really the 4.3V supply.

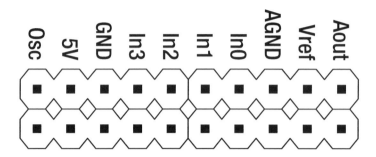

Figure A-24. *PCF8591 connector area*

APPENDIX B

■ ■ ■

References, Links, and Sources

This appendix provides links to go beyond the information presented in the book. The links are categorized by chapter, with an additional "General Interest" category. Some of the links are to the web sites of manufactures of electronic parts, and others are to companies that sell them. The book web site at http://www.apress.com will maintain an updated list of links.

General Interest

Digi-Key: http://www.digikey.com/

LEGO Education: http://www.legoeducation.com/store/

LEGO MINDSTORMS: http://mindstorms.lego.com/

LEGO page with NXT Developer Kits: http://mindstorms.lego.com/Overview/NXTreme.aspx

LEGO Store: http://shop.lego.com/

Michael Gasperi's LEGO page: http://www.extremenxt.com/lego.htm

Mindsensors: http://www.mindsensors.com/

MINDSTORMS-related newsgroup: http://news.lugnet.com/robotics/

Nxtbot.com blog: http://www.NXTBot.com

The NXT STEP blog: http://www.thenxtstep.blogspot.com

Nxtasy.org NXT news: http://www.nxtasy.org/

Philippe (Philo's) LEGO page: http://www.philohome.com/

Radio Shack: http://www.radioshack.com/
Robot construction plans: http://engk12.ece.missouri.edu/program.htm

SensorWiki.org: http://sensorwiki.org/

Chapter 1

Comparison of LEGO motors: http://www.philohome.com/motors/motorcomp.htm

Homebrew Sound Sensor: http://www.extremenxt.com/sound.htm

Human vision information:
http://www.onr.navy.mil/sci_tech/31/312/ncsr/devices/led/•ch_11_human_vision.pdf

Koerner, Brendan I. "Geeks in Toyland." *Wired Magazine*, February 2006.

MIT MindFest: http://www.media.mit.edu/mindfest/

Mindell, David, et al. "LEGO Mindstorms, The Structure of an Engineering (R)evolution":
http://web.mit.edu/6.933/www/Fall2000/LegoMindstorms.pdf

Papert, Seymour. *Mindstorms: Children, Computers, and Powerful Ideas.* New York: Basic Books, 1993.

Russell Nelson's LEGO MINDSTORMS Internals web site: http://www.crynwr.com/lego-robotics/

Chapter 2

Bricx Command Center: http://bricxcc.sourceforge.net/

Java: http://lejos.sourceforge.net/

LabVIEW: http://www.ni.com/academic/mindstorms/

LEGO page with Legacy Blocks: http://mindstorms.lego.com/Support/Updates/

NXC: http://bricxcc.sourceforge.net/nbc/

NXT-G Book: http://www.apress.com/book/view/9781590598719

PBLua (another alternative language): http://www.hempeldesigngroup.com/lego/pbLua/

RobotC: http://www.robotc.net/

Chapter 3

Philo's plug: http://www.philohome.com/nxtplug/nxtplug.htm

Chapter 5

Braitenberg, Valentino. *Vehicles: Experiments in Synthetic Psychology.* Cambridge, MA: The MIT Press, 1986.

Braitenberg Vehicles: http://people.cs.uchicago.edu/~wiseman/vehicles/

Cadmium sulfide photoresistors: http://www.selcoproducts.com/CFM/photocell_toc.cfm

GE Infrastructure Sensing: http://www.thermometrics.com/

Human comfort zone: http://www.p2pays.org/ref/08/07692.pdf

The Rotronic Humidity Handbook: http://www.rotronic-usa.com/Ref/Rotronic%20Humidity%20Handbook.pdf

Theremin: http://www.thereminworld.com/

Chapter 6

Bourns: http://www.bourns.com/

Inverted pendulum: http://en.wikipedia.org/wiki/Inverted_pendulum

Chapter 7

Batteries: http://www.duracell.com/oem/primary/alkaline/alkaline_manganese_prod.asp

Chapter 8

2N3906 datasheet: http://www.fairchildsemi.com/ds/2N/2N3906.pdf

Acroname: http://www.acroname.com/

DN6849SE datasheet: http://www.ortodoxism.ro/datasheets/panasonic/SPC00004CEB.pdf

Sharp GP2D12 datasheet: http://document.sharpsma.com/files/GP2D12-DATA-SHEET.PDF

Chapter 9

1230-030D-3L datasheet: http://www.meas-spec.com/product/t_product.aspx?id=2828

1N4148 datasheet: http://www.fairchildsemi.com/ds/1N/1N4148.pdf

LM324 datasheet: http://www.national.com/ds.cgi/LM/LM124.pdf

Lamp filament resistance: http://www.ee.bgu.ac.il/~pel/pdf-files/conf104.pdf

Chapter 10

2N3904 datasheet: http://www.fairchildsemi.com/ds/2N/2N3904.pdf

Chapter 11

The Clapper: http://www2.jeiusa.com/index.php/je-products/the-clapper.html

Etch-A-Sketch: http://www.ohioart.com/etch/

Chapter 12

1N400X datasheet: http://www.diodes.com/datasheets/ds28002.pdf

1N4733 datasheet: http://www.fairchildsemi.com/ds/1N/1N4744A.pdf

Dyanalloy and Flexinol: http://www.dynalloy.com/

Globe pencil sharpener:
http://rinovelty.com/index.cfm/fuseaction/products.detail/item/STSHGLO/globe_pencil_sharpe
ner

IRF510 datasheet: http://www.irf.com/product-info/datasheets/data/irf510.pdf

IRF520 datasheet: http://www.irf.com/product-info/datasheets/data/irf520.pdf

IRF9530 datasheet: http://www.irf.com/product-info/datasheets/data/irf530.pdf

Jameco Robotic Store: http://www.robotstore.com/

Potter and Brumfield: http://relays.tycoelectronics.com/pnb.asp

PS2501-4 datasheet: http://www.cel.com/pdf/datasheets/ps2501.pdf

The Robot Shop: http://www.robotshop.us/

STTH2R06RL datasheet: http://www.st.com/stonline/products/literature/ds/10757.pdf

TLC555 datasheet: http://focus.ti.com/lit/ds/symlink/tlc555.pdf

Chapter 13

Cadmium sulfide photoresistors: http://www.selcoproducts.com/CFM/photocell_toc.cfm

Grayhill keypad datasheet:
http://lgrws01.grayhill.com/web/images/ProductImages/Series%2096%20Standard%20Keypads.pdf

I^{2}C manual: http://www.nxp.com/acrobat_download/applicationnotes/AN10216_1.pdf

Linear stepper motor datasheet:
http://media.digikey.com/pdf/Data%20Sheets/Portescap%20Danaher%20PDFs/35DBM-L.pdf

PCF8574 and PCF8574A datasheet:
http://www.nxp.com/acrobat_download/datasheets/PCF8574_4.pdf

PCF8591 datasheet: http://www.nxp.com/acrobat_download/datasheets/PCF8591_6.pdf

Reed Relays: http://www.cotorelay.com/html/reed_relay_8l_series.htm

Simon game: http://www.dieterkoenig.at/ccc/english/se_story_simon.htm

Tact switch datasheet: http://www.e-switch.com/pdf/TL1105.pdf

ULN2003 datasheet: http://focus.ti.com/lit/ds/symlink/uln2003a.pdf

Chapter 14

Galvanic Skin Response: http://www.extremenxt.com/gsr.htm

Hand warmers: http://www.warmers.com/

Light sticks: http://science.howstuffworks.com/light-stick.htm

NxtRICedit download: http://ric.dreier-privat.de/Docu/index_eng.htm

NXT-remote: http://www.norgesgade14.dk/index.php

Panoramic photography: http://www.shortcourses.com/how/panoramic/panoramic.htm

Pong: http://www.pong-story.com/

Razix and NXT Director: http://www.razix.com/nxtdirector.htm

RoboDNA and Dashboard Designer: http://robodna.com/roboDNA/

Appendix A

Global Specialties: http://www.globalspecialties.com/

1N4148 datasheet: http://www.fairchildsemi.com/ds/1N/1N4148.pdf

LM324 datasheet: http://www.national.com/ds.cgi/LM/LM124.pdf

■ ■ ■

Code Listings

Arranged by chapter, here are the complete listings of the NXC programs. You can also download them from the book website, in the Source Code/Download area at http://www.apress.com.

Chapter 13

Listing C-1. *blinkall.nxc*

```
#define I2Cport S1        // Port number
#define I2CAddr8574 0x70 // I2C address x040 8574 or 0x70 for 8574A
byte WriteBuf[]={I2CAddr8574,0x00}; // write buffer is addr and data

task main() {
  int nbytes;
  SetSensorLowspeed (I2Cport);        // Configure I2C port
  while (true) {
    WriteBuf[1]++;                     // update data byte
    I2CWrite(I2Cport, 0, WriteBuf);   // send buffer
    while(I2CStatus(I2Cport, nbytes)==STAT_COMM_PENDING); // wait
  }
}
```

Listing C-2. *low2high.nxc*

```
#define I2Cport S1 // NXT sensor port 1
#define I2CAddr8574 0x40 // 0x40 8574 or 0x70 for 8574A
byte WriteBuf[] = {I2CAddr8574, 0xFF}; // Sent to 8574
byte ReadBuf[];     // Receive from PCF8574
int RdCnt=1;        // Number of bytes to read
```

```
task main (){
  SetSensorLowspeed (I2Cport); // Configure NXT port
  while (true){
    // write output data and read back port value
    I2CBytes(I2Cport, WriteBuf, RdCnt, ReadBuf);
    // shift left 4 bits and make lowest 4 bits 1
    WriteBuf[1] = (ReadBuf[0] << 4) + 0x0f;
  }
}
```

Listing C-3. *simon.nxc*

```
#define MaxNotes 50
#define ToneDuration 300
#define IntervalDuration 100

#define I2Cport S1
// I2CAddr8574 = 0x40 for PCF8574
// I2CAddr8574 = 0x70 for PCF8574A
#define I2CAddr8574 0x40

// Write buffer to send to PCF8574
byte WriteBuf[] = {I2CAddr8574, 0xFF};

// Read buffer that receives byte read from PCF8574
byte ReadBuf[];

// Number of bytes to read
int RdCnt=1;

// Notes buffer
int notes[];

byte LedVal[] = {0xef, 0xdf, 0xbf, 0x7f};
int Tone[] = {TONE_C4, TONE_E4, TONE_G4, TONE_C5};

//*****************************************
// Plays a tone and light matching LED.
// LED are on higer half of PCF8574 data byte
// Parameter is LED number (0..3)
void LedTone( int Led)
{
   if(Led < 0 || Led > 3 ) return;
   WriteBuf[1] = LedVal[Led];
   I2CWrite(I2Cport, 0, WriteBuf);
   PlayTone (Tone[Led], ToneDuration);
   Wait(ToneDuration);
   WriteBuf[1] = 0xff;
   I2CWrite(I2Cport, 0, WriteBuf);
   Wait(IntervalDuration);
}
```

```
//*******************************************
// Read the I2C button state and returns button number
// The buttons are on lower half of PCF8574 data byte
// Rightmost button have priority.
int GetButtons()
{
  WriteBuf[1] = 0xff;
  do
  {
    I2CBytes(I2Cport, WriteBuf, RdCnt, ReadBuf);
  }
  while (ReadBuf[0] == 0xff)
  for(int i=0; i<4; i++)
  {
    if((ReadBuf[0] & 1) == 0) return i;
    ReadBuf[0]>>=1;
  }
}

task main ()
{
  int i;
  // Configure NXT port
  SetSensorLowspeed (I2Cport);
  TextOut(8, LCD_LINE3, "NXT Simon");
  TextOut(8, LCD_LINE4, "Press orange");
  TextOut(8, LCD_LINE5, "button to start");

  // Wait for orange button and seed random generator
  do
  {
    Random();
  }
  while (! ButtonPressed (BTNCENTER, true))
  TextOut(8, LCD_LINE4, "              ");
  TextOut(8, LCD_LINE5, "              ");
  Wait(1000);

  // Initialise notes buffer, without repetition
  ArrayInit(notes, 0, MaxNotes);
  int Val=Random(4);
  notes[0]=Val;
  for(i=1; i < MaxNotes; i++)
  {
    do
    {
      Val=Random(4);
    } while (Val == notes[i-1]);
    notes[i] = Val;
  }
```

317

```
  for(i=1; i < MaxNotes; i++)
  {
    // Play tune
    int fail=false;
    for(int j=0; j<i; j++)
    {
      LedTone(notes[j]);
    }

    // Check if players correctly reproduce melody
    for(int j=0; j<i; j++)
    {
      int button=GetButtons();
      LedTone(button);
      if(button != notes[j])
      {
        fail=true;
        break;
      }
    }
    Wait(1000);
    if(fail) break;
  }
  ClearScreen();
  TextOut(10, LCD_LINE3, "Game Over!");
  TextOut(10, LCD_LINE4, "Level Reached");
  NumOut(10, LCD_LINE5, i);
  PlayTone(TONE_C6, 100);
  Wait (100);
  PlayTone(TONE_G5, 120);
  Wait (120);
  PlayTone(TONE_E5, 150);
  Wait (150);
  PlayTone(TONE_C5, 170);
  Wait (170);
  PlayTone(TONE_G4, 200);
  Wait (5000);
}
```

Listing C-4. *magicwand.nxc*

```
#define I2Cport S1
#define Touch S4
#define Motor OUT_A
// I2CAddr8574 = 0x40 for PCF8574
// I2CAddr8574 = 0x70 for PCF8574A
#define I2CAddr8574 0x40
```

```
// Display patterns
// Each byte represents a column of dots
// Bit set to 1 means lit LED.
// Least significant bit is at top of column.
// Last byte must be all 0
// Maximum number of bytes par pattern: 15

byte L_[] = {0xff, 0x80, 0x80, 0x80, 0x80, 0x80, 0x80, 0x80, 0};
byte E_[] = {0xff, 0x89, 0x89, 0x89, 0x89, 0x81, 0x81, 0};
byte G_[] = {0x7e, 0x00, 0x81, 0x81, 0x81, 0x81, 0x91, 0x90, 0x72, 0};
byte O_[] = {0x7e, 0x00, 0x81, 0x81, 0x81, 0x81, 0x81, 0x00, 0x7e, 0};

byte N_[] = {0xff, 0x01, 0x02, 0x04, 0x08, 0x10, 0x20, 0x40, 0x80, 0xff, 0};
byte X_[] = {0x80, 0x41, 0x22, 0x14, 0x08, 0x14, 0x22, 0x41, 0x80, 0};
byte T_[] = {0x01, 0x01, 0x01, 0x01, 0xff, 0x01, 0x01, 0x01, 0x01, 0};

void WaitTouch(void)
{
  // Wait for pressed
  while(Sensor(Touch)==0);
  // and release
  while(Sensor(Touch)==1);
  return;
}

void DispLetter (const byte & letter[])
{
  int nbytes;
  // Wait for the end of previously sent data
  while(I2CStatus(I2Cport, nbytes)==STAT_COMM_PENDING);
  // Write buffer to send to PCF8574
  byte WriteBuf[];
  ArrayBuild(WriteBuf, I2CAddr8574, letter);
  for(int i=1; i<ArrayLen(WriteBuf); i++)
  {
      WriteBuf[i] ^= 0xff;
  }
  I2CWrite(I2Cport, 0,  WriteBuf);
}

task main ()
{
  // Configure NXT I2C port
  SetSensorLowspeed (I2Cport);
  // Configure Touch sensor
  SetSensorTouch (Touch);
  // Start Motor, full power
  OnFwd(Motor, 100);
  while (true)
```

```
{
    // display LEGO during 5 sweeps
    for (int i=0; i<5; i++)
    {
      WaitTouch();
      // wait a little to center display in linear part of sweep
      Wait(20);
      DispLetter(L_);
      DispLetter(E_);
      DispLetter(G_);
      DispLetter(O_);
    }
    // Display NXT
    for (int i=0; i<5; i++)
    {
      WaitTouch();
      Wait(20);
      DispLetter(N_);
      DispLetter(X_);
      DispLetter(T_);
    }
  }
}
```

Listing C-5. *keypad.nxc*

```
#define I2Cport S4        // keypad connected to port 4
#define I2CAddr8574 0x70 // 0x40 for 8574 or 0x70 for 8574A
byte WriteBuf[] = {I2CAddr8574, 0x00}; // write buffer
byte ReadBuf[]; // read buffer
int RdCnt=1; // read one byte

long GetKey() {// returns the key value or -1 if no key
  WriteBuf[1]=0xEF; // Col 1
  I2CBytes(I2Cport, WriteBuf, RdCnt, ReadBuf);
  if(ReadBuf[0]==0xEE) return(1); // Row 1
  if(ReadBuf[0]==0xED) return(4); // Row 2
  if(ReadBuf[0]==0xEB) return(7); // Row 3
  if(ReadBuf[0]==0xE7) return(14);// Row 4
  WriteBuf[1]=0xDF; // Col 2
  I2CBytes(I2Cport, WriteBuf, RdCnt, ReadBuf);
  if(ReadBuf[0]==0xDE) return(2); // Row 1
  if(ReadBuf[0]==0xDD) return(5); // Row 2
  if(ReadBuf[0]==0xDB) return(8); // Row 3
  if(ReadBuf[0]==0xD7) return(0); // Row 4
  WriteBuf[1]=0xBF; // Col 3
  I2CBytes(I2Cport, WriteBuf, RdCnt, ReadBuf);
  if(ReadBuf[0]==0xBE) return(3); // Row 1
  if(ReadBuf[0]==0xBD) return(6); // Row 2
  if(ReadBuf[0]==0xBB) return(9); // Row 3
  if(ReadBuf[0]==0xB7) return(15);// Row 4
```

```
    WriteBuf[1]=0x7F; // Col 4
    I2CBytes(I2Cport, WriteBuf, RdCnt, ReadBuf);
    if(ReadBuf[0]==0x7E) return(10); // Row 1
    if(ReadBuf[0]==0x7D) return(11); // Row 2
    if(ReadBuf[0]==0x7B) return(12); // Row 3
    if(ReadBuf[0]==0x77) return(13); // Row 4
    return(-1); // no keys pressed
}

task main () {
    long Value = 0, Key;
    string TextValue, FileName="X.TXT";
    char FileHandle, Count;
    SetSensorLowspeed (I2Cport);  // config I2C Port
    NumOut(0,0,Value,true); // show inital value
    while (true) { // loop forever
        while(GetKey()<0); // wait for key to be pressed
        Key=GetKey();  // get key value
        PlayTone(1000,5); // make key pressed sound
        switch(Key) {  // case based on key value
            case -1:  // no key = do nothing
            break;
            case 15:  // # = negate value
                Value = -Value;
            break;
            case 14:  // * = clear value
                Value = 0;
            break;
            case 13: // 10-13 write value to file and quit
            case 12:
            case 11:
            case 10:
                FileName[0] = Key + 55; // fix name to A, B, C, or D
                DeleteFile(FileName); // delete any old file
                CreateFile(FileName,16,FileHandle); // open file
                TextValue=NumToStr(Value); // convert value to string
                WriteLnString(FileHandle,TextValue,Count);// write it
                CloseFile(FileHandle); // close file
                Stop(true); // done
            break;
            default: // 0-9 = just build up value
                if(Value>=0) Value=Value*10+Key;
                else Value=Value*10-Key;
            break;
        }
        NumOut(0,0,Value,true); // show current value
        while(GetKey()>=0); // wait for key to be unpressed
    }
}
```

321

Listing C-6. *read4.nxc*

```
#define port S1                          // sensor port 1
#define I2CAddr8591 0x90                 // PCF8591 address
byte WriteBuf[] = {I2CAddr8591, 0x04}; // write buffer
byte ReadBuf[];                          // read buffer
int RdCnt=5;                             // read 5 bytes

task main(){
  SetSensorLowspeed(port);              // make port I2C
  while(true){
    // Write config byte and read back 5 bytes
    I2CBytes(port, WriteBuf, RdCnt, ReadBuf);
    NumOut(0,24,ReadBuf[1],true);       // Chan 0
    NumOut(0,16,ReadBuf[2]);            // Chan 1
    NumOut(0,8,ReadBuf[3]);             // Chan 2
    NumOut(0,0,ReadBuf[4]);             // Chan 3
  }
}
```

Listing C-7. *readhue2.nxc*

```
#define I2Cport S1
// I2CAddr8574 = 0x40 for PCF8574
// I2CAddr8574 = 0x70 for PCF8574A
#define I2CAddr8574 0x40
#define BLUE 1
#define RED 4
#define GREEN 0x10

// Write buffer to send to PCF8574
byte WriteBuf[] = {I2CAddr8574, 0xFF};

struct rgb
{
  int Red;
  int Green;
  int Blue;
};

void ReadRawColor(int port, rgb &RawRGB )
{
  SetSensorLowspeed (port);
  WriteBuf[1] = RED ^ 0xff;
  I2CWrite(port, 0,  WriteBuf);
  Wait(20);
  SetSensorTouch (port);
  Wait(80);
  RawRGB.Red = 1024 - SensorRaw (port);
```

```
    SetSensorLowspeed (port);
    WriteBuf[1] = GREEN ^ 0xff;
    I2CWrite(port, 0,  WriteBuf);
    Wait(20);
    SetSensorTouch (port);
    Wait(80);
    RawRGB.Green = 1024 - SensorRaw (port);

    SetSensorLowspeed (port);
    WriteBuf[1] = BLUE ^ 0xff;
    I2CWrite(port, 0,  WriteBuf);
    Wait(20);
    SetSensorTouch (port);
    Wait(80);
    RawRGB.Blue = 1024 - SensorRaw (port);
}

int Raw2Hue(rgb &RawRGB)
{
  int max, min;
  int d;
  rgb normalized;
  int hue;

  //find the color with max intensity
  max = (RawRGB.Red > RawRGB.Green) ? RawRGB.Red:RawRGB.Green;
  if(RawRGB.Blue > max ) max = RawRGB.Blue;
  //find the color with min intensity
  min = (RawRGB.Red < RawRGB.Green) ? RawRGB.Red:RawRGB.Green;
  if(RawRGB.Blue < min ) min = RawRGB.Blue;
  //diff of max and min also scale
  d = (max-min)/60;
  //normalize color intensity
  normalized.Red = (max - RawRGB.Red)/d;
  normalized.Green = (max - RawRGB.Green)/d;
  normalized.Blue = (max - RawRGB.Blue)/d;
  //compute hue based on max color
  if(RawRGB.Blue == max) hue = 240 + normalized.Green - normalized.Red;
  if(RawRGB.Green == max) hue = 240 + normalized.Red - normalized.Blue;
  if(RawRGB.Red == max) hue = normalized.Blue - normalized.Green;
  if(hue < 0) hue = hue + 360;
  return hue;
}

task main ()
{
  // Configure NXT port

  rgb RawRGB;
  int hue;
```

```
  while (true)
  {
    ReadRawColor(I2Cport, RawRGB);
    hue = Raw2Hue(RawRGB);
    ClearScreen();
    TextOut (0, LCD_LINE2, "Red:  ");
    NumOut (36, LCD_LINE2, RawRGB.Red);
    TextOut (0, LCD_LINE3, "Green:");
    NumOut (36, LCD_LINE3, RawRGB.Green);
    TextOut (0, LCD_LINE4, "Blue: ");
    NumOut (36, LCD_LINE4, RawRGB.Blue);
    TextOut (0, LCD_LINE5, "Hue:  ");
    NumOut (36, LCD_LINE5, hue);
  }
}
```

Chapter 14

Listing C-8. pong.nxc

```
#define port S1                       // sensor port 1
#define I2CAddr8591 0x90              // PCF8591 address
byte WriteBuf[] = {I2CAddr8591, 0x04}; // write buffer
byte ReadBuf[];                       // read buffer
int RdCnt=5;                          // read 5 bytes

task main(){
  byte lpadx,lpady,rpadx,rpady,bx,by,bxv,byv,lscore,rscore;
  lpadx=5;
  lpady=0;
  rpadx=95;
  rpady=0;
  lscore=0;
  rscore=0;
  bx=6;
  by=30;
  bxv=1;
  byv=1;
  SetSensorLowspeed(port);            // make port I2C
  while(true){
    I2CBytes(port, WriteBuf, RdCnt, ReadBuf);
    NumOut(78,60,rscore);
    NumOut(20,60,lscore);
    GraphicOut(lpadx, lpady, "N.ric");
    lpady=ReadBuf[3]/4;
    GraphicOut(lpadx, lpady, "P.ric");
    GraphicOut(rpadx, rpady, "N.ric");
    rpady=ReadBuf[4]/4;
```

```
        GraphicOut(rpadx, rpady, "P.ric");
        GraphicOut(bx, by, "W.ric");
        bx=bx+bxv;
        by=by+byv;
        GraphicOut(bx, by, "B.ric");
        if (bx>94){
          GraphicOut(bx, by, "W.ric");
          lscore=lscore+1;
          bx=6;
          by=30;
          PlayTone(100,500);
          Wait(500);
        }
        if (bx<3){
          GraphicOut(bx, by, "W.ric");
          rscore=rscore+1;
          bx=94;
          by=30;
          PlayTone(100,500);
          Wait(500);
        }
        if (by>60) byv=-1;
        if (by<1) byv=1;
        if (bx==5){
          if(abs(lpady+6-by)<10){
            bxv=1;
            PlayTone(600,50);
          }
        }
        if (bx==93){
          if(abs(rpady+6-by)<10){
            bxv=-1;
            PlayTone(600,50);
          }
        }
        Wait(10);
      }
    }
```

Index

▓ C

Made in the USA
Lexington, KY
15 January 2012